MW01614505

THE LAST
WORD

SOPHIE TRACE TRILOGY

THE LAST
WORD

A NOVEL

KATHY HERMAN

David C Cook®
transforming lives together

THE LAST WORD
Published by David C. Cook
4050 Lee Vance View
Colorado Springs, CO 80918 U.S.A.

David C. Cook Distribution Canada
55 Woodslee Avenue, Paris, Ontario, Canada N3L 3E5

David C. Cook U.K., Kingsway Communications
Eastbourne, East Sussex BN23 6NT, England

David C. Cook and the graphic circle C logo
are registered trademarks of Cook Communications Ministries.

This story is a work of fiction. All characters and events are the product of the author's
imagination. Any resemblance to any person, living or dead, is coincidental.

All Scripture quotations, unless otherwise noted, are taken from the *Holy Bible,
New International Version®. NIV®*. Copyright © 1973, 1978, 1984 by International
Bible Society. Used by permission of Zondervan. All rights reserved.

ISBN 978-1-61793-421-6

Published in association with the literary agency of Alive Communications,
Inc, 7680 Goddard St., Suite 200, Colorado Springs, CO 80920

The Team: Don Pape, Diane Noble, Amy Kiechlin, Caitlyn York, and Karen Athen
Cover Design: DogEared Design, Kirk DouPonce

Printed in the United States of America

To Him who is both the Giver and the Gift

ACKNOWLEDGMENTS

THE Great Smoky Mountains and rolling hills of East Tennessee provide the stunning backdrop for this story, though the town of Sophie Trace exists only in my imagination. How I have enjoyed lingering there during the writing of this series.

I drew from several resource people, all of whom shared generously from their storehouses of knowledge and experience. I did my best to integrate the facts, as I understood them. If accuracy was compromised in any way, it was unintentional and strictly of my own doing.

I owe a debt of gratitude to Commander Carl H. Deeley of the Los Angeles County Sheriff's Department for responding so quickly to my many questions and for reading various scenes and offering suggestions and valuable input. It's been fun working with you, Carl. I've learned a lot. And I love it that you've read every book I've written.

I want to extend a heartfelt thank you to my friend Paul David Houston, former assistant district attorney, for helping me understand sentencing and parole, and what is involved when an inmate is released from prison. As always, Paul, thanks for being so accessible and quick to respond. You've been a lifesaver.

I'd like to say thank you to my sister Caroline Berry, for receiving these chapters via email and saving them so I'd have a copy "off premises." I appreciated the effort and the peace of mind it gave me.

A special word of thanks to those whose prayers seemed, at times, almost tangible: my tenacious prayer warrior and sister Pat Phillips; my online prayer team—Chuck Allenbrand, Judith Depontes, Jackie Jeffries, Joanne Lambert, Adrienne McCabe, Susan Mouser, Nora Phillips, Kim Prothro, Will Ray, Kelly Smith, Leslie Strader, Carolyn Walker, and Sondra Watson; my dear friends Mark and Donna Skorheim, Susie Killough, Judi Wieghat, Don and Pearl Anderson; my friends at LifeWay Christian Store in Tyler, Texas, and Nashville, Tennessee; and my church family at Bethel Bible Church. I cannot tell you how much I value your prayers.

To the retailers who sell my books and the many readers who have encouraged me with personal testimonies about how God has used my words to challenge and inspire you. He uses *you* to fuel the passion that keeps me writing.

To my novelist friends in ChiLibris, who allow me to tap into your collective storehouse of knowledge and experience—what a compassionate, charitable, prayerful group you are! It's an honor to be counted among you.

To my agent, Beth Jusino, and the diligent staff at Alive Communications. Your standard of excellence challenges me to keep growing as a writer. I only hope that I represent you as well as you represent me.

To Cris Doornbos, Dan Rich, and Don Pape at David C. Cook Publishers for believing in me and investing in the words I write; and your hardworking staff for getting this book to the shelves. What could be more exciting than being colaborers "on the same page" for Him?

To my editor, Diane Noble, for being a trusted encourager, advocate, and friend. Your insightful suggestions resulted in a stronger inspirational message and a tighter story line. You always make me look better than I am. Thanks!

To my husband, best friend, partner (and roadie), Paul, who has carried my books when they were light and when they were heavy; when the distance was short and when it was far—and still looked out for my interests every step of the way. Your servant attitude brings tears to my eyes. Surely a special crown awaits you.

And to my Lord and my God, who saved me by grace and called me into relationship with You, breathe life into my words and motivate Your people to proclaim the gospel boldly and without shame—whether on distant shores or in our own neighborhoods.

PROLOGUE

I AM NOT ASHAMED OF THE GOSPEL,
BECAUSE IT IS THE POWER OF GOD FOR THE
SALVATION OF EVERYONE WHO BELIEVES:
FIRST FOR THE JEW, THEN FOR THE GENTILE.
ROMANS 1:16

THE shadow of death seemed to suck the life out of Vanessa Jessup as she pushed open the glass door at Planned Parenthood and staggered across College Boulevard. She slid behind the wheel of her old Honda Accord and locked the door as if that would somehow keep out the stark reality that threatened to rewrite her future.

Abortion would be the easy way out, though everything in her screamed in defiance. How was she going to take care of a baby? Did she even want to? What about getting her teaching degree? Backpacking across Europe after graduation? Spring break! By then she would look as if she'd swallowed a basketball.

This just couldn't be happening. Not now. Not when she was halfway through her sophomore year in college and had a clear direction for her life. The words of Psalm 139 reverberated in her mind.

For you created my inmost being; you knit me together in my mother's womb. I praise you because I am fearfully and wonderfully made.

Not this child. According to the Bible, it was conceived in sin. But the chemistry between Ty and her was so magnetic and overpowering that making love to him didn't seem wrong. They were soul mates—a perfect match. How could she have foreseen this? They had been so careful. It wasn't fair.

Did she even have the courage to tell her parents that she had redefined her Christian ideals and slept with her psychology professor—and not because she wanted a good grade? Would they understand that her relationship with Ty was electric, and that she loved him more than she ever dreamed she could love anyone?

She laid her head on the back of the seat and sighed. So much for the white dress and church wedding her parents always dreamed of. She dreaded their tears of disappointment and the lecture that would follow. But right now, it mattered more to her what Ty thought.

She sat for a minute and tried to relax, then opened her cell phone and pressed auto dial. She listened as it rang three times. *Come on. Pick up. I know you're finished lecturing for the day.*

"Professor Nicholson."

"Ty, I need to see you. It's really important."

"I'm with someone at the moment. Is this concerning your grade?"

"Look, I get it," Vanessa said. "You can't talk. But I know you have a faculty meeting tonight, and this can't wait till tomorrow."

"I could meet you in my office in forty-five minutes."

"I'd rather meet at Chelsea Park at our usual spot."

"That should work fine. I'll be glad to discuss whatever details are concerning you then."

"Okay, thanks."

Vanessa disconnected the call, another verse of Psalm 139 barging into her thoughts.

Your eyes saw my unformed body. All the days ordained for me were written in your book before one of them came to be.

She groaned. How was she supposed to think of this "positive pregnancy test" as a human being whose steps had been preordained by God? This pregnancy was a mistake—an incredible inconvenience that would ruin her chance to get her teaching degree.

Perhaps allowing the child to be adopted was the best course of action. But if she carried this baby to term, could she bear to part with it? Could Ty? And if they decided to keep the baby and take on the rigors of parenting, were they ready for marriage? As much as she loved Ty, the thought of having the rest of her life nailed down was both suffocating and terrifying. But choosing just to live together and raise the baby would alienate her parents. Caring for a baby alone was unthinkable. How was she supposed to make all these decisions? She needed time to process.

She blinked away the raw disappointment she knew she would see in her parents' eyes. They expected better from her. Hadn't she promised herself and the Lord that she would save her virginity for her husband? How would they react when they realized she had broken her promise unashamedly—and with an unbeliever?

Then again, wasn't she the child who always seemed to disappoint? How was she supposed to compete with a pre-law scholar like her older brother, Ryan? Or a gifted and talented math whiz like her little sister, Emily? It wasn't as though her grades weren't satisfactory. And she was working diligently toward her elementary teaching degree—a worthy, achievable goal if she didn't lose her momentum. A baby would change everything. How could she find time to study if she was caring for an infant?

Her mind flashed back to when Emily was born. So tiny. So perfect. So *demanding*. Each person in the family took turns holding her, feeding her, changing her, rocking her, and it seemed never ending.

Vanessa felt as if her lungs were in a vise and she couldn't breathe. She rolled down the windows and let the crisp January breeze flood her face. She took a slow, deep breath. And then another. And another.

She started the car, pulled onto College, and drove toward Chelsea Park. At least she had just been home for Christmas break, and her parents wouldn't be expecting to see her again for a while. That would give her time to think through her situation and make a decision.

Vanessa sat under a gigantic oak tree on the wrought-iron bench closest to the bandstand in Chelsea Park. Despite the biting north wind, she was uncomfortably warm and sticky under her wool peacoat.

She looked up just as Professor Tyson Nicholson got out of his yellow Corvette and strolled across the brown, crunchy lawn toward her. He waved, looking handsome in his tan London Fog and black trousers, his thick, dark hair a striking contrast to his reddish beard.

He hurried over to her and pressed his warm lips to her cheek, then sat next to her on the bench and warmed her hand with both of his.

"Sorry I'm late," he said. "I was with Professor Roberts. The man doesn't know how to end a conversation. What's up? You look stressed."

Vanessa felt robotic, almost as if someone had pushed a button to make her speak. "I've tried to think of an easy way to tell you this, but there isn't one … I'm pregnant." She stopped breathing.

The silence that followed seemed charged, like those seconds between a flash of lightning and the boom of thunder.

Ty leaned forward, his elbows resting on his knees, and combed his fingers through his hair. "How could this happen when we always used protection? Are you absolutely sure?"

"I just left Planned Parenthood. There's no question. I'm about eight weeks along. I'm as shocked as you are."

Ty's silence sent a chill crawling up her spine.

Finally he said, "Okay. What's done is done. Set up the abortion, and I'll pay for it. Let's get this out of the way."

Vanessa felt as if her tongue was a lead weight and her stomach was falling down an elevator shaft. That's it? Couldn't he at least *think* about it? Consider the options? Ask to hear her thoughts on the matter?

Ty slipped his arm around her. "You'll hardly skip a beat. Set it up for a Thursday or Friday and give yourself the weekend to recuperate." He put his lips to her ear. "It's the best solution, honey. You've got your education to think about. And I have to guard my reputation."

"Are you ashamed people will find out we're together?"

"This isn't about shame. You know how I feel about us. But we agreed to keep our relationship a secret as long as you're my student.

That's one issue. The other is I have zero interest in being a dad, now
or in the future. You know that. Why do you look surprised?"

Tears welled, and Vanessa couldn't see anything. "I-I don't know.
I guess I was hoping you might change your mind."

"I've been completely honest with you from day one. I live from
day to day. I'm just not into permanent."

"Does this mean you're breaking up with me?"

"What it *means*"—Ty cupped her cheek in his hand—"is that a
baby would require a permanent commitment that I have no interest
in and that you shouldn't even consider until you get your teaching
degree."

Vanessa realized she was shivering. "I'm not … I don't think …
I-I'm just not sure I can handle getting an abortion."

"Of course you can. You're an intelligent young woman. It's the
best option."

"It's the convenient option." Vanessa fiddled with the button on
her coat. "But it's not the only option. We have others."

"No, *we* don't. I'm sorry this happened, but under no
circumstances am I taking on the role of dad. And you're not
equipped to be a single mom."

"Abortion just seems wrong, especially when there are couples
waiting to adopt babies."

"Vanessa, honey, look at me." He tilted her chin, his evocative
brown eyes reaching to her very soul. "What's wrong is letting all that
religious nonsense you grew up with strong-arm you into carrying
this baby to term and then giving it up. I refuse to be a party to that.
There can't be any doubt in your mind how I feel about you. But if
you want us to be together, there's only *one* option."

Ty's pronouncement came like the clanging of cymbals and reverberated in her heart with stark finality.

Vanessa wiped the runaway tear that trickled down her cheek. She couldn't lose Ty. She just couldn't. She glanced up through the bare branches that swayed in the wind like bony hands applauding her demise and noticed that gray winter clouds had hidden the sun. A sense of utter desolation came over her, and she thought it fitting for one who was about to sell her soul to the devil.

CHAPTER 1

POLICE Chief Brill Jessup pored over the department's budget for the rest of the fiscal year and couldn't see any way she could afford to hire another patrol officer without going to the city council. She sighed. The last time she asked those tightwads for additional funds she practically had to beg.

A strange noise interrupted her thoughts. She peered through the blinds on the glass wall into the bustling detective bureau and listened intently. There it was again.

A burly man appeared in the doorway. He bumped off either side, then staggered into her office. Facedown. Hands dripping with blood, clutching his abdomen.

"What in the world …?" She jumped to her feet, frozen in place.

Detective Sean O'Toole looked up and stretched out his hand toward her, his eyes screaming with pain. He collapsed in front of her desk and hit the floor.

"Officer down!" she shouted. "I need an ambulance—now!"

She hurried around the side of her desk, grabbed the clean hand towel next to the coffeepot, and got down on her knees. She laid the towel over the bloody wound and applied pressure.

"Sean, talk to me. What happened?"

The detective's face was ashen. "He c-came from behind … put me in a choke hold … stuck a knife in my gut … said he was coming after you—to f-finish the job."

"You never saw his face?"

"No. Hairy arms. White guy. Navy blue short sleeves. Smelled like c-cigarettes. Deep voice."

"Where did this happen?"

"Hallway. Watercooler."

Sean moaned, his face pallid and contorted with pain, his eyes slits of icy blue.

"Come on, Sean, stay with me."

Detective Captain Trent Norris burst into her office. "I'll take it from here, Chief."

"How did he get from the watercooler to my office without someone in the DB seeing he needed help?"

"I guess we were all focused on other things. It's been crazy."

Trent got down on the floor and swapped places with her, his palms pressed over the wound. "Hang in there, buddy. The paramedics are just down the block. They'll be here any second. You're going to be fine. Stay with me. Talk to me."

Brill sprang to her feet and hurried over to the officers who crowded outside her door. "O'Toole was just stabbed by some lowlife who snuck up behind him at the water cooler. We're looking for a white man wearing a short-sleeve, navy blue shirt, possibly bloodstained."

She locked gazes with Sean's partner. "Detective Rousseaux, secure the scene and make sure it's not compromised.

"Captain Dickson, lock down the building and search every corner of every room.

"Sergeant Chavez, set up a containment for two blocks around the building.

"Sergeant Huntman, clear the route to St. Luke's and make sure we have officers in radio cars ready to escort the ambulance. Come on, people, move it!"

The officers scrambled in all directions, and she ran out to the restroom.

She tore off paper towels until she had a stack, folded them in half and held them under the faucet, then pressed out the excess water and rushed back to her office.

She got on her knees and gently pressed the wet towels onto Sean's forehead, all too aware he was sweating profusely and still bleeding despite the pressure Trent was keeping on the wound. "We need something to elevate his legs."

She went over to the bookshelf and grabbed several thick books and put them under Sean's feet, hoping he wouldn't die of shock before the paramedics arrived.

Lord, don't take him now. He's young. He's got a wife and three kids.

"Come on, buddy, talk to me." Trent patted Sean's cheeks. "What else do you remember about this creep?"

"Tell Jessica I love her. The kids, too. Promise me."

"You're not going to die," Trent said. "The bleeding's slowing down. Talk to me, Sean. We want whoever did this to you."

"He's coming after the chief. Going to kill her."

"Who's going to kill her?" Trent's dark eyes shot Brill a glance. "Give us something else. You're too sharp of a detective to have missed anything."

"Had a mark. Top of right hand."

"What kind of mark?"

"A tattoo. Or b-birthmark. Size of a quarter."

Brill heard voices and heavy footsteps in the DB, and seconds later two paramedics glided through the door and asked her to stand aside with Trent.

She observed in disbelief as the pair worked to save her detective's life, heartsick that she might have to tell his wife and children he'd been murdered on her watch—and just feet away from armed police officers.

She started to brush the hair out of her eyes and realized her hands were bloody. She shuddered with the realization that whoever thrust a knife into Sean O'Toole had threatened to finish the job when he got to her.

Five hours later Brill sat at the conference table in her office with Detective Captain Trent Norris, Detective Beau Jack Rousseaux, Patrol Captain Pate Dickson, and Sheriff Sam Parker trying to assess where they were in the case.

"It's a miracle Sean made it through surgery." Brill looked from man to man. "We could be sitting here planning his funeral."

"He's too stubborn to die," Beau Jack said.

"Stubborn's no match for a knife blade, Detective. I want this animal locked up."

"Don't forget he threatened to come after you," Trent said. "How'd he get in here, anyway?"

Pate's face turned pink. "One of my sergeants, Tiller, reported that a white man dressed in navy blue coveralls with the Miller's Air Conditioning logo on the pocket was standing outside the door when he arrived this morning. The guy said he was here to fix the AC. He had a toolbox and a big smile. Dark hair and mustache. Big guy. Looked fifty to fifty-five."

"So the sergeant just keyed in the combination and let him in without checking with maintenance?" Beau Jack said. "Real smart move."

Pate stroked his chin. "Come on, Miller's service people are in here all the time. The sergeant let down his guard. We've all done it."

"Yeah, well, my partner nearly died because Sergeant Tiller let down his guard."

"What's done is done," Brill said. "It's not like we have a precedent for this kind of thing in the Sophie Trace PD."

Beau Jack stuck a Tootsie Pop in his mouth. "I guess we do now."

"We definitely need to tighten security," Trent said. "Since we have no idea who this guy is, everyone we bring into the DB to be interviewed will be suspect."

"I can't spend the rest of my life in fear of this nutcase coming after me," Brill said. "I have a job to do. Trent, you take charge of tightening security. All of us need to heighten our awareness of our surroundings. Anything or anyone that doesn't feel right, check it out."

Sam's white eyebrows came together. "I can't believe y'all were that trusting. My deputies would never let unauthorized individuals into a secured area. They're trained to follow protocol."

"So are my officers." Brill forced herself not to sound defensive. "But those of you in the county sheriff's department deal with a broader range of criminals. Until now, the Sophie Trace PD had no reason to fear an officer being attacked in a secured area."

"I'll cover it in each briefing," Trent said. "From this day forward, no one gets in the secured area until he has clearance. I don't care how inconvenient it is to check him out."

Brill looked over at Pate. "Tell me about your search of the building."

"No evidence was found in the building, ma'am. My officers searched every nook and cranny and checked the sinks for hair and blood. Doesn't appear the attacker stopped to clean up."

"How'd Chavez do with the containment?" she said.

"He contained a two-block area around city hall, checked license plates, and talked with pedestrians. That yielded one female witness who passed the suspect on the sidewalk around 10:45—just after O'Toole was stabbed. The suspect was headed down First Street at a pretty good clip. Our witness says he was overweight, average height, dressed in navy blue coveralls and a black windbreaker and carrying a gray toolbox. She said he was wearing sunglasses and did *not* have a mustache. She's working with Tiller and our sketch artist. We ought to have something soon."

"Did she see which way he went?" Trent said.

Pate shook his head. "Once he passed her, she didn't give him a second thought until Chavez questioned her."

"Well," Brill said, "I'm eager to see the sketch. If this man has threatened to come after me, I'd sure like to see if I recognize him."

A short time later, Brill sat at her desk and studied the artist's sketch of the man who stabbed Sean O'Toole. Sergeant Tiller was the only one who saw the suspect's eyes, and the female witness was the only one who saw his mouth without the mustache. He looked vaguely familiar, but she couldn't put a name to the face or even explain what it was about him that looked familiar.

Her cell phone vibrated, and she read the display screen.

"There you are," she said. "I guess you got my message?"

"Honey, I'm so sorry," Kurt Jessup said. "I've been following the news. I'm glad Sean pulled through. Must've been horrible for you."

"I thought we were going to lose him."

She told Kurt everything that had happened from the time Sean O'Toole staggered into her office until the paramedics took him to St. Luke's in an ambulance—except that the assailant told O'Toole he was coming after her to "finish the job." Why get into that over the phone?

"Sounds intense. You must be emotionally drained."

"I don't think it's caught up with me yet. It was surreal washing Sean's blood off my hands, and I had to throw away my uniform shirt. Beau Jack lent me the extra shirt he had in his locker so Emily wouldn't have to see the mess. Does she know about the stabbing?"

"Yes, but I made sure she's not planted in front of the TV, listening to the gory details. It'll just trigger thoughts of the hostage ordeal, and we both know she's not over it."

Are any of us? Brill glanced up at the clock. "I'll be home in forty-five minutes. Is Vanessa there yet? I can hardly wait to see her."

"She'll be here between seven and eight. Said not to plan on her for dinner."

"By the time I get home, it'll be too late to cook anything," Brill said. "And you know what Friday night is like. If we go out, we'll have to wait forever, and I don't want Vanessa to come home to an empty house."

"I've got it covered, honey. I bought a baked chicken and a quart of potato salad at the grocery store. We've got stuff here for a green salad. That should work."

"What would I do without you?"

Kurt laughed. "I have no idea."

"I'll see you soon. I love you."

"Love you, too."

Brill hung up the phone and looked out the window. Through the leafy trees and beyond the ridges of hazy green foothills, the blue gray silhouette of the Great Smoky Mountains dominated the early evening sky. She sat for a moment and just enjoyed the beauty and the calm.

Lord, thank You for letting Sean pull through.

Her office phone rang, and she picked it up. "Yes, LaTeesha."

"Captain Donovan from the Memphis PD is on line one for you."

"Thanks." She pushed the blinking button. "Hello, John."

"Hey. It's great to hear your voice. Saw you on the news last fall. I figured you'd make a name for yourself, but I didn't think you'd go to such extreme measures."

She smiled. "Things got pretty crazy, all right. So are you enjoying my old office?"

"Not today. I've got bad news … Zack Rogers was stabbed night before last. Happened in his driveway. Some worthless piece of garbage came up behind him and stuck a knife in his gut, and said to tell District Attorney Cromwell he was coming after him. I didn't call you because the doc said Zack was going to be all right. But his heart gave out …"—John's voice cracked—"an hour ago. No one saw it coming. His kids are still in high school, and with their mother dead … well, it's a tragic loss. I knew you'd want to know since you and Zack were partners for so long."

Brill felt a wave of nausea sweep over her, a decade of memories flashing through her mind in an instant.

"The thing is," John said, "we knew Zack was being targeted because one of my detectives was stabbed last week, and the perp told him he was coming after Zack. We offered Zack protection, but you know how independent he was—bound and determined he could take care of himself."

Brill's heart pounded so hard she was sure he could hear it. "John, one of *my* detectives was stabbed today just outside the detective bureau. The attacker told him he was coming after me, to finish the job. This can't be a coincidence."

There was a long moment of dead air, and she figured John was processing the implications.

"You and Zack helped put away lots of perps, Brill. And Jason Cromwell was district attorney during the time you two were partners. Did anybody ever threaten you?"

"Are you kidding? All the time. We blew it off."

"Well, looks like one of them was dead serious. Anybody in particular stand out?"

"Sure, Bart and Sampson Rhodes. But they're lifers and not eligible for parole. Zack and I busted them what, nine or ten years ago? If they had been serious about taking us out, they could've snapped their fingers and gotten it done in nine or ten *minutes*."

"Maybe they're patient,"

"Or maybe this is someone else," Brill said. "Someone who was forced to wait a long time for the chance to get even—someone who served out his sentence. Someone who wouldn't think of hiring a hit man, but rather delights in the systematic elimination of the people who put him away. Someone who enhances his enjoyment by first stabbing a person who is close to the intended victim and making sure that person lives long enough to tell the intended victim that he or she is next."

"You've worked with the FBI profilers so long you actually sound like one."

"Unfortunately, John, I think I'm right."

CHAPTER 2

BRILL Jessup combed her hair with her fingers, pinched her cheeks, then pushed open the front door of her home, the pleasing fragrance of flowers wafting under her nose. She came inside, chagrined to see blood drops on her shoes. How had she missed that?

Kurt came out of the kitchen and pulled her into his arms, his longer-than-usual embrace saying more than words could have.

"It's great to be home," she finally said. "What a horrible day."

"Hi, Mom."

Emily Jessup skipped down the stairs and ran over to her mother, her ponytail swaying, and threw her arms around her waist.

"I made up Vanessa's bed and opened the window so her room would air out, and I borrowed three of the flowers Dad got you and put them in a bud vase. I even put a square of chocolate on her pillow like they did at the hotel we stayed in with Grammy and Poppy."

Brill pushed back and memorized the joyful expression on Emily's face. "Where did you get a square of chocolate?"

"Well, it's really just a Hershey kiss. But she'll get the idea."

Brill stroked her baby's cheek and realized how fast she was growing up. "Vanessa will be tickled you went to all this trouble."

"I made the salad for dinner," Emily said. "And we get to have that yummy bread Tessa made us."

Kurt smiled. "She just brought it over. It's still warm."

"She is *the* most thoughtful neighbor. I'm starved. Things were so hectic down at the station that I forgot to eat."

"Come on, Chief. The table's set and we're ready to go."

Kurt put his arm around her and walked her into the kitchen.

Brill noticed the blood drops on her shoes again and had a flashback of kneeling on the floor, pushing with all her might on Sean O'Toole's midsection, trying to stop the bleeding and thinking he was going to die. She would have to pick a time to tell Kurt about the threat on her life. But not before they had time to rejoice in Vanessa's coming home for the summer.

"She's here!"

Brill smiled as Emily brushed past her, pulled open the front door, and raced out to the driveway.

Brill took Kurt's hand and stepped outside on the stoop, surprised to see a young man in the driver's seat of Vanessa's car. "Well, well. She's not alone."

Kurt curled his lip. "Why didn't Vanessa mention she was dating someone? I'm not ready for her to bring some guy home to meet us."

"She's twenty years old. You and I were practically engaged at her age."

"Why did I feel older than she looks?"

"Because she's your little girl. Come on, let's go see if we can help her bring her things in."

Brill walked over to the car, her heart pounding, and looked at Vanessa's face through the window. She'd grown her hair longer since Christmas. She looked radiant.

The car door opened, and Vanessa slowly climbed out and then stood up straight, her cheeks flushed, her belly ... *round*. She lifted her eyes and looked nervously from Brill to Kurt to Emily and back to Brill.

"Hi, everybody."

The young man got out of the car, and Brill grabbed Kurt's arm and squeezed before he could take a step. "Don't."

Emily looked questioningly at Vanessa, then gingerly placed her hands on her big sister's protuberance. "You're having a *baby*?"

Vanessa glanced at her parents sheepishly.

Brill studied the size of her daughter's bulging middle and said, "In the not-too-distant future, I gather."

"My due date is July twenty-eighth."

Brill felt every ounce of excitement drain from her heart, as though someone had pulled the plug on her hopes and dreams for Vanessa. She felt at the same time cheated, deceived, and strangely terrified. She moved her gaze to the young man who stood leaning on the open driver's side door.

"Are you the baby's father?" she asked.

Brill could tell by Kurt's tight grip on her hand that he was exercising great restraint.

"No. I'm Ethan Langley, a friend of Vanessa's from college."

The nice-looking young man with a-little-too-long, dark, curly hair and round glasses came over and stood next to Vanessa, offering Kurt his hand.

"I didn't think she should drive all that way by herself. I live in Maryville and thought I'd take the bus home from here. My aunt and uncle live just across town. I can stay with them tonight."

"Hey," Emily said. "If Vanessa's having a baby, does that mean I'll be a sister-in-law?"

"No, silly." Vanessa took her index finger and tapped her sister on the nose. "You're going to be an aunt."

Emily seemed to be processing, and then a grin slowly stole over her face. "Like on *Wizard of Oz*. Auntie Em. Auntie Em."

"Well, now we know the *real* reason you didn't come home for spring break," Brill said flatly. "It's unconscionable that you kept this from us for seven months. You think this isn't going to affect *us*?"

"There never seemed to be a right time."

"You deceived us, Vanessa."

"I'm sorry. I didn't want to disappoint you." Vanessa's eyes brimmed with tears. "I kept thinking I would wake up one day and it would all be a bad dream."

"Let's go inside," Kurt said. "We can get your things later."

"I should go." Ethan turned and hugged Vanessa. "I'll get my stuff out of the car tomorrow. If you need me for anything, call my cell."

Vanessa nodded.

"Nice to meet all of you." Ethan pushed his glasses higher on his nose. "I hope next time it will be under more relaxed circumstances."

As Ethan slipped on his backpack and jogged across the street and toward downtown, the four Jessups stood motionless, as if their feet were cemented to the ground.

"So who *is* the father?" Kurt finally said.

"Someone I loved with all my heart." Vanessa's eyes were blue pools. "He didn't want the baby. He said if we were going to stay together, I had to end the pregnancy. I couldn't do that. I just couldn't." She wiped the tears off her cheeks.

"What's the guy's name?" Kurt said.

"Tyson Nicholson. He was my psychology professor. We agreed not to tell anyone because he was faculty and I was a student."

"How *old* is this guy?"

"Thirty … nine."

Kurt rolled his eyes. "For crying out loud, Vanessa."

"He has an *obligation* to help you financially," Brill said.

"Ty moved and didn't leave a forwarding address. I checked with the post office."

"I'm sure the university knows where he is."

Vanessa stared at her hands. "A month ago, we suddenly had a substitute psychology professor. No one gave us an explanation, other than 'Professor Nicholson is no longer with us.' Ethan convinced me to go to the dean and explain my situation. I did, but he couldn't help me. He said that Ty had left without giving notice or a forwarding address. I could tell he was really disgusted."

"Nicholson can kiss his career good-bye," Kurt said. "No university is going to hire him after he acted so irresponsibly."

Vanessa's lower lip quivered. "I'm sorry I couldn't get up the courage to tell you about the baby till now. I thought the least I could do was finish out the school year and try to make passing grades so I wouldn't waste the tuition money." Vanessa put her face in her hands. "Please help me get my life straightened out. Everything's such a mess. I've never felt so lost."

Kurt pulled her into his arms, Vanessa quietly sobbing.

Brill looked out at the mountains and swallowed the emotion that tightened her throat. She didn't dare let her emotions rule her head while there was someone out there who wanted to kill her.

Brill sat at the kitchen table with Kurt and both daughters, trying not to look as devastated as she felt and wanting to get this confrontation over with.

"Emily, why don't you go read your book and let us talk to Vanessa?" Brill said.

"Why can't I stay?"

"Because this is an adult matter."

"But I already know everything."

Kurt tilted her chin. "You're very grown up for ten. But what we want to talk to Vanessa about is her business, and she can decide who she wants to tell and who she doesn't."

"I'll be glad when everyone doesn't think I'm a big baby."

Vanessa reached over and gave Emily's ponytail an affectionate tug. "You won't be the baby much longer."

As Emily left the kitchen, Brill's mind flashed back to when she was pregnant with Emily and Vanessa was the ten-year-old.

The room was suddenly uncomfortably quiet.

"I don't have to tell you how shocked and disappointed we are," Brill said. "I'll spare you the lecture. I'm sure you've already beat yourself up."

Vanessa avoided eye contact. "I can imagine what's going through your minds, but I want you to know that what happened between Ty and me was special. We really loved each other."

"If you felt that way," Brill said, "why did you keep it from us?"

"I told you, we couldn't make it public because he was a professor and I was a student."

"And you knew it was wrong." Brill looked into her daughter's eyes. "Vanessa, he used you. You're a beautiful, desirable young woman. If this man *loved* you, he wouldn't have abandoned you because you couldn't destroy the child you made together."

Kurt gently squeezed Brill's arm, and she stopped talking and let him have his say.

"Vanessa, I certainly can't talk to you as if *I've* done everything right." Kurt's face turned bright pink, and he reached over and took Brill's hand. "But I can tell you there *are* consequences when we choose not to abide by the laws God's put in place for our protection. I love you, and it hurts me that you're already experiencing some of those consequences. Your mother and I will help you any way we can. But it's not going to be easy."

"Since you have no way to support the baby," Brill said, "I assume you're leaning toward adoption?"

Vanessa took a lock of hair and twisted it around her finger. "Actually … I'm thinking seriously about keeping him. I know I have two more years of college to get behind me," she added quickly, "and keeping him will require sacrifices. But I'll find a way to do it."

"With what, honey?" Kurt said. "Do you know how much it costs to raise a child?"

"No, but I'm not the first mother to keep her baby."

"You know for sure it's a boy?"

Vanessa nodded, her hands massaging her round abdomen. "I saw the ultrasound." She smiled, and her whole face lit up. "I saw him kick. I think he knows my voice."

"You're no more equipped to raise a child right now than I am." Brill sighed. "Honey, think long term. Raising a child is an enormous responsibility. Once he's yours, there's no turning back. You've got your entire future ahead of you. There are hundreds of childless couples that would give anything for a chance to raise this baby. I don't want you to rule out adoption without careful consideration."

"I haven't ruled out anything, Mom." Vanessa hugged her belly. "But no one could love him more than I do. You've always said where there's a will, there's a way."

"Yes, but this isn't just about *you*. It's about what's best for that little boy and what kind of a life you can offer him. Do you have any idea what it's like to struggle to make ends meet month after month after month?"

"No, but you and Dad did it when you had me and Ryan thirteen months apart."

"There were *two* of us helping. Doing it alone is different."

"Your mom has a point," Kurt said. "Raising a child is hard work. It can be tough for a single parent."

Vanessa's eyes brimmed with tears, and she shook her head. "I'm not ready to have this discussion. We're talking about my *son*. I know I could give him up for adoption and make some couple very happy. I'm sure they'd love him. But I *already* love him."

Brill brushed the hair out of Vanessa's eyes. "What in the world were you and this man thinking? Didn't you ever consider you might get pregnant?"

"No. We took precautions." A tear spilled down Vanessa's cheek. "This shouldn't have happened. But it did. And *it* is a little boy that I don't want to grow up wondering if his mother loved him."

"Adoptive parents stay in touch with birth parents these days," Brill said. "You would always know how he's doing. And he would always know the sacrifice you made in allowing him to be adopted."

Vanessa put her hands over her ears. "I can't listen to this right now."

"Look, why don't we all sleep on it"—Kurt reached over and took Vanessa's hand—"and let the magnitude sink in. There's a lot to consider, and we've still got plenty of time. It's a huge decision, and we really need to pray about it. We didn't plan on this child, but he's no surprise to God. And God's the one we need to turn to for direction."

Vanessa nodded.

Brill wondered if she'd ever seen her daughter so adamant, and for the first time it occurred to her that this child she was so quick to dismiss was also her grandson.

Brill turned out the light in the bathroom and climbed into bed and into Kurt's waiting arms, her back against his chest. Was she ready to hit him with a second whammy?

Neither of them said anything for a long time.

"How could I not have known?" Kurt finally said.

"A fairer question might be, 'How could Vanessa have deceived us?'"

Kurt pulled her closer, and she could feel his warm breath on her neck. "I should've known something was wrong when she didn't come home for spring break. I should've pursued it."

"We *did*. Vanessa never gave us any reason to doubt that she was going to stay on campus and work on a research paper. It made sense. She'd been struggling to keep her grades up. We didn't know she was seeing anyone. Why don't you seem the least bit angry with her?"

"It'll probably hit me later." He stroked her hair. "At the moment, I'm scared to death for Vanessa, and for us. She seems set on keeping this baby. And she sure doesn't have the resources to support a child—not without us. I don't know about you, but I'm not too hot on the idea of having a baby around the house twenty-four/seven. I'm too old to start over."

"I couldn't agree more. But we have something else to pray about that's even more imminent. I debated on the timing, but I think you need to know now. The man that stabbed Sean O'Toole threatened to come after me."

She turned over and looked into Kurt's eyes, which were wide in the light of the moon shining through the window.

"He already got to Zack Rogers."

"*What?*"

"Zack died today."

She told Kurt every detail of her phone call from Captain John Donovan of the Memphis PD.

"I can't believe this," Kurt said. "Zack's *dead?*"

"John thinks the killer's someone Zack and I collared and helped convict. I agree. But over the course of ten years, we put away a lot of criminals."

"Tell me again why he went after O'Toole?"

"Probably for kicks … so O'Toole would make sure I knew he was coming after *me*."

"Good grief, Brill. Can't you get some kind of protection?"

"Yes. I'm not going to make the same mistake Zack did. I've got officers outside, watching the house. And we've stepped up security at city hall. We just need to figure out who he is and lock him up." *Before he can strike again.*

CHAPTER 3

THE next morning, Brill sat at the conference table in her office with Trent Norris, Beau Jack Rousseaux, Pate Dickson, and Sheriff Sam Parker, finishing up her briefing on yesterday afternoon's disturbing phone conversation with Captain Donovan from the Memphis PD.

"Now that we've established the perp's motive is to get to me and DA Cromwell," she said, "let's make it impossible for him to do that. The Memphis PD will do their part to protect Cromwell. And this department, along with Sheriff Parker's deputies, will do everything in our power to ensure that this vicious cop killer can't penetrate our defenses."

"He won't, Chief," Trent said. "Not as long as I have anything to say about it."

"I appreciate your confidence, though I can't stress strongly enough that each officer needs to be on high alert regarding his or her own personal safety. I don't want anyone else getting hurt because of this man's quest to get to me."

"We're going to need more manpower," Trent said.

"Sam's offered to provide deputies to beef up security for the city offices in this building and maintain a visible law enforcement presence in the area. This will enable the Sophie Trace PD to function at full capacity."

Sam flashed a patronizing grin.

"In the meantime," Brill continued, "Captain Donovan is pulling together all branches of law enforcement in the Memphis area to help go through old case files that involved me, my former partner, and the former district attorney. We put away a lot of dangerous criminals when I was working vice back in the nineties. This could be someone newly released from prison that wants to get even."

"Don't we have the security camera footage from yesterday?" Trent said.

"We do. We're going to review it with Sergeant Tiller and our female witness in hopes we might get a good look at our cop killer. I'm sure each of you shares my outrage and absolute commitment to getting this scumbag, no matter what it takes. Let's show him what happens when he brings a knife to a gunfight. Any questions?"

Sam Parker puffed out his chest and leaned forward, a manufactured grin exposing a gold tooth. "Since the time you stepped into this position, Chief Jessup, my deputies and I have spent a disproportionate amount of the county's time assistin' y'all. Of course, there have been unprecedented circumstances. And we are only too glad to be of assistance."

In other words, the "little lady" is no match for the big boys. She held Sam's gaze and didn't react. What she wouldn't give to wipe that obnoxious grin off his face. Nothing she said or did, not even her stellar career on the Memphis PD, was going to make him change his sexist view of a female police chief. Why give him the satisfaction of knowing he'd annoyed her?

She folded her hands on the table and smiled graciously. "Thank you, Sheriff. I think I speak for every officer in my department when I say we are truly grateful for your assistance."

Trent looked down at the table, almost as if he were reading her mind.

"All right, then. If there are no questions, let's go to work. Trent, would you mind staying for a minute?"

Brill got up and walked the others to the door, then went back and sat at the table across from Trent, his bright smile a striking contrast to his dark skin.

"What's so funny?" she said, and then burst into laughter at the same time he did.

"You handled that starchy redneck better than I would've, Chief. I'm not sure I could take that hit without firing back."

"Sure you could've. You've turned a deaf ear to racial overtones from Sheriff Parker that were more demeaning that his 'little woman' inferences. But as condescending as Sam can be, I can't think of anyone else outside this department that I would trust to cover our backs. He'll do a thorough job, if for no other reason than to get the credit."

"Good point. But I don't mind telling you that I'm feeling extremely protective right now. I was totally caught off guard by what happened to Sean. There's no way I'm letting this guy get to you."

"I appreciate that, Trent, but don't forget you're at risk too—maybe more than anyone else in the department because you're my right-hand man. This perp has already attacked two officers on the Memphis PD and hasn't gone after the DA yet. It's hard to say what his next move will be. We know that yesterday, at least, he was on *this* side of the state."

Vanessa Jessup sat at the kitchen table with Emily and her dad, finishing up breakfast and trying to come to grips with the shocking
threat on her mother's life.

"I wish Mom would get out of police work," Vanessa said. "After
what that nutcase put Emily through, I know bad things *can* happen
to anyone."

"As I already explained to Emily"—Kurt handed her the jelly—
"your mother has her entire police force and the sheriff's department
protecting her. They weren't expecting what happened yesterday.
Now they're ready for anything."

"Well, Mom even had the FBI on her side last time, and that
didn't stop the guy."

Vanessa felt a kick under the table and lifted her eyes. Her dad
had a let's-change-this-conversation look on his face.

"Seems kind of weird having deputies parked across the street,"
Emily said. "But I'm glad."

Kurt nodded. "Me, too. Just to be on the safe side."

Emily craned and peered outside, an orange-juice mustache
framing her mouth. "It's so cool they're just in a regular car. Like on
TV. Dad, do you have to work today?"

"No way. I closed the door to my office, didn't you notice? All
five of my stores are open, but I'm taking off the entire Memorial
Day weekend."

"That's a first," Vanessa said. "Is Mom?"

"She's probably not going to take off until she gets the guy who
stabbed Detective O'Toole. And her former partner."

Emily stuck out her lower lip. "That means we don't get to go anywhere or do anything fun for Memorial Day."

"That's not true," Kurt said. "We could drive over to Gatlinburg and surprise your brother."

"Tell me again what his job is." Emily popped the last of a bagel into her mouth.

"He's the assistant manager of a restaurant called the Whistlin' Dixie. He gets to stay in the apartment upstairs for free and save the money he makes for a trip to Costa Rica after he graduates next year."

"Ryan told me they serve awesome ribs," Vanessa said, "and have really great jazz music. I'd love to see it."

"I hate going without your mom, but she'd probably rather we didn't just sit around over the long weekend anyway. It's supposed to rain today, and we've got church tomorrow. Monday's supposed to be sunny. Why don't we plan to go then?"

"Hurray!" Emily said. "I'll wear my new pink crop pants and my sandals with the jewels on the straps. And Vanessa can give me a pedicure and paint my toenails. She knows how to get the color on perfectly."

Kurt opened his phone and seemed to be studying his calendar. "If I stop at the SpeedWay store in Pigeon Forge and check on my manager, I could write off most of the mileage. That'd sure save on gas."

Emily sat back in her chair and let out a dramatic sigh. "You'll talk and talk and we'll never get to have any fun."

"I'll only need an hour. You can give Vanessa a demonstration of what the new color printer can do. Afterwards, we can find a fun place to have lunch, play some miniature golf, let you girls do some shopping. Then we'll drive into Gatlinburg and have dinner at the Whistlin' Dixie. How's that sound?"

Vanessa smiled. "Great."

Kurt's eyebrows came together. "That was an easy sell. I guess that means your brother already knows you're pregnant."

Vanessa looked at her hands. She might as well get this over with. "Don't be mad, but I talked to Ryan when Ty and I broke up. He insisted I tell you and Mom everything," she quickly added, "but I made him promise to let me do it when I got up the nerve."

"It just hurts me that you didn't think you could come to us."

"You and Mom were just getting back together," she said. "I didn't think you needed a new family problem to deal with."

"Nice try, Vanessa. But we've already established the real reason."

"All right, I'm a coward. I didn't want to disappoint you. And yet"—her eyes filled with tears—"I'm the kid who always *does*."

Her dad put his hand on hers. "I love you, honey. I have no trouble making the distinction between you and the mistakes you've made."

Vanessa wiped the tear off her cheek. "That's why I love you so much."

Kurt's cell phone rang and he glanced at the number. "It's one of the deputies who's watching the house. I'd better answer it." He put the phone to his ear. "This is Kurt … what's his name … ? All right, hang on."

Kurt looked out the kitchen window. "Yeah, that's Ethan. I'll let him in."

Brill stood at the window in her office, her hands clasped behind her back, and looked out at the dark, rolling bank of clouds that had formed a shroud over the Great Smoky Mountains. How fitting it seemed that this day should be gloomy. Everything about it felt dark. She could reconcile being on someone's hit list easier than the fact that Vanessa had kept her pregnancy a secret from her family for seven months.

She heard a knock at her door and jumped, her hand over her heart. She composed herself and turned around, a smile pasted on.

"It's just me," Trent said. "I'm planning to go to Nick's Grill and meet my wife for lunch at eleven. Can I bring you back a veggie burger and some sweet potato fries?"

"I'd appreciate that. Thanks."

"You okay?"

"No." Brill leaned against the window. "But it's not because someone's out to get me. Vanessa dropped a bomb on us last night."

"So she made it home okay?"

"Yes, seven months pregnant. I've never been so shocked in my life."

Trent's face went blank. "Wow. She never gave you a hint?"

"Not really. She didn't come home for spring break. Said she was working on a research paper. Her grades were slipping. We had no reason to doubt her."

"What reason did she give for waiting so long to tell you?"

Brill already wished she hadn't said anything. Why did she want Trent knowing something this private?

"Hey, it's none of my business," he said. "I just hate to see you stuff your emotions."

"Is that what I'm doing?"

"Takes one to know one. I just thought it might help to talk."

Brill looked into Trent's eyes and saw genuine caring. He was going to find out soon enough. "Vanessa said she dreaded disappointing us. It took her this long to get up the courage to tell us."

"Well, you can imagine how hard it must be for a girl from a strong Christian family to face her parents with something like this."

"Yeah, well … it gets worse. The father is her thirty-nine-year-old psychology professor."

"Whoa. What does he have to say for himself?"

"Oh, the plot gets thicker," Brill said. "He walked away from his job at the university a month ago without giving notice and with no forwarding address. No one knows where he is. So Vanessa is not only emotionally devastated, she has no financial help."

Trent sighed. "So what happens now?"

"Kurt and I suggested adoption. She got teary and said she wasn't ready for that conversation. Well, she'd better *get* ready with only two months left."

"Maybe she doesn't want to give it up."

"That's what I'm afraid of. She saw the baby kick during the ultrasound and already refers to him as her son." Brill brushed the hair out of her eyes. "It's like she's convinced she can keep him and they'll both live happily ever after."

"Stranger things have happened."

"You sound like you're siding with her."

Trent folded his arms. "Aren't we *all* on her side?"

"Of course we are. I can't be objective at the moment. All my hopes and dreams for my beautiful daughter are down the toilet."

"Yeah, that's a tough one."

Brill looked down at the cars parked at the meters. "Call me old-fashioned, but I always imagined the boyfriend coming to ask for her hand. Kurt walking her down the aisle. Vanessa radiant in a white dress and her grandmother's diamond pendant. The handsome prince waiting at the altar."

"No one can blame you for having a dream. But I guess this is where you go to Plan B."

Brill swallowed the emotion that threatened to steal her composure. "What Plan B? For heaven's sake, we didn't even know she was seeing anyone, let alone sleeping with him."

There was a flash of lightning and then a loud boom of thunder that shook the building and reverberated for what seemed like a quarter of a minute. The rain began to fall and then fall harder, blowing in sheets against the window until it was hard to see out.

"I didn't intend to dump on you," Brill said. "It's just that I've been hit all at once with Sean's stabbing, Zack's death, the threat against me, and now the crisis with Vanessa. I'm not even sure what I'm supposed to feel."

"Maybe you just need to feel whatever you feel and not try to analyze it."

"You're probably right. I tend to work problems to death. Listen … I'd appreciate it if you'd keep this to yourself for now."

"Sure, no problem. I'm here if you need to vent."

Implode is more like it.

CHAPTER 4

VANESSA took Ethan's hand, pulled him into her parents' house, and closed the front door.

"What's with the cops giving me the third degree?"

Vanessa glanced out the window at the officers getting back into the unmarked car parked across the street. "You can't say anything, but the guy who stabbed that detective yesterday also threatened my mom. They're trying to keep it quiet, but someone will probably leak it to the press. They always do."

"You okay?"

Vanessa nodded. "Come out to the kitchen. You want something cold to drink? We've got Coke, Diet Dr Pepper, green tea, and bottled water."

"Water's fine, thanks."

She reached into the refrigerator, took out two bottles of water, and handed one to Ethan, then sat across from him at the table.

"How'd it go after I left?"

"My folks and I had a serious discussion." She took a sip of water, and then told Ethan about the previous night's conversation with her parents.

"I didn't hear a plan in all that."

"I haven't really decided anything." She sighed. "I can tell they want me to put the baby up for adoption."

"Did you tell them which way you're leaning?"

"Kind of. I didn't push very hard since things were so tense. But they got the idea." She put her hand on his. "Thanks again for driving me home. I was really dreading facing my parents alone."

"No problem. I enjoyed talking with you. And I'm glad if my being there helped."

"It did. But my parents were much calmer than I expected."

"It's obvious they care a lot about you."

"I know. Did you come to get your things out of the car?"

Ethan took a sip of water. "Yeah, my bus doesn't leave till five. I wanted to see how you were doing first."

"I'm okay."

He seemed to study her, and then said, "You're better than okay. You are *the* most beautiful pregnant woman I've ever seen."

Vanessa rolled her eyes.

"I'm serious. Your skin is flawless … and those gorgeous blue eyes and that dark, shiny hair … you're awesome."

"Ethan, I look like a hippo."

"An incredibly *stunning* hippo."

They both laughed.

"I happen to think pregnant is beautiful," he said.

"I'm not sure I share your enthusiasm for the *look,* but it is amazing carrying this little life inside me. I can't imagine letting someone else raise him."

"Then stand your ground. Don't agree to anything you're not absolutely sure about."

"How can I be absolutely sure about anything right now?" She looked out the window. "This is the biggest decision of my entire life, and I honestly don't know what's the right thing to do."

"Maybe all your options are right, and it's just a matter of picking the one that works best for you."

Vanessa looked over at the young man whose admiring brown eyes made her squirm. "Is it selfish for me to want to raise my son?"

"I think 'selfish' is an unfair label to slap on a mother who doesn't want to part with her own flesh and blood."

"But I can't offer him any of the advantages his adoptive parents could."

"You're his mother. That says a lot. And you don't know that you won't get married down the road."

"Down the road could be a long time." She put her hand on her middle and felt the baby move.

"Is he kicking?"

"Like a punter. Come feel."

Ethan came around the table, and she put his hand on her tummy. A smile spread across his face, and he laughed like a little boy holding a lightning bug for the first time. "Wow. That is so incredible."

"It is, isn't it?"

"Too bad Professor Nicholson is such a deadbeat. You deserve better."

"I keep hoping he'll come back," she said.

"Any man who took off like that should make you nervous. Would you marry him, if he asked you?"

"I don't know. I still love him. I keep trying to talk myself out of how I feel."

"The guy's too old for you—"

Her father came into the kitchen and took a Coke out of the fridge. "So are you headed to Maryville?"

"Yes, sir. My bus leaves at five. I came to get my things out of Vanessa's car." He glanced at his watch. "I should probably hit the road."

"You don't have to rush off," Vanessa said.

"I should go before it starts raining again. I have to transfer everything to my uncle's car, get it to the house, and pack it for the bus ride."

"I'll bet your parents will be glad to see you."

"Yeah, it works both ways."

Vanessa steadied herself with the table and rose to her feet. "Why don't I walk you out so the cops on stakeout won't have a stroke?"

"Hey, be glad they're out there," Kurt said. "The threat to your mother is no joke."

Later that afternoon, Brill and Trent trudged down the east corridor of St. Luke's Hospital, their wet shoes squeaking on the tile, rain dripping off their jackets, and stopped at room 109.

Officer Rick Ulman was standing at the door and flashed a big smile. "Detective O'Toole will be glad to see you."

Trent rapped on the door. "Sean, it's me. The chief's with me. Okay to come in?"

"Come," said a raspy voice.

Brill followed Trent into the private room and went over to the bed where Sean lay hooked up to two IVs, one filled with clear liquid and the other with blood. He was also hooked up to a machine that digitally displayed his vital signs and another that gave him oxygen.

"How're you feeling?"

"Like a puppet." Sean held up one hand and the tube with it. "Good thing I'm … not going anywhere."

"How's the pain level?"

"Morphine took the edge off. By the way, Chief … I apologize for *dropping in* … on you that way." Sean started to smile and then winced instead. "Did you find out anything … on the scuzz who knifed me?"

"We don't have an ID, but we think we're dealing with the same perp that stabbed my former partner, Zack Rogers, on Wednesday night." Brill ran her finger along the bedrail. "Zack died yesterday of a heart attack."

She told Sean about her phone conversation with Captain Donovan and explained how the Sophie Trace PD and county sheriff's department had beefed up security.

"This spineless coward has stabbed three cops," she said. "We aren't going to let him get to anyone else."

Sean nodded, more with his eyes than his head. "Good. Nobody needs this."

"And don't worry about work," Trent said. "Beau Jack and I have got you covered. Just concentrate on getting back on your feet—and not *too* soon."

"Now you sound like … my wife."

Trent laughed. "So listen in stereo. Maybe it'll sink in."

Sean seemed far away for a few moments as if he were about to nod off, and then moved his gaze to Brill. "I'm sorry about Zack. How long were you partners?"

"Ten years. Five before I became pregnant with Emily. And five after she was born." Brill smiled without meaning to. "Zack was so proud of me when I got promoted to detective captain. He was as qualified as I was but couldn't say enough to support me. I got assigned to another precinct, but we stayed in touch. I got a birthday card from him just last month. I don't think it's hit me yet that he's dead."

"Tough break, Chief."

"The real victims are his son and daughter," she said. "They're still in high school, and their mother died of ovarian cancer five years ago. I *really* want to get this guy, lock him up, and throw away the key."

A male nurse came into the room and opened a cabinet that had all sizes of what appeared to be prepackaged bandages and gauze. "Sorry to be a party pooper, but I need to change Detective O'Toole's dressing, and then he really needs to rest. Doctor's orders."

"Yeah, we're leaving," Trent said.

Brill let go of the bedrail. "Sean, we'll check on you tomorrow. Hang in there. Every officer in the department is committed to getting the guy who did this."

"If you need to ask me anything else … you know where to find me."

Brill left the room and nodded at Officer Ulman as she and Trent walked toward the exit.

Vanessa stuck her head into the car and looked in the backseat for anything Ethan might have left behind.

"The backseat's empty," she said.

Ethan slammed the trunk shut and brushed his hands together. "Okay, then. Consider me officially out of your hair."

"Who said you were in my hair?"

"I did. You and your folks need to work things out. You don't need an outsider hanging around."

Vanessa leaned on the car and realized she really wanted Ethan to stay.

"I'm glad I got to know you this year," she said. "You've been a good friend."

"So it's okay if I call once in a while?"

"You'd better. I thought you said you were going to come visit."

"I will." Ethan pushed back the dark curls that kept falling on his forehead. "But you need time to think."

"I've got more time than I want *or* need."

"Not necessarily. The next two months will fly by and could be the most important in your life. You need to have a clear head."

Vanessa took his hand and held it. "I think clearly when I can run things by you. You're a good sounding board."

"I'll just be a phone call away. I start my summer job on Wednesday, so leave a message if you get my voice mail."

"I will."

Ethan stepped closer and put his arms around her. "I'll be praying that the Lord will open and close doors so you'll know what to do."

"Thanks."

"One more thing … just for the record … I've never seen a "hippo" as lovely as you."

Vanessa laughed and pushed him away. "Go get your things packed or you'll miss your bus."

Brill surveyed her surroundings, then folded her umbrella and got in the passenger side of Trent's plain DB car, glad to feel less conspicuous.

"It's a relief to see Sean looking so good," Trent said.

"It really is." Perhaps *good* was overstating it, though he was on the mend. She couldn't quite shake the sight of him sprawled on the floor in her office, his chest gushing blood despite the pressure she applied.

"Sean's a great detective." Trent started the car, backed out of the parking space, and headed for downtown. "It's sobering to think how close we came to losing him."

Brill listened to the rhythmic sound of the windshield wipers and fought to stay awake. Depression had been creeping around all day, just waiting for her to give in to it. When she left the police station, there would be another crisis at home that demanded her attention.

"When is Zack's funeral?" Trent said.

"Not till Wednesday. I'll fly to Memphis Tuesday and stay someplace."

"Not without protection, you won't."

Brill nestled in the seat and closed her eyes. "Maybe I should ask Officer Howell to go with me."

"Rachel? Sure, that makes sense. You two could share a room."

"I know Captain Donovan will make sure we're well protected while we're on his turf."

"Yeah, I almost wish this good-for-nothing would make a move. The Memphis cops would be all over him like red ants on a piece of garbage."

Her phone beeped and she looked at the name on the screen, then put it to her ear. "Yes, Sergeant Tiller."

"Ma'am, the security camera at the west entrance of city hall gave us a good picture of the perp. Our lady witness confirmed that he's the guy she saw outside on the sidewalk after O'Toole was stabbed. I literally just sent the picture to the Memphis PD and to your phone. Take a look."

"Thank you, Sergeant." She glanced over at Trent. "Tiller got a good shot of the perp off the security camera. I'm pulling it up now."

Brill studied the photograph; the perp's facial features were more pronounced than in the artist's sketch. Where had she seen those eyes before? The instant it hit her, she felt as if her heart were falling down a deep well. "Trent, turn the car around and go back to the hospital—now!"

She hit the auto dial on her phone. "Come on, Rick. Pick up."

"Ulman."

"This is Chief Jessup. Go in and check on O'Toole."

"The nurse just left a few minutes ago. He's asleep."

"Check his pulse. Hurry! I'll wait."

"Yes, ma'am …"

She heard the shuffling of feet and turned to Trent—"I think the nurse that ran us out of there is—"

"Chief, he's not breathing! There's no pulse! Nothing!"

"Get a doctor and secure the room as a crime scene. The nurse that was in there is our perp."

CHAPTER 5

BRILL leaned against the wall outside room 109 in the east corridor of St. Luke's Hospital, reluctant to put her full weight on her legs for fear they wouldn't hold her up. The tightness in her chest threatened to spill over the dam of her defenses.

As Dr. Yang Cho came out of Sean's room, clipboard in hand, his expression was grave. He walked over to Brill, his straight dark hair falling in bangs, his thick glasses magnifying the apprehension in his eyes.

"The coroner's on his way," Dr. Cho said. "The cause of death appears to be anaphylactic shock. The medical examiner will have to confirm with blood and skin tests, but the rash and sudden loss of blood pressure certainly suggests it. This patient is highly allergic to peanut."

Brill shifted her gaze to Trent. "Did you know that?"

"Beau Jack and I both knew. Sean always carried an EpiPen with him, but he never had to use it."

Dr. Cho pointed to the clipboard. "The allergy is properly noted in red at the top of the patient's chart. And also by the red band around his wrist. Everyone on the medical staff would know."

"Since we've established that the nurse was bogus," Brill said, "what could this man have done to cause Detective O'Toole to go into anaphylactic shock?"

Dr. Cho dabbed his face with a handkerchief. "This patient was *extremely* allergic. If he were given a capsule filled with peanut butter or peanut oil, or given a teaspoon of peanut oil, it would be sufficient to cause anaphylactic shock. And without an epinephrine injection, it would be fatal."

"So if Detective O'Toole was tricked into ingesting anything made from peanut, he could have died within minutes?"

Dr. Cho avoided eye contact. "Yes. The patient would've reacted immediately with wheezing, tightness in his chest, and nausea. His blood pressure would drop. Without immediate medical attention, he could not survive."

Brill felt as if she were going to throw up and took a slow, deep breath. And then another. How could this be happening? Twenty minutes ago Sean O'Toole was alive and talking and on the mend.

She held up her phone so Dr. Cho could see the picture. "We're looking for this man, only his hair's been dyed blond. He was dressed in blue scrubs and posing as a nurse."

"I don't recognize this man. I'm sorry. The hospital will launch a full investigation."

"All right, doctor. I'm sure my investigators will want to talk to you as well."

"I'll gladly answer questions," Dr. Cho said. "I'm deeply sorry for this loss. The coroner should be here shortly."

Brill put more of her weight against the wall and watched Dr. Cho make a quick exit down the long corridor. She was suddenly aware of someone talking to her and realized it was Officer Rick Ulman, who had the look of a scared little boy.

"Chief, the nurse had a hospital ID," he said. "I admit I didn't look at the photo that closely, but he had blond hair. I swear the guy never flinched when I checked his name against the list of approved employees."

"What happened after we left?"

"He came out and said he was going to change O'Toole's dressing and give him some medication the doctor ordered to help relax him. He was only in there a few minutes. Smiled when he left and said O'Toole was sleeping like a baby. I never thought a thing of it." Ulman seemed to stare at nothing. "How'd he get the ID?"

"He tied up the nurse in the mop closet and stole his uniform and ID."

Ulman shook his head. "I should've caught it."

Brill saw the remorse in his eyes. Why make him feel any worse than he already did? He would have to face the DA's investigators soon enough. She knew she had to suspend him in the meantime. But she wasn't going to ask for his badge and his gun with his peers watching.

"Rick, wait here."

She walked around the corner, looking for Trent, and saw him pacing along the wall, his fists clenched, his head down, seemingly lost in a world of his own. He mumbled angrily, and she figured he was calling Sean's killer every foul name he could think of. She coughed to make her presence known.

Trent looked up, his eyes wide, and she sensed that if his skin weren't black, his face would be scarlet.

"Sorry, ma'am. I can't believe that animal just stood there and watched Sean die."

"The animal's name is Merrick Fountain. He's fifteen years older than the last time I saw him, and the blond hair is dyed, but I recognized him the minute I saw the security camera photo. He abused his wife for years. Zack and I responded to numerous domestic abuse calls from his wife, son, and neighbors. The wife wouldn't press charges, and Merrick always went home, and the cycle started all over again. We tried to get his wife into a women's shelter, but she was too afraid to leave him."

"So did he kill her?"

"No, one day Mrs. Fountain called 911 and said her husband had stabbed her brother. The brother bled out before we could get there. Merrick swore it was self-defense, and the wife changed her story and backed him up. But DA Cromwell didn't buy it and charged him with second-degree murder and subpoenaed the son and Zack and me to testify for the prosecution. He was able to convince the jury of a pattern of abuse and violence, and Merrick was convicted. As he was led away, he was screaming and hollering that we would all pay in blood."

"What happened to the wife and son?"

"They finally went into a battered women's shelter and disappeared."

"So you and Zack and Cromwell are the three targets he can get to."

"Looks that way. But he's taking a few other people down in the process. I guess it's his way of twisting the knife—literally."

Trent glanced over her shoulder and sighed. "Here comes Jessica O'Toole. Let me tell her."

"No," Brill said. "Sean died because of me. I'll do it."

Brill pushed open the door of her house and went inside, the fragrance of flowers a welcome change from the antiseptic hospital smell that lingered in her senses. She laid her keys on the entry hall table and turned around just in time to fall into Kurt's arms.

She yielded to his embrace until she was sure the tears she was saving for a private moment were dammed securely. She pushed back and looked into Kurt's eyes and saw fear.

"What a day," he said softly.

"Unreal. What did you tell the girls?"

"Everything about Zack, though there's not a whisper about it on the regional stations. And they're reporting that O'Toole died of complications from the stabbing, so I decided to leave it at that until it's confirmed that he was poisoned. The kids are scared enough for you as it is. Ryan called a few minutes ago. It was all I could do to convince him not to drive home."

Brill sensed two pairs of eyes studying her from the living room. She took Kurt's hand, walked over to where Vanessa and Emily sat on the love seat, and flopped on the couch across from them.

Vanessa sighed. "I'm really sorry about what happened."

"Me, too," Emily said.

"Me, three." Brill forced herself not to frown. "I don't think I can handle talking about this all evening; so if you have any questions, ask now before I shut it off."

"We pretty much know everything," Vanessa said.

Brill could tell Emily was working up the courage to ask something.

Finally her youngest said, "Did they have kids?"

The question pierced her to the heart, but she didn't flinch. "Yes, Detective O'Toole had two in grade school and one in middle school. And Zack had two kids in high school, who had already lost their mom. We need to pray for them. This was a huge shock."

Kurt slapped his knees and then stood. "Homemade chicken and noodles for dinner."

"I used your recipe, Mom," Vanessa said. "I hope it tastes as good as yours."

Emily took her mother's hand and pulled her to her feet. "Come on. You've had a hard day. I made chocolate pudding for dessert, and Dad set the table. We decided to pamper you."

Brill looked at Vanessa's round tummy. She hadn't even had time to process the repercussions of her daughter's pregnancy. Or how to locate Tyson Nicholson and hold him financially responsible.

"Pamper me, eh?"

"It was *my* idea," Emily said. "But I can't cook as well as Vanessa, so she got to do the hard part."

"So what am I now, chopped liver?" Kurt winked. "I admit it's nice having girls in the house. I actually had time to read the newspaper."

Brill kissed Emily good night, then went downstairs, where Vanessa was sitting on the couch looking as radiant as she'd ever seen her, thumbing through the latest issue of *Expecting* magazine.

"You should be on the cover," Brill said.

"Thanks." Vanessa turned the page. "I didn't expect to hear that from *you*."

Brill sat on the couch next to her. "I'm disappointed, honey. I'm not blind."

There was a moment of uncomfortable silence, and then a tear spilled down Vanessa's cheek. "I'm so sorry, Mom. Ty and I really tried to be responsible. This wasn't supposed to happen. You don't need this with everything else that's going on."

"Looks like we both have a full plate right now. Have you thought any more about the future?"

"Are you kidding? That's all I think about."

"And ...?

"I'm not ready to talk about adoption, if that's what you mean."

Brill took her hand. "Vanessa, you have two months. It's going to fly by. We have to be realistic about the options. If you don't want to consider making this child available for adoption, then come up with a plan."

"I will. Give me a little time. I just got here."

"And whose fault is that?"

"Mine, all right?" She yanked her hand away. "I admit it. I messed up. I always mess up. Isn't that what you're thinking?"

"No, that's not what I was thinking. Why do you assume that I expect you to fail?"

"Because you do."

"That's not true."

"Mom ..." Vanessa sighed. "You probably don't even know you're doing it. But I'll never be as smart as Ryan and Emily. I'll never bring home A's. I'll never get a scholarship. Or get on the dean's list. Or do anything brilliant or clever. You're always bragging on everything they do. Nothing I do is worth bragging about."

"That's nonsense, Vanessa." Brill turned to her and tried to hide her annoyance. "You're loved because you're ours. Your accomplishments are different from Ryan's and Emily's. It's not a contest."

"What accomplishments, Mom? Name one. My whole life I've been average in every way. I have to work hard just to make passing grades in college. And now I'm pregnant without a husband or a job or any way to raise this baby. Just one more disappointment for you and Dad."

How did Vanessa expect her to respond? It was true that she'd been a disappointment many times. To say she hadn't would be disingenuous, and Vanessa would see right through it. But Brill didn't love her less than Ryan and Emily.

"First of all, your father and I love you because of who you are, not what you do. And second, I don't think it's productive to start comparing accomplishments with your siblings. You're all of twenty years old. Most of what you'll accomplish in your life hasn't even happened yet. God's got a unique plan for you."

"He sure didn't intend for me to get pregnant."

"Well, He certainly wasn't surprised by it. Every choice you make He already knew about before you were born. You know that."

Vanessa wiped the tears off her cheeks. "Great. Then He can be disappointed in me too."

"Why don't we stop using the word *disappointment* and start thinking of positive ways we can deal with your situation?"

"There's nothing positive about my *situation*. But I have this miracle growing inside me, this wonderful little boy that I should probably give to someone else to raise, but I don't want to."

"Then come up with a plan, Vanessa. If you want to raise your son, fight for him. You're not going to get very far if you keep thinking of yourself as a victim."

"I can't believe Ty left me to deal with this alone."

"Well, he did, and you're going to have to deal with it." *And I'm going to use every resource I have to find this loser and hold him responsible.*

CHAPTER 6

NICK Phillips dipped his tasting spoon into the simmering pot of tomato basil soup and brought it to his mouth, savoring the tangy, spicy flavor. He winked at the cook, put his spoon in the dishwasher, and went out to the dining area of Nick's Grill just as Tessa and Antonio Masino came in through the glass door.

He put his hand on Tessa's shoulder and shook Antonio's hand. "Hey, you're early. Gus is saving your places at the counter."

"We went to early church, thinking we'd get here before noon and miss the crowd," Antonio said. "We could hardly find a place to park."

Nick looked out at the packed-out tables and booths and smiled. "Yeah, Memorial Day weekend seems to be the official kickoff of the tourist season. The numbers are probably higher because of the media hype last fall surrounding the red shadows legend."

Tessa rolled her eyes. "Please don't get Gus on *that* subject."

"Not to worry." Nick followed the Masinos over to the counter. "The specials are written up there on the chalkboard. The tomato basil soup will knock your socks off. Low fat, too. All you can eat for six ninety-five. Comes with a grilled-chicken garden salad and all the cracker bread you want."

"Sounds tasty," Tessa said. "That's what I'll have."

Antonio nodded. "Make it two."

"Maggie, two specials for the Masinos," Nick hollered.

Antonio slid onto the stool next to Gus Williams and patted him on the back. "How's it going, friend?"

"Really can't complain, but I always do." Gus chuckled and rubbed the Coke off his white mustache. "Your next-door neighbor is sure back in the thick of things."

Antonio nodded. "Tessa took a loaf of bread over to the Jessups' last night. The chief wasn't home yet, but Tessa talked to her husband. He as much as said that when a cop gets killed, the earth stands still till they get whoever did it."

Nick stepped closer to the end of the counter so he didn't have to strain to hear the conversation. "Has Sophie Trace ever lost a police officer before now?"

"Fifty years ago," Tessa said, "in a shootout after a bank robbery. But it gives me cold chills to think of someone sneaking into the police station and stabbing a detective. It's dreadful. Just dreadful."

Gus planted his elbows on the counter. "Guess we're gonna have to start usin' metal detectors like big city police departments."

"Not sure that would've made any difference," Nick said. "A source inside the police department told the TV station that the suspect was disguised as a workman—toolbox and all. They're not saying *how* he got in the detective bureau, but obviously, his disguise was key."

"Looked mean as a junkyard dog in his mug shot." Gus took a sip of Coke. "Merrick Fountain. That's a name for you. The brute was a wife beater before he went to prison for stabbin' his brother-in-law."

"Your orders are up next." Maggie Cummings put two mugs on the counter for the Masinos and filled them with coffee. "You know, my sister's ex used to beat the tar out of her, just because he felt like it. Guys like them are criminals. I'm sorry someone had to get killed before this Fountain character got what he deserved. They should've never let him out." Maggie's eyes turned to slits. "But why would a wife beater from Memphis, who just got out of the state pen, come all the way to Sophie Trace to get inside our police department and stab a detective?"

"Hmm …" Nick draped a bar towel over his shoulder. "Good question. Must've had a personal beef with Detective O'Toole."

"How?" Maggie took packets of coffee creamer out of her uniform pocket and set them next to Antonio's mug. "I doubt O'Toole was a cop fifteen years ago when this Fountain character was convicted. So what's the connection?"

Gus hooked his thumbs on his suspenders, his eyebrows two white arches. "Since our new police chief is from Memphis, I'm bettin' *she's* the connection."

Brill Jessup climbed in the backseat of Kurt's Dodge Caravan, next to Emily, and let Vanessa have the passenger seat. What had Pastor Gavin preached on? She hardly heard a word of it. Her mind was reeling with thoughts of burying cops and getting through the birth of Vanessa's baby.

"I thought that went well," Kurt said.

Vanessa sighed. "That's because you weren't the one everyone was staring at."

Kurt started the van, backed it out of the space, and drove toward the church exit. "People were very nice, Vanessa. They were surprised, that's all. When they met you at Thanksgiving, you didn't look pregnant. Your mother and I share prayer requests with the people in our Sunday school class. They had to be wondering why we never mentioned it."

"Yeah, Pastor Gavin and his wife looked totally freaked out," Emily said.

Brill tugged on Emily's skirt, her index finger to her mouth, and said, "I'm sure they were surprised too."

"Actually, they seemed more concerned about your detective that died." Vanessa seemed to be studying something in the side mirror. "Are the police going to follow us everywhere we go?"

"It's just a precaution till we arrest Merrick Fountain," Brill said. "We've had such an overwhelming response for help from law enforcement all over the region that I'm not going to feel guilty using some of that manpower to make sure Fountain can't get near anyone in my family."

"I'm *glad* the police are following us," Emily said. "Are you going to work this afternoon?"

"I need to, sweetie. I'm flying to Memphis on Tuesday so I can go to Zack's funeral on Wednesday. And my whole department will be out on Thursday afternoon for Sean O'Toole's funeral." Brill wondered if her family could hear in her voice the sadness that weighed down her heart.

"I liked Uncle Zack," Vanessa said. "He was really nice. He always told Ryan and me knock-knock jokes and gave us Life Savers."

Emily's eyes grew wide. "I remember the picture of him holding me after I was born. I had one of those little pink stocking caps on my head."

"Zack kept calling while I was in labor with you. Remember that, Kurt?"

"Yeah. I think he called more times than my mother."

Brill looked out the window. "He was a good friend and a great cop. Besides your dad, he was my closest friend for ten years. I don't think it's hit me yet that he's gone."

"Mom, are you going to cry?" Emily said.

Brill blinked several times and swallowed the emotion that tightened her throat. "Crying won't get the job done." She forced a smile and locked gazes with Kurt in the rearview mirror. "I envy that you all get to go see Ryan tomorrow. I wish things weren't so crazy so I could go with you."

Brill greeted two of Sam Parker's deputies posted at the back entrance of city hall and keyed in her combination. She pushed open the door and was hit with a gust of cold air. She strode down the hall into the police station, crossed the detective bureau, and went into her office, tempted to pull the blinds on the glass wall and just sit and stare.

Instead she opened her cell phone, looked up a phone number, and pressed the Talk button. The phone rang once. Twice. Three times. Should she hang up? Had she really given this enough thought?

Come on, Dexter. Pick up before I change my mind.

"Well, well, well. If it isn't a blast from the past." There was a smile in Dexter Babbitt's voice. "How are you, Brill? I guess I should say, 'Chief.'"

"I'm fine, thanks. How about you?"

"Couldn't be better. You and Kurt doing okay?"

"We're fine. But the rest of my world is falling apart."

"Yeah, I heard on the news that a detective in your department got stabbed and died of complications."

"I'm afraid it's even worse than that." Brill took a few minutes and told Dexter how Detective O'Toole was poisoned, and how she recognized Merrick Fountain on the city hall security tapes and determined he was the nurse at the hospital. She told him about her phone call from Captain Donovan on the Memphis PD and about her former partner dying. And about Vanessa's circumstances.

"Wow. You've got some serious stuff going on. How can I help?"

"I want to hire you to find Tyson Nicholson. Interested?"

"Sure. It'd do my heart good to nail the professor and make him pay."

Brill sat at her desk and picked up a pencil. "How soon can you get on it?"

"Right away, actually. I just finished up on another job and was going to take a couple weeks off. But I really don't have anything planned, so it can wait."

"You sure?"

"Absolutely. I'm flattered you thought of me."

"Why? You're the best PI I know."

"I'm probably the only PI you know."

Brill chuckled. "I'm looking at quality, not quantity. Can you start Tuesday, after the holiday weekend?"

"Sure."

"Okay. Let me talk to Kurt and get back to you ASAP. I already browsed your Web site, so I know what your fees are."

"Sounds good. I'll wait to hear from you. Say hello to Kurt for me."

"I will. And I'd appreciate it if you didn't discuss the details of O'Toole's death with anyone. The details will come out soon enough."

"You got it."

Brill laid her cell phone on her desk just as Trent came into her office and flopped into the chair next to her desk.

"City hall is secured. The only thing we don't have is a moat." Trent grinned. "There's no way Merrick Fountain is going to get in here again."

"Are Sam's deputies letting you take the lead?"

"They're great as long as he isn't around. You know what a control freak Sam is."

Brill arched her eyebrows. "The sheriff is definitely a force to be reckoned with."

"Gripes me the way he patronizes you, ma'am."

"I thought you were going to call me Brill."

Trent smiled with his eyes, and she decided he was a dead ringer for Denzel Washington.

"I'm working on it," he said. "Hard to break old habits. Some of it's just southern manners my mama drilled into me. Before I forget, I went by the house to see Jessica O'Toole this morning."

"How's she holding up?"

Trent shook his head. "She's devastated. If she had to lose her husband, she at least wanted him to die in the line of duty as a hero—not in a hospital bed from anaphylactic shock."

"Sean *was* a hero. He staggered all the way to my office to warn me. He could've bled to death." Brill sighed. "I can't believe I was in that hospital room with Merrick Fountain and didn't recognize him."

"Are you kidding? He doesn't look anything like the man in the mug shot. I can't believe you recognized him on the security tape."

"I had a lot of time to study his face at the trial," Brill said. "I thought he looked like a weasel. Still does. He's just older. When the nurse came into O'Toole's hospital room, I remember thinking he looked harsh with bleach blond hair, but I didn't pay much attention to him."

"Why would you? We had no reason to consider him a suspect when we thought Ulman had screened the nurses. I just hope it doesn't end up with Ulman's getting canned when the DA's office does their investigation."

Brill looked through the blinds into the detective bureau. "Hopefully, they'll give Ulman credit for what he did right. After all, Merrick Fountain *was* wearing a hospital ID badge that matched a name on the list of approved employees. But Ulman should've paid closer attention to the photo."

"Doesn't make him a bad cop."

"I agree. But O'Toole is dead and the city council wants someone's head on a stick. I have a feeling it's going to get ugly."

That night, Brill sat at the vanity in the master bathroom and let her face soak up the expensive moisturizing cream that promised to erase the appearance of wrinkles. She bemoaned the tiny lines that fanned out from her eyes and the creases around her mouth. Were they due to the stress of the past two years? Or just the fact that she had turned forty-five?

She was glad she had saved the birthday card Zack sent her. How could she have known it would be the last time she ever heard from him? His death didn't seem real to her yet, but she imagined his orphaned teenagers were feeling the deep, agonizing void that would hit her soon enough.

Death. So final. So unchangeable. Her parents and in-laws had crossed over into the very presence of God. But had Zack? Had he ever come to the realization that he was a sinner and needed God's mercy and grace for himself? Or had he continued to question how God could let criminals prey on the innocent and then forgive even the most depraved offender just because he was sorry and vowed never to do it again?

Zack certainly wasn't the first cop to balk at the idea that God would let "a piece of worthless garbage" off the hook. He just couldn't accept God's willingness to forgive a remorseful criminal, regardless of the offense, but not a cop who thought he was good enough in his own right and didn't need to be forgiven. The whole concept of mercy and grace seemed lost on him.

Brill sighed. Law enforcement was a tough mission field to plow. How grateful she was to have been raised in a Christian home. If it weren't for that, the dregs of humanity and their unspeakable acts might cause her to be cynical too.

"You still breathing?"

Kurt's voice caused her to jump.

"For heaven's sake. Give me some warning, will you?"

Kurt came up behind her and gently massaged her shoulders. "Sorry, honey. I just wondered if you were okay. You've been sitting here a long time."

"I was thinking about Zack. I don't know if he was saved. It really bothers me."

"He had the choice to trust Christ as his Savior, same as everyone else."

"I'm just not sure that he ever did. Zack was disgusted that God would extend His mercy to criminals who didn't deserve it. He was never able to see *himself* as an undeserving sinner."

"That we know of. I'd like to think he did." Kurt stroked her hair. "You said you wanted to talk to me about something."

She nodded and looked at his face reflected in the mirror. "I called Dexter Babbitt this afternoon. I want to hire him to find Nicholson."

"I don't know, Brill ... the guy's a deadbeat. Do we really want to open Vanessa up to more hurt?"

"I just want him to help with child support. She can't do this by herself."

Kurt stopped rubbing her shoulders and met her gaze. "So you've just thrown in the towel and agreed she's going to keep the baby? End of discussion?"

"Her *heart's* already decided, Kurt. We can have all the discussions we want, but I know our daughter. She made her decision before she ever came home. We need to help her prepare for the inevitable."

Kurt put his hands to his temples. "Let me get this straight. You actually agree with Vanessa's decision?"

"No. But I *am* willing to support Vanessa. I don't want her or this child to suffer. Therefore, I want Nicholson to do his share."

"The creep skipped out on her. I don't think it's smart to get Vanessa's hopes up that he's going to lift a finger to help her, even if you find him."

"The court can force him to."

"He'll just run again. He's a loser. And Vanessa will get hurt."

Brill sighed. "I wish you'd at least give it a chance. We won't tell Vanessa that Dexter is searching for Nicholson. If we find him, we'll see how he responds and assess the situation. Fair enough?"

"All right, you're the chief. But a man doesn't profess to love a woman and then abandon her when she's carrying his child unless he's a loser."

"Or has something to hide."

CHAPTER 7

ON Memorial Day afternoon Brill sat at her desk, reviewing the preliminary coroner's report and the crime scene reports made in the detective bureau where Sean O'Toole was stabbed and also the hospital room where he later died.

The coroner found a significant level of peanut oil in Sean's stomach, but none in his mouth or throat, and determined he had swallowed a capsule of peanut oil, which resulted in anaphylactic shock and death. An autopsy was under way to confirm his findings.

The crime scene reports showed no fingerprints or DNA that could be linked to Merrick Fountain. But not all the trace evidence had been analyzed yet.

A knock on the door startled her, and she turned.

Sheriff Sam Parker stood in the doorway. "I just came to check on you, Chief Jessup."

He flashed an annoying grin, his gold tooth more obvious than his badge. He could have called. Why was he really here?

"Come in, Sheriff. I didn't expect you to be working on a holiday."

"Well, we've got a *situation* now, don't we?"

Sam, tall and arrogant, strutted over to her desk and sat in the vinyl chair next to it, his hands clasped behind his head. What she wouldn't give to wipe the smirk off his face.

"I see you've got a copy of the coroner's prelim," he said. "Detective O'Toole's death was a tragedy that could've been prevented. But then I don't need to tell you what sloppy police work looks like."

Oh, but I'm sure you will. She didn't bother to hide her irritation. "Knowing what we know now, Officer Ulman should have examined the photo on the ID badge more closely, but the impostor did have blond hair, as did the nurse in the photo. And the name on the badge was on the approved list of employees."

"The impostor was a decade older than the staff nurse, Chief Jessup."

"Photographs can be flattering, Sheriff Parker."

"The impostor's hair was bleach blond, not sandy blond like the man's in the photo."

"People mess with their hair color all the time. Officer Ulman noted the hair was blond and didn't stop to question what shade it was when everything else checked out."

Come on, Sam. Give me a break.

"He should've been attuned to any man who appeared to have changed his hair color. I can see the word *sloppy* doesn't set well with you." Sam stared at her and didn't blink.

"What doesn't set well with me, Sheriff, is not giving a good cop the benefit of the doubt. Hindsight is always twenty-twenty. But the fact is, Officer Ulman made eye contact with the impostor, and he didn't flinch. The man was dressed in scrubs and wearing a hospital ID with a name that was on the approved list. He had blond hair, as did the man in the photo. He had what appeared to be the patient's medication in hand. Ulman will regret this tragic oversight for the rest of his life. But any one of us could've made that mistake."

"Is that so?"

"It is."

"What if this Merrick Fountain had attacked *you* in O'Toole's room? You're the ultimate target."

"There's no way Fountain could've known I was in O'Toole's room until he arrived. Frankly, it was gutsy of him to come in while I was there, since he didn't know if I would recognize him. And we can speculate all day about what might have happened. But the only thing Officer Ulman is guilty of was not seeing the need to further scrutinize the photo ID."

Sam stared at her for several more seconds before the tautness left his face and he said, "You stand by your officers. I respect that."

"I have good people in my department. They're not perfect. But they're committed to protecting this community. I think if Sean O'Toole had been in Rick Ulman's place, he might well have made the same call."

"The DA's office may beg to differ."

"We'll see. In the meantime, why don't we work together and try to catch the *real* criminal?" Brill clasped her hands together and softened her tone. "I'm positive it was Merrick Fountain who posed as the nurse. Fountain was alone with O'Toole for several minutes after Trent and I left. He's our killer."

Vanessa looked out at the quaint shops and eateries that lined the main highway through Gatlinburg, aware that the squad car with the two police officers assigned to watch them was still following closely behind.

"I've enjoyed the day," Vanessa said, "even if *Shortcake* back there did beat us at miniature golf."

"I always win," Emily said. "I wish Mom could've seen my hole in one. It seems weird she's not with us. I miss her."

Vanessa nodded. "Me, too."

"Me three," Kurt said as he stopped the van at the red light at Crandall Street. "This is where we hang a left."

"I like this town," Emily said. "There're a million people here for Memorial Day. Hey, I see an ice-cream parlor. Can we go there after we have dinner at Ryan's restaurant?"

Vanessa pulled down the visor and looked in the mirror at her baby sister. "We're going to be too full."

"You maybe, but not me." Emily pointed to herself. "I'm never too full for ice cream. Right, Dad?"

Kurt laughed. "That's been my experience. I think you're in another growth spurt." The light turned green, and he made a left. "The Whistlin' Dixie should be a block up this way."

Vanessa was surprised at how steep the road was and kept her eyes peeled for the trombone Ryan said would be obvious. She finally saw a two-story brick building with a huge trombone mounted above the entrance. The words "Whistlin' Dixie" were displayed on a red, blue, and yellow neon sign that filled the glass window in front.

"What a cool place!" Emily exclaimed. "I can hear the music playing."

"It's packed out already." Vanessa scanned the parking lot. "Dad, I don't see *any* parking spaces."

"We may have to go back to that pay-and-park we passed," Kurt

said. "Kills me to spend eight bucks just to park my van, but hey …
it's not every day we get to surprise your brother."

"Eight dollars?" Emily mumbled. "There goes my ice cream."

As they drove back down the hill, Vanessa saw the police car
make a U-turn and noticed Emily kept her eye on it.

Kurt paid the fee to park in the lot, and then the three of them
walked over to the sidewalk.

The police car pulled alongside them. "We'll park across from the
Whistlin' Dixie," the officer said. "Y'all just go about your business
when you get inside. We've got you covered."

"Thanks," Kurt said. "Okay, girls. Let's hike up the hill. You'll
probably wish you had on tennis shoes instead of sandals."

Emily got behind Vanessa and pushed, and the sisters giggled all
the way to the top of the hill.

"Wow. I'm out of breath." Vanessa put her hand over her heart.

"You? I'm the one who did all the work," Emily said.

"Well, the baby can tell I exerted myself. He's kicking up a
storm."

"Can *I* feel him?"

"Sure." Vanessa took Emily's hand and placed it on her round
tummy. "You should feel a series of thuds, kind of like when someone
flicks you with their fingers."

Emily's bright blue eyes grew wide, and a grin slowly stole across her
face. "I feel it. He's kicking. Dad, you've got to feel this. It's amazing."

"I'm sure there'll be plenty of chances. I'm going to go put us on
the waiting list."

Vanessa hid the sting of her father's dismissive tone. Would it
have taken any more than a few seconds to feel his grandson kicking?

His attitude brought her back to the harsh reality that her dad probably didn't want to get attached.

"Vanessa! Wait up!"

Vanessa turned toward the deep voice and saw a young man with round glasses talking to the police. It was Ethan Langley.

"Ethan?" She laughed. "What are *you* doing here?"

He ran up to where she and Emily were standing, his dark curly hair windblown and noticeably shorter than the last time she saw him.

"I didn't have anything going on for Memorial Day," he said, sounding short-winded, "so I decided to come here to your brother's place and try the ribs. You said they were a bigger draw than the jazz band."

"That's what Ryan said."

"You here to see him?"

"Uh-huh. My mom had to work, so Dad took care of some business at his store in Pigeon Forge and then the three of us spent the afternoon playing miniature golf and shopping. We came here to have dinner and surprise Ryan."

"Well, it's great to see you. You look pretty as ever."

"Vanessa thinks she looks like a blimp," Emily said.

Ethan smiled. "She told me a hippo." He took Emily's hand and shook it. "We didn't get formally introduced the other night."

"I'm Emily."

"So you're the little sister I keep hearing about?"

"Well, I used to be the baby, but now Vanessa's having one, so I get to be the aunt."

"Yes, Auntie Em. I remember you saying that."

Kurt came over and stood behind Emily, his hands on her shoulders. "Ethan … what a surprise seeing you here."

"Vanessa told me about this place, and I thought I'd check it out before I start my summer job on Wednesday."

"I see …"

Vanessa caught her father's dubious expression. Did he think she had secretly planned for Ethan to show up? She wanted to disappear.

"Have you put your name on the list yet?" Kurt said.

"No, sir. I just got here. How long is the wait?"

"Thirty to forty minutes, but you're welcome to sit with us. The place is packed out, and I doubt they're going to be too keen on finding a table for one."

Vanessa felt the heat flood her face. If Ethan had come to enjoy the band by himself, there was no gracious way for him to bow out now.

Brill heard a commotion in the detective bureau and jumped to her feet, her hand on her gun. She peeked through the blinds on the glass wall, relieved to realize the ruckus was just the sound of Mayor Lewis Roswell barking at Trent, his mouth moving faster than his hands.

She walked out to Trent's desk and tapped the mayor on the shoulder.

"Is there something I can help you with, Mr. Mayor?"

"There you are. I need to speak with you in private."

Mayor Roswell brushed past her and headed for her office.

She looked at Trent, rolled her eyes, then followed the mayor into her office and closed the door.

The mayor stood facing the window, his hands clasped behind his back. She could tell from his demeanor that he didn't want a cup of coffee or a place to sit.

"Chief Jessup … I don't think I need to tell you how upset the city council is over Sean O'Toole's death."

"As well they should be," she said. "Every officer in this department is devastated."

He spun around, his hands deep in his trouser pockets. "Would you mind telling me why we're just now finding out that O'Toole died because the guy who stabbed him got past your security at the hospital?"

"I'm not going to make excuses—"

"Good, because there aren't any."

"Fair enough. But you need to see the bigger picture."

The mayor lifted his eyebrows. "Please," he said sarcastically, "enlighten me."

Brill told him everything related to the case that had happened from the time Detective O'Toole, wounded and bleeding, stumbled into her office, until she recognized Merrick Fountain's face on the security tapes and called Officer Ulman at the hospital.

The mayor's eyebrows formed a bushy line. "Why did you give the public the impression that O'Toole died of complications from the stabbing?"

"*That*, sir, was purely media speculation. We consistently declined to comment on the cause of death until this morning, after we got the preliminary autopsy report."

"Well, it's what you're *not* saying that's fueling the rumors."

"If you're referring to the threat on my life, the sheriff and I agreed when O'Toole was stabbed that there was nothing to be gained by making the threat on my life public."

The mayor's eyes turned to slits. "Well, somebody leaked everything, Chief Jessup. Now my phone is ringing off the hook. People want to know why this town has been turned upside down since you took office. They want to know if you've been involved with the mafia. Some are even trying to connect this crime with the disappearances last fall."

"That's ridiculous and you know it. Until three days ago, we hadn't had a serious crime here since we cleaned house of the gangs last December. I would think it would behoove you to defend this department's record." *You arrogant, self-serving coward.*

"What I'm *behooved* to do is answer to the city council. A police officer has been murdered on your watch."

"I'm painfully aware of that."

"The first cop killing here in half a century."

"I know that, too."

The mayor raked his hands through his perfectly styled hair. "Then you also know there's going to be a very dramatic, heartrending funeral here on Thursday. A young widow is going to receive the flag that was draped on her husband's coffin, and three grieving kids are going to be captured on film and exploited by the media. People will be screaming for justice."

"No one louder than *I*." Brill lowered her voice. "Look, this department, along with the sheriff's department and the Memphis PD, is doing everything in its power to get Merrick Fountain. His picture was released to the media, and we have a warrant for his arrest."

"What about the officer who let the killer into O'Toole's hospital room?"

"Rick Ulman has been temporarily suspended and is currently under investigation by the DA's office. But in fairness to him, the impostor wore the nurse's ID and was on the approved list. Any one of us could have made that error in judgment."

"Do you *all* need your eyes checked?"

Lord, don't let me lose it. That's just what he wants. Brill looked at the floor and slowly counted to ten. "I'm confident that Ulman will be cleared. Posting him outside the door was just a precaution. We had no reason to suspect that the assailant would go after O'Toole a second time. Everyone thought I was the target."

"You thought wrong."

"And I have to live with that." Brill caught the mayor's gaze and held it. "The best tribute we can pay to Sean O'Toole is to go after the suspect, lock him up, and not become despondent over what didn't go as planned."

"Tell that to O'Toole's wife."

"I *did.* I'm the one who had to look Jessica in the eyes and tell her Sean was dead." Brill paused and swallowed the emotion. "We're working around the clock to get O'Toole's killer."

"That's what we're paying you for."

"That's right. And you can sleep in safety tonight because my officers have done a great job of keeping the peace in this town. I assure you I'll be wide awake, not because I'm on Fountain's hit list, but because I'm burdened with the responsibility of having lost one of my men. With all due respect, Mr. Mayor, you have no idea what it's like to wear this badge."

"I didn't come over here with the intention of getting confrontational."

"And yet here we are *again*." Brill paused, her temples throbbing. "Last fall when the disappearances had the entire community baffled, you and I had a similar confrontation. I would think my performance then, in the midst of the worst crisis this town has ever faced, would be sufficient to earn your trust."

"Each situation is unique, Chief Jessup. I don't mind telling you, I have doubts. How can you run this department efficiently with a threat hanging over your head?"

"The same way I would run it if there were no threat—only more cautiously."

"Ah, like you did at the hospital?"

That did it. Brill stiffened and glared at the mayor, summoning the full authority denoted by the four stars on her collar. "As long as *I'm* chief of police, I'll conduct this department in the way I think will best secure the safety and quality of life in this community."

"Is that what you want me to tell the city council?"

"Word for word. They can remove me if they want and throw the entire department into disarray. I'm sure many of my officers would resign in protest."

"Oh, so now you're threatening *us*?"

"I'm just telling you the facts, Mr. Mayor. With the media zeroed in on O'Toole's death, the firing of the police chief and the ensuing disruption would do nothing to prolong your or the city council's political careers. Stay out of my way until we get O'Toole's killer caught and convicted. If the city council wants me out after that, they won't have to ask twice."

Sweat popped out on the mayor's forehead, and perspiration soaked the armpits of his starched Ralph Lauren shirt. Had she hit a nerve?

He let out an exaggerated sigh. "I'll relay this conversation to the city council. Watch your step, Chief Jessup. You would not be hard to replace."

Mayor Roswell made a beeline for the door and didn't bother to shake her hand on the way out.

Brill went across the detective bureau and down the hall to the women's restroom. She stood at the sink and splashed cold water on her face, trying to regain her composure. Wasn't it hard enough dealing with the fact that Sean died on her watch without the mayor attacking her judgment and threatening her job?

CHAPTER 8

KURT sat next to Emily and across from Ethan and Vanessa in a booth at the Whistlin' Dixie, his head buried in the menu. He had decided five minutes ago what he wanted. Why was it that suddenly no one seemed to have anything to say?

"Sorry it took me so long." Ryan Jessup, dressed in khaki shorts and a red Whistlin' Dixie polo shirt, appeared at the booth looking very managerial in his square glasses.

He gave Emily's ponytail a tug. "How's our favorite baby sister?"

"Good. I won at miniature golf. I made a hole in one."

"Keep that up and Dad'll have to take you out on a *real* course."

Ryan stood back and gave Vanessa the once-over. "And how's Miss Piggy?"

She giggled and threw a straw at him. "This is my friend Ethan Langley. He and I were in the same psychology class this past year."

"Nice to meet you." Ryan shook Ethan's hand.

"Same here. Vanessa told me about this place and that you were assistant manager for the summer. I spent the day at Cades Cove and Roaring Fork. As long I was this close, I thought I'd check it out. Can't believe I ran into your family."

Me either. Kurt tried not to show his irritation. Was it too much to ask to have a day alone with his kids? Why had he felt obligated to ask Ethan to join them?

"I assume Vanessa told you the ribs are to die for?"

Ethan nodded. "Absolutely."

"But *I* came for the corn on the cob." A slow grin took over Emily's face. "Mom is going to hate it that we got to see you and she didn't."

"Speaking of Mom …" Ryan turned to Kurt. "How's she holding up?"

"Your mother's not going to show it, but I think she feels somewhat responsible for Detective O'Toole's death."

"Why?" Emily said. "She didn't do anything."

"She was in charge. That means she gets credit when things go well. And she gets blamed when they don't."

Ethan's eyebrows furrowed. "I know you all told me that the threat to Mrs. Jessup is being kept out of the news. But I heard it talked about on the radio on my way here."

Kurt squeezed a slice of lemon into his water. "You actually heard them say that she's been threatened?"

"Yes, sir. They also said that detective, who was in the hospital recovering from stab wounds, was poisoned. Apparently he was highly allergic to peanut oil. They gave the suspect's name, but I don't remember it. Said it was someone that Chief Jessup helped put away years ago. I'm sorry. I thought you knew."

Kurt took a sip of water. Who leaked the story? And why hadn't Brill told him so he could fill the kids in?

"Hey," Emily said. "Nobody told me the detective was poisoned."

"Me, either." Vanessa looked questioningly at Kurt.

He held up his palm. "Your mother and I decided not to say anything until the coroner confirmed it and the information was released to the media. It's odd that she didn't call and tell me, but she probably didn't think we'd hear about it while we were out having fun."

"Was the killer the same man who threatened to hurt Mom?" Emily's eyes were wide and fearful.

"Why don't we go ahead and order?" Kurt said. "This isn't exactly dinner conversation."

Ryan glanced at his watch. "Uh, the band should be back from their break any second. I'll send a waitress to take your orders, and I'll be back later. Glad you guys came to check the place out."

Kurt resumed his hiding place behind the menu and stole a few well-spaced glances at Vanessa. She had seemed distant ever since they sat down. Was she as annoyed as he was that Ethan had intruded upon their evening? Or was she just preoccupied with her mother's situation?

Brill nodded at the officers parked across the street and pushed open the arched wood door. She breathed in the fragrance of roses and spotted a bouquet on the entry hall table. Would she ever grow tired of Kurt's weekly ritual of bringing her fresh flowers as a promise that she was the one and only lover in his life? For a split second, she remembered what she had chosen to forget and blinked it away. She and Kurt had renewed their wedding vows. Why dredge up what couldn't be changed?

She went into the living room and set her briefcase on the coffee table, then slumped on the new couch and yielded every muscle in her body to its firm and unfamiliar touch. When her eyes were closed and she couldn't see the floral fabric that tied together all the colors in the room, she missed the comfort of the plaid couch that was older than Emily. Yes, Pouncer had sharpened his claws on the side. And Kurt had spilled mustard on the arm and never could get the stain completely out. And the kids had used it for a trampoline, for timeouts, and for watching TV. It was well seasoned and *comfortable*. She wondered if whoever had bought it from Goodwill would appreciate it as much as she had.

Her cell phone buzzed, and she groaned. Not now. All she wanted was a few minutes of quiet to clear her head. She fumbled for the phone and saw Kurt's number on the screen.

"Hi," she said.

"Hi, yourself. Where are you?"

"On the couch with my eyes closed. How about you?"

"I'm standing in the alcove outside the men's room at the Whistlin' Dixie."

Brill smiled. "How's Ryan?"

"He looks great. This place is right up his alley. He's going to give us a tour of his apartment after we're done eating."

"Well ... was he shocked to see Vanessa pregnant?"

"Are you kidding? Ryan's known about it for months." Kurt's voice was flat. "Vanessa called him right after she found out she was pregnant. He thought she should tell us."

"For heaven's sake, Kurt. What does that say about us?"

"Don't even get me started. Oh ... you'll never guess who showed up just when we did: Ethan Langley."

"What a coincidence."

"More like a pain. I felt obligated to invite him to join us, though I really wanted the time alone with the kids."

An uncomfortable moment of dead air caused her to think the connection had been lost.

"Kurt … you there?"

"Yeah. Why didn't you call and tell me that the media had been advised about the threat on your life and the real cause of O'Toole's death?"

"I didn't think you'd be listening to the news while you were enjoying your day with the kids."

"I wasn't. We found out from Ethan, who heard it on the radio."

Brill sighed. "I'm sorry. The media was advised about the murder after the preliminary autopsy report came in, but I didn't know till later that someone leaked the part about the threat to me. I thought it could wait till your outing was over."

"Well, I sure didn't appreciate something that sensitive coming from someone else. You should've seen Emily's face."

Brill winced. "I'm sorry, Kurt. Is she just terrified?"

"Probably. Vanessa and Ryan seemed shaken too. After what happened to Zack and his detective, it is a bit sobering that this same guy stabbed Sean O'Toole and then poisoned him to make sure he died. The threat to your life affects us, too, you know."

"Of course it does." *So does the threat to my job, but I haven't got time to deal with that right now.*

"Emily doesn't know how to verbalize everything she's feeling, but it's obvious she's still experiencing Post Traumatic Stress Disorder from the hostage ordeal last fall."

"I should've called." Brill turned on her side and faced the fireplace. "I just figured the girls would talk your ear off and you wouldn't turn on the radio. I didn't think about you running into someone else who'd heard it. How was the rest of your day?"

"Good."

Brill listened as Kurt told her about their miniature golf adventure and shopping spree, and also about their brief time with Ryan when they arrived at the Whistlin' Dixie.

"So did Ryan seem okay with Vanessa being pregnant?"

"Downright jovial. And Emily's enthralled with the baby's kicking. They act like we're getting a puppy. They don't seem to realize how serious this is."

Brill moved her gaze to the family portrait on the bookcase. "How can they? They've never raised a child."

"Well … all that aside, it's been a fun holiday outing for the girls. Just feels odd without you."

"You sound down."

"I'm always a little lonesome without you. You know that. Maybe when the case is solved, we can get away for a weekend—just the two of us."

Brill sighed. "I'd love that. But we still have the crisis with Vanessa. I know she just got home, but she's got to do some serious decision making. The next two months will go fast. If she's set on keeping the baby, we have to be realistic about how much we're willing and able to help her." *Especially if we're living on one salary.*

Vanessa savored the barbecued ribs, corn on the cob, coleslaw, and scrumptious homemade rolls. She enjoyed the sound of the jazz band as she listened to Ethan talk to her dad about the stock market. Emily kept glancing over at two Hispanic men who were standing at the bar.

"Your dinner's getting cold," Vanessa said.

Emily pushed her plate away. "I'm full."

"Did you save room for ice cream?"

"Not really."

"What? I thought you were the one who always had room for ice cream."

One of the Hispanic men left the bar and walked past the booth, and Emily clutched her dad's arm tightly.

"Can we go now?" she said.

Kurt took a sip of iced tea. "Sweetie, we're not finished eating yet. How come you didn't finish your corn on the cob?"

"I'm not hungry anymore."

He felt her forehead with the back of his hand. "You feeling okay?"

"My tummy hurts. I want to go home."

Kurt cupped her cheek in his hand, looked into her eyes. "Emily, you're safe here. You don't have to be afraid. And Mom is safe. Two armed officers are posted outside our house and here in the restaurant. No one is going to hurt you or her."

Emily glanced over at the Hispanic man at the bar and then at Kurt, her bright blue eyes round and filled with uncertainty.

"That detective wasn't safe." Her voice sounded uncharacteristically babyish.

"That's because the officer outside his room wasn't paying close attention. Look over there." He pointed to the doorway. "Those officers are watching every move we make. We're the safest people on the planet." Kurt put his arm around her, took another bite of coleslaw, and continued talking to Ethan about foreign stocks with high yields.

Vanessa felt invisible and didn't like the feeling. She missed Ty and was sad all over again that he had left without saying good-bye. His disapproval of her carrying the baby to term was no excuse to disappear without an explanation. Didn't he know how much she loved him? Did he even care? The thought that he might be with another woman was more than she could bear.

"What's wrong with you?" Emily said. "Are you going to cry?"

Don't you ever miss anything? "I was just thinking about someone."

"The baby's father?"

"Uh-huh."

"What was he like?"

"Oh … smart. Handsome. Witty. Creative. Gentle. A great listener—"

"Don't forget insensitive and a deadbeat," Ethan added.

Vanessa felt her face get hot. "I was talking to Emily."

"Excuse me for interrupting. But we talked about this all the way from Memphis. Don't lose your perspective."

"Ethan's right," Kurt said. "No matter how wonderful the professor was, there's no excuse for him leaving you high and dry."

"He wouldn't have left without a good reason."

"The good *reason* is he didn't want to support this child," Ethan said.

"Do you really believe he'd throw away his entire teaching career to avoid paying child support?"

Ethan folded his hands on the table. "Vanessa, Professor Nicholson was obviously not the man we thought he was. I liked him too. But we have to face reality. He skipped out."

"He wouldn't do that. You don't know him like I do."

"You're right. I don't." Ethan downed the last of his Coke. "I need to get on the road. I've got a long drive ahead of me." He looked up at Kurt and shook his hand. "Thanks for inviting me to share your table. Emily, next time I'm in Sophie Trace, I'll take you to The Scoop for a banana split. I promise you, you've never had anything like it."

Emily smiled and cocked her head. "Come *soon*."

Ethan patted Vanessa's hand and slid out of the booth. "It was great seeing you. You all have a safe trip back."

She watched Ethan walk past the police officers and disappear through the doorway.

"He likes you," Emily said.

"I like him, too. We're good friends."

"No, he *really* likes you."

Vanessa turned her attention to Emily. "*No*, he really doesn't. We're good friends. That's all. He respects that I'm in love with Ty."

Emily arched her eyebrows, her lips pressed tightly together, and had that annoying if-you-say-so look on her face.

Vanessa sighed. She suddenly felt lonely and wished they didn't have such a long drive home.

CHAPTER 9

BRILL got out of her squad car and nodded at the two officers in the plain DB car that had pulled up to a meter across the street from Nick's Grill.

She paused a moment and marveled at how dawn's streaks of orangey pink and purple contrasted with the haze that was draped across the top of the foothills like a sheer white veil. She leaned against the car and soaked in the beauty, knowing the fiery colors would quickly fade to pastels once Tuesday's sun cleared the horizon.

The sound of someone coughing distracted her, and she looked up just as Trent Norris dropped a cigarette in the middle of the street and crushed it. He smiled sheepishly, then walked over to her.

"Don't look at me like that," he said. "I'm *trying* to quit."

"You might get it done if you could see how black your lungs are."

"Last time I checked, I was black all over." He put his hands in the pockets of his suit pants and avoided eye contact. "Sorry, bad joke. I know you really care."

"My grandfather died of lung cancer. He smoked three packs a day for years."

"We're all going to get old and die of something."

"He wasn't old, Trent. He was fifty-two. It happened when I was a little kid."

"Okay … maybe I'll bum a few Tootsie Pops off Beau Jack. They keep him from lighting up." Trent glanced at his watch. "By the way, I told him to be here at seven. You said you wanted to talk to me first."

"I do. Let's go inside."

Trent held open the glass door, and Brill went inside, hit with the wonderful smells of bread baking and coffee brewing.

The waitress led them to a booth by the windows.

Brill slid in opposite Trent and looked through the blinds at the snapshot view of the old-fashioned gaslights, historic brick buildings, and striped awnings that characterized Third Street.

"Would you like coffee?" The waitress handed them each a menu.

Brill nodded. "Yes, and someone will be joining us shortly. We'll order after he arrives, if that's okay."

"No problem. I'll be right back with your coffee."

Brill folded her hands on the table. "I wanted to talk to you about my conversation with Mayor Roswell. How much did you hear?"

"Pretty much all of it."

"Great. I suppose everyone in the detective bureau did."

"I don't see how. There was a lot going on. My desk is closest to your office, and I had to strain to hear what was said." The corners of Trent's mouth twitched.

"Well, thanks for that." Brill fiddled with the silverware, feeling both relieved and embarrassed.

"Just between you, me, and the fencepost," Trent said, "I was proud of the way you stood your ground."

"Thanks. I'm just getting started. I'm not going to sit back and let the DA's investigators trash a good cop because the city council wants his head on a stick."

"It's hard to say what they'll do since there was a death involved."

"Yes, but it was nothing more than cookie-cutter protocol that Ulman was posted outside O'Toole's door. No one thought O'Toole needed protecting. Everyone, including me, thought I was the next target."

Trent held her gaze. "Go on."

"Ulman is squeaky clean, has a decade of experience and a relationship with the community. He's not the kind of cop I want to replace."

"Maybe he'll get off with a slap on the wrist."

"Regardless, this kind of investigation can crush an officer's spirit. He'll need a great deal of moral support to stay in law enforcement after it's over."

"With all due respect, ma'am, I'm more worried about you." Trent scanned the room and spoke just above a whisper. "Mayor Roswell's as self-serving as they come. He'll back you if it works in his favor. And he'll sell you out if it doesn't. The guy's spineless."

"It's not my intention to bad-mouth the mayor. After all, he was instrumental in hiring me. But you'd think he'd want to give me every break so I could prove myself and make his decision look good."

"How much proof does he need? All he has to do is point to the way you handled the disappearances. Your hunches were right on. You didn't learn to think like that at the police academy."

"Thanks, Trent. My hunches have served me well in law enforcement. But according to the mayor, I wouldn't be hard to replace."

A row of lines formed on Trent's forehead. "You're doing a
bang-up job, Chief. The city council's blind if they can't see it.
And you were *right on* when you told the mayor they're going to
have a bunch of angry cops on their hands if they try to replace
you."

Brill spotted the waitress coming with the coffee. "I love my job,
Trent. But if my best isn't good enough, then maybe I'm the wrong
person to run the department."

Vanessa tried for the third time to snap her robe, then wiggled out
of it and threw it on the chair. Should she be surprised that the hurt
and disappointment she had seen on her dad's face kept her up most
of the night?

She stared at the ballerina music box he had given her after some
boys in the fifth grade had made fun of her long legs. Her dad said
she was perfect, just the way God made her. She wondered what he
thought of her now.

Vanessa stood, vaguely aware of the pink sky outside her window.
She walked downstairs and into the kitchen, where her dad sat at the
table, one hand clutching a coffee mug, the newspaper open in front
of him.

"I didn't expect to see you up this early." Kurt nodded toward the
counter. "There's fresh coffee in the pot."

"Thanks, but I'm not supposed to have caffeine."

"It's been a while. I'm a little rusty."

Vanessa poured herself a glass of orange juice and sat at the table next to him. The baby's kicking reminded her of what she had come to say.

"Could we talk for a minute?"

"Sure." Kurt folded the newspaper and set it aside. "What's on your mind?"

Vanessa breathed in slowly and let it out. She could do this. She had to do this.

"It's obvious things are not okay between us. We need to get it out in the open."

"All right. I think you know that nothing you do will ever cause me to stop loving you. That said, I'm deeply disappointed on a number of levels."

"Because I slept with Ty and got pregnant and you don't get to walk me down the aisle?"

"It's much *deeper* than that. You missed an enormous blessing."

"You can't expect me to apologize for loving Ty."

"How about for concealing your pregnancy from your mother and me for seven months?"

"I already said I was sorry for that."

Kurt laced his fingers together. "Yes, you did. My emotions haven't caught up yet. I'm struggling to understand how you could even think of keeping something of this magnitude from us."

"Because I knew you would react this way."

"Would you rather I just pretended that what you did was okay?" His dark eyes bore into her conscience and then filled with tears.

He turned and looked out the window. "What happened to your promise ring?"

"I still have it. Dad, I know I made a vow to save myself for marriage. But I fell in love with Ty, and it didn't seem important anymore."

"With him out of the picture, it just might."

"My generation isn't hung up about all that."

"And you can see where that thinking has gotten you and thousands of other girls."

"What right do you have to get on my case, after you cheated on Mom?"

Kurt turned and looked her squarely in the eyes. "I have every right. And the responsibility. I'm your father. The fact that I broke the rules doesn't change them."

"Why *did* you?"

Kurt twisted his wedding band around his finger. "The same reason you did—because I put my own wants and desires ahead of what God says is right. I deceived myself. And I paid a hefty price for it. I almost lost your mother." He paused and seemed to be collecting himself. "I wouldn't have gotten myself into that mess if I'd done what I promised. And that's what I thought we had helped you do. You made a vow to God to save yourself for your husband. You wore a ring to seal the promise. Your mother and I thought you took it seriously."

"I did, at the time." Vanessa drew a heart in the condensation on her glass. "I felt differently when I met Ty. It honestly didn't seem wrong."

"You missed out on the blessing of the two becoming one. It goes way beyond the physical. But regardless, that decision will impact you for the rest of your life. You're about to bring a human being into the world."

She choked back the emotion. "It's not like I planned it."

"That's beside the point, Vanessa. No matter how responsible you tried to be, it was irresponsible to get involved in the first place. What seemed to you like an adult decision was *sin*."

"I hear you. But I have trouble seeing my relationship with Ty as sinful. It seemed so right and natural."

"Sex *is* right and natural. It was ordained by God—but for marriage. The world's so messed up about sexuality, there are no boundaries anymore. But God's Word hasn't changed. Your mother and I had this conversation with you when you were in high school. You know right from wrong."

Vanessa did know. And hadn't she known then, the first time she was consumed with passion and ended up in Ty's bed, with candles flickering and some romantic CD playing in the background? She wasn't sure how she was supposed to feel about "becoming a woman," but later, she dismissed the feelings of remorse and told herself how special it was that, of all the women on campus, Ty had picked her.

She had put her promise ring in a drawer and decided she was old enough to do what she wanted as long as no one got hurt. But how could she have ever anticipated *this?*

The baby kicked, almost as if he understood her anguish, and a tear spilled down Vanessa's cheek.

Her father wiped it away with his thumb. "I will say this: I'm proud of you for not aborting this baby. That took amazing courage since you knew it would cost you your relationship with the man you love."

"You always look for the positive in me." Vanessa swallowed a sob. "That's why I listen to you, Dad. You've always understood and accepted me and tried to make me live up to my potential. You and Mom drilled the Bible into my head. It's in there, even when I wish it wasn't. I knew my affair with Ty was wrong, but I wouldn't admit it to myself. It hurts so much that I've disappointed you."

"I'm just disappointed that you settled for so little, Vanessa. You are such a prize."

A prize. Vanessa's eyes clouded over, and the tears streamed down her cheeks. No one besides her dad would ever think that now.

Brill packed the last of her incidentals in her cosmetic case and put it in her overnight bag.

"About ready?" Kurt said.

"I'm just waiting for Rachel. We've got plenty of time. Our flight doesn't leave till four."

"Are you sure you'll feel safe with her watching your back?"

"She's a black belt in karate and the best shot in the department. We'll have a radio car follow us to the Knoxville airport, and I'll have a wall of blue around me in Memphis." She sat on the bed and combed her hands through her hair. "I can't believe I'm going back to my hometown to bury Zack."

Kurt sat on the bed and put his arm around her. "I wish I could be with you. I really don't like this."

"I'll be fine. Just don't let the girls out of your sight. Officers will be watching the house. I'll be home tomorrow night."

"And then you can do it all over again on Thursday. O'Toole's funeral's being televised on WSTN."

"It'll be tough on everyone." Brill stood at the same time Kurt did.

He put his hands on her shoulders and smiled. "You're going to look classy in your dress uniform, Chief. I wish the reason for your packing it were different."

"Me, too. It's overwhelming. I haven't had the mental or emotional space to process Vanessa's situation, and I really need to."

"She and I had a candid discussion at breakfast. Caught me completely off guard."

Brill listened as Kurt relayed the details of that conversation and its emotional conclusion.

"The dialogue was about as honest as it gets," Kurt said.

"I wondered how long it would take her to throw the affair in your face to try to justify her actions. You said all the right things. You've always been able to get through to Vanessa on a level I can't. She's convinced I expect her to fail, and I don't know where that's coming from."

"It's just that you, Ryan, and Emily are brainier and more competitive than she and I. It can be intimidating."

"I don't mean to come across that way. I'm glad you and Vanessa aren't Type A personalities. I don't think this family could handle any more."

Kurt pressed his lips to her cheek. "We're a good mix. I love you, honey. I'll miss you."

"Same here. I really dread watching them fold the flag and hand it to Zack's kids. I hope my knees don't buckle."

CHAPTER 10

NICK Phillips finished visiting with the new customers in booth one and, through the window, spotted the Masinos getting out of their car. He glanced at his watch: twelve noon, straight up.

Half a minute later, the front door opened and Nick walked over to Antonio and shook his hand, then put his other arm around Tessa.

"Good to see you," he said. "You actually arrived before Gus for a change. Come on, I've got your seats reserved at the counter."

"You treat us so well," Tessa said. "Eating lunch here is the highlight of our day."

"Works both ways, my friends."

Nick followed them over to the counter and said, "Today's specials are written there on the blackboard. I highly recommend the grilled veggie burger with Swiss cheese, avocado, sweet onions, and tomatoes on your choice of homemade sourdough, wheat, or rye. Comes with potato salad made with low-fat mayo that's to die for. My wife's recipe."

Antonio helped Tessa onto a stool and then straddled the one next to her. "I don't suppose there's any chance my sweetheart is going to let me order a triple cheeseburger and onion rings?"

Tessa hummed a tune Nick wasn't familiar with.

Antonio smiled. "All right. I'll have the veggie burger," he said to Maggie, who was already standing on the other side of the counter with her green pad and pencil. "On rye. With coffee."

Tessa nodded. "Make it two. With a side order of sweet potato fries." She turned to Antonio and batted her eyelashes, an angelic smile on her face. "We've been really good. Let's splurge a little."

Nick chuckled. "You two crack me up."

"Hey, everybody." Gus slid onto the stool at the end of the counter.

Antonio patted him on the back. "How's it going, friend?"

"Really can't complain, but I always do." Gus laughed. "Maggie, you sweet thing, I'll have my usual."

Maggie blew him a kiss and went through the swinging doors to the kitchen.

"So," Nick said, "was anybody else shocked to find out the police detective who got stabbed was poisoned at the hospital—with peanut oil? How bizarre is that?"

Gus shrugged. "Why are you surprised? The cops don't tell us everything. I've been tryin' to tell you that since the disappearances. Not that y'all listen to me."

"I didn't know a person could be that allergic to peanuts," Antonio said.

Nick nodded. "Peanut and shellfish allergies aren't that uncommon. Restaurant owners have to be on top of things like that. We don't do much frying here, but when we do, we use pure vegetable oil, not peanut oil."

"Hmm … peanuts as a murder weapon," Antonio said. "Whodathunk?"

Gus chuckled. "Jimmy Carter's worst nightmare."

"Will you guys be serious?" Tessa planted her elbows on the counter. "Some young widow is planning her husband's funeral. And don't forget the rodent who killed him has threatened to come after our Chief Jessup, whose family happens to be dear to me."

Gus waved his hand. "Aw, I didn't mean any disrespect, Tessa. It's just ironic the detective was murdered with somethin' natural like *peanut oil* after he survived a brutal stabbing."

"Well," she said, "having been victimized myself, I'm probably overly sensitive about—"

"Hi, everybody." Clint Ames sat on the stool next to Tessa and took off his sunglasses. "Man, is it warming up out there."

Nick walked over behind the counter and stood, his arms folded. "I didn't expect to see *you* again till after Labor Day. Are you filled up out at Hazy View?"

"Every cabin and RV space. But my boys have just about mastered Resort Management 101. I thought I'd get out of their hair for a while. So what'd I miss?"

Nick draped a bar towel over his shoulder. "We were just saying how shocked we are about that detective dying of peanut oil."

"Well"—Clint raised his eyebrows—"I found out from a friend who's a sheriff's deputy that Chief Jessup's former partner was stabbed to death last week in Memphis."

"What?" Tessa said. "There was nothing in the news about that."

Gus turned and looked over the top of his glasses. "There's nothing in the news about *a lot* of things. I keep tellin' y'all."

"You think everything's a conspiracy," Clint said. "There's no cover-up here. The media hasn't connected the dots yet. But they will."

"What dots?"

"Apparently, way back when Chief Jessup was a detective on the Memphis PD, the DA subpoenaed her and her partner to testify at Merrick Fountain's trial. He was convicted of second-degree murder for stabbing his wife's brother and left the courtroom shouting that he was innocent and they would all pay in blood. Looks like he wasn't kidding."

"Wait a minute," Gus said. "How does Detective O'Toole fit into this?"

Clint turned and looked down the counter at Gus. "This Fountain freak goes after a subordinate who lives long enough to tell the real target that he or she is next. At least, that's what happened with the partner."

"You're sayin' O'Toole was stabbed to scare Chief Jessup?" Gus said.

"Actually to warn her. Maybe Fountain came back and finished off the detective just to terrorize her. Look, I've said way too much. You guys keep this to yourselves until it all comes out."

Tessa wrung her hands. "This is shocking. Just shocking. Haven't the Jessups been through enough? Poor Emily. I wonder if she knows all this? She's still so fragile."

Antonio put his arm around Tessa. "I thought we agreed we weren't going to relive what we can't change."

"You know what?" Nick threw his hands in the air. "I just remembered Tuesday is No Bad News Day."

"First I heard of it," Gus said.

Nick caught Gus's gaze and nodded toward Tessa. *Come on, bud. Help me out here.*

"Oh, yeah." Gus winked, a smile beneath his white mustache "That's right. I thought we called it All Good News Day, but it's the same thing."

Vanessa sat with Emily on the glider on the back porch, sharing a bunch of seedless grapes.

"I wish Mom's partner from Memphis hadn't died," Emily said.

"Me, too." Vanessa patted her sister's arm. "But losing Uncle Zack made Mom mad enough to go after the guy who stabbed him. The guy's a loser."

"He's smart, though."

"It doesn't take intelligence to stick a knife in someone."

Emily picked a couple grapes off the bunch and popped them into her mouth. "But he knew how to sneak into the detective bureau with all those cops and not even get caught. That's really hard to do."

"Don't give him credit."

"Well, he stole an ID and got in the hospital room too. This perp is a very sly trickster."

Vanessa fought not to smile at her little sister's choice of words. "Don't worry. Mom will get him."

"What if she doesn't?" Emily said, her mouth stuffed full of grapes.

"She will." Vanessa dismissed the uneasiness that her sister's words had aroused.

There was a prolonged silence, and then Emily said, "What if he gets to her first?"

"He won't. Mom knows what she's doing." Vanessa put her arm around Emily. "Her officers will keep her safe."

"I wish I could believe that, but I don't."

"Because of what almost happened before?"

Emily cocked her head. "What do you think?"

"But you're still alive. And the police knew exactly what to do. Right?"

"I guess so."

"I wasn't there, so I can only imagine how afraid you were. But think of all the times Mom has been in the middle of something scary and put her police skills to work. She's an amazing cop. And if she says she's going to get this guy—she will."

Brill sat with Captain John Donovan at a corner table at Hal's All Night Diner, with Officer Rachel Howell sitting at a nearby table, reading a magazine and sipping a cherry Coke.

"I'm glad you made it to Memphis without incident," John said. "We've all been on pins and needles here, trying to keep DA Cromwell safe. He's seventy now. Active. Determined to play golf and go about his life. Sometimes I think he should just draw a big target on his head."

Brill pursed her lips. "He knows this ape's on a mission and isn't going to stop till we lock him up. I still remember the look of resignation in Mrs. Fountain's eyes—like a whipped puppy's. I remember thinking no human being should ever be reduced to that."

John poured her another cup of decaf. "Why don't we change the subject? You look great in four stars. What's it like being police chief in Sophie Trace? I thought the job seemed too tame for you, but after last fall, I can't say that anymore."

"No, but things have been amazingly calm since the disappearances. Overall, crime's under control. We've cleaned house of a few homegrown gangs and a couple metro gangs that tried to move in. We've had our share of robberies, drug dealing, assaults—aggravated and non—but surprisingly few rapes. And no murders."

John smiled. "Sounds wonderfully boring."

"Actually, it isn't boring at all. It takes work to keep things tidy. My detective captain, Trent Norris, is invaluable. Wish I could say the same for the mayor and city council."

"A real pain, eh?"

"That's putting it mildly. They demand results but aren't patient with the process. They want everything solved yesterday. Of course, Detective O'Toole's death has them foaming at the mouth."

"They need to blame someone."

Brill sighed. "I know. But the truth is, none of us were expecting Fountain to come at O'Toole a second time." She told John what had happened at the hospital that resulted in Rick Ulman's suspension. "He's devastated by the whole thing. You know how hard it is to revive an officer after they crush his spirit."

"I do. I'm sorry."

Brill took her thumb and wiped the lipstick off the rim of her cup. "So ... how does it feel to head up the detective division?"

"*You* know. There's good and there's bad. I don't always sleep at night."

"I remember. But it was four years of good experience. There are those who would argue that taking the job of police chief in a town of thirteen thousand is a comedown. But I like it. I've got great people in the department, and not really much gender bias. I was worried about that, since I'm the first female to take the helm there."

John grinned. "Not to worry. You've *earned* their respect. The disappearances made headline news, and you cracked that case wide open—like you always do. You're a tough act to follow, I'll tell you that."

"I hear you're doing just fine." Brill took a sip of coffee, focusing again on the reason for her visit. "I guess you should fill me in on the plan for tomorrow."

"We've assigned officers to guard you and DA Cromwell. We'll keep you surrounded and out of view as much as possible. I don't see Fountain getting anywhere near the cemetery, but I almost wish he'd try. There'll be several hundred officers there who'd love to take him out."

Brill lay in bed at the Southern Manor Inn, Rachel out in the living room, watching TV, John's two officers keeping watch outside. She opened her cell phone and pressed the auto dial for home. She hadn't even looked at the clock when she requested a 6:00 a.m. wake-up call, and she hoped Kurt hadn't gone to bed yet.

"Well, there you are," he said. "How was your time with John?"

"Good. After Rachel and I got checked in here, we met for dinner at Hal's and caught each other up on the past nine months."

"How does he like your old job?"

"So-so. I think the stress is worse than he thought. He didn't say it, but I think he envies my decision to head up a smaller-town department."

She told Kurt the details of the conversation and nodded off for a second in the middle of the last sentence.

"Honey, go to bed," Kurt said. "You sound exhausted."

"Actually, I'm under the covers as we speak."

"I'm almost there myself. The DB car is outside, so Emily finally relaxed enough to fall asleep."

Brill sighed. "This is so hard on her."

"She's handling it. Are you sure you're safe?"

"Rachel is in the other room watching a movie, and John's officers are nearby. I'm fine. I just called to say good night."

"I'm glad you did. I wish I were with you."

"Ditto."

She could hear Kurt breathing into the phone.

"Honey, I'll be thinking of you tomorrow," he said. "I'll be praying the funeral goes well and isn't too hard on everyone. You cops seem to have mastered the art of not showing emotion. But something tells me there won't be a dry eye when they fold the flag and give it to Zack's kids. See you tomorrow night. Call me when you land. I love you."

"I love you, too. Hug the girls for me."

"I will."

Brill set the phone on the bed, her eyes closed, and let her body go limp as if she were floating on water … buoyant as a lily pad … under the shade of a cypress tree … utter peace … and stillness …

A loud, piercing scream shattered the tranquility into a million shards of raw terror.

Brill's eyes flew open, her heart pounding, and she groped until she found her gun on the nightstand. She jumped to her feet and moved stealthily to the bedroom door and listened. Nothing.

She cracked the door and peeked into the living room. The couch was empty. Where was Rachel? Had someone broken into the room? She started to go out but, instead, closed the door and locked it.

She grabbed her cell phone off the bed and dialed Rachel's number and could hear it ringing.

"Yes, Chief."

"Where are you?"

"In the kitchen. You need something?"

"Are you all right?"

"I'm fine. Why?"

"I heard a woman scream."

"When?"

"One minute ago. Are you alone?"

"Absolutely. Well, unless you count Ben and Jerry."

Brill unlocked the bedroom door and opened it ever so slowly, her gun held in front of her.

Rachel, her eyes wide and questioning, sat at the kitchen table, a spoon in one hand, a pint of Ben and Jerry's Rainforest Crunch ice cream in the other.

Brill exhaled and lowered the gun, a hollow feeling in the pit of her stomach.

"I've been right here, Chief. I didn't hear anyone scream."

Brill collapsed on the couch. "Sorry, Rachel. I must've been dreaming. The scream sounded so real. For a minute, I thought Merrick Fountain had gotten to *you*."

CHAPTER 11

WEDNESDAY'S temperatures were on the rise as scores of law enforcement officers filed onto the grounds of Our Redeemer Cemetery, the Mississippi River snaking in the distance, and the state of Arkansas stretched beyond it as far as the eye could see.

The turnout for Zack Rogers's funeral had been even greater than anticipated. Countless officers from various law enforcement agencies around the state came to pay their respects. And afterward they lined up their vehicles and formed a seemingly endless caravan that processed from the church to the cemetery, passing by Memphis citizens who lined the predetermined route in somber silence.

Brill stood with John Donovan and other officials of the Memphis PD just a few yards from the green awning that marked the burial site, and listened to the officiant say the final prayer.

She glanced over at Zack's son and daughter, who sat arm in arm near their father's flag-draped casket, and could hardly believe how grown up they were. She turned away and tried to think of something else. Her mind flashed back to Zack's visit the day Emily was born …

There'd been a knock on her hospital room door, then Zack had stuck his head in the room.

"Any chance I can see the little dickens who's kept my partner out of the field for six months?"

"Sure, come in," Kurt said. "She's a keeper."

Zack, his eyes wide with wonder, came over to the bed, holding a bouquet of pink roses.

"Isn't she something?" he whispered.

"Emily Patrice," Brill said. "Six pounds, eight ounces."

"She looks like you."

"Think so?"

"Yeah, minus the red hair."

Vanessa tapped him on the shoulder. "Uncle Zack, *I* get to help babysit."

"Not me." Ryan pinched his nose. "I'm not changing diapers."

"Maybe Zack would like to hold her," Brill said.

"You trust me?"

She laughed. "You've had as much practice as I've had. And if I can put my life in your hands, I think I can trust you to hold my daughter."

"Good point."

Zack laid the roses on the bedside table, and Brill ever so carefully transferred Emily into his arms, impressed with how relaxed he seemed.

"Here we go, cutie." He stood up straight. "Your uncle Zack's got you now. And you're about the prettiest thing I've ever seen in that little pink hat."

Kurt grabbed the camera. "Say cheese."

Zack turned, Emily looking like a china doll in his arms, and the camera flashed …

The sound of bagpipes playing "Amazing Grace" brought Brill back to the present, and the words resounded in her mind.

> *Amazing grace, how sweet the sound*
> *That saved a wretch like me.*
> *I once was lost but now am found,*
> *Was blind but now I see …*

She looked out to the Mississippi, her eyes stinging, and pictured Zack strolling the streets of gold with his wife. Had he ever been able to work through his doubts about God's fairness? About his own sinfulness? Had he ever trusted Jesus Christ as his Savior? It was easier to believe he had than to say good-bye forever.

The bagpipes stopped playing, and an eerie silence settled over the gathering. Brill held her breath. On cue, seven officers lifted their rifles and fired three times in perfect sync, the shots echoing across the wide Tennessee sky.

She felt emotion tighten her throat as white-gloved officers removed the flag from the casket and folded it ceremoniously, then presented it to Zack's children. A tear rolled down her cheek, and she quickly wiped it away and dug her feet more firmly into the grass, determined to find Merrick Fountain and lock him up for the rest of his life.

Vanessa walked into the kitchen. Emily had her elbows planted on the table, her chin resting in her palms, and seemed to be studying something.

"What are you looking at?"

"A picture of Mom's partner that died."

Vanessa went over to the table and picked up the photo and smiled.

"Where'd you find this?"

"In the photo album."

"I was there when it was taken. Uncle Zack had come to the hospital to see you. He brought Mom flowers and Ryan and me pink bubblegum cigars."

"Was he nice?"

Vanessa handed the photograph back to Emily. "Very. And funny."

Emily was quiet for a few moments, and then said, "I can tell Mom's really sad that he died."

"Of course she is. You can't be partners with someone for ten years and not be close."

"I don't like it when Mom cries. It makes me want to cry too."

Vanessa sat in the chair next to Emily and put her arm around her sister's shoulder. "Listen, Shortcake. Mom's fine. She's a rock."

"What if she's not fine? She might be sad all by herself."

"She's not by herself. Half the cops in the state are attending the funeral."

"Well, she's not a rock," Emily said. "She just pretends to be."

"We already had this conversation. You don't need to worry about Mom. If she wasn't tough, she'd have gotten out of law enforcement a long time ago."

"Zack was tough too. And he's dead."

Vanessa gave Emily a reassuring squeeze. "Don't you worry about that creep getting to Mom. Now that everyone knows what he's up to, her officers can protect her." *I hope.*

"But she seems sad again." Emily sighed. "Like when she was angry about the adultery."

Vanessa fiddled with Emily's ponytail. The poor kid had learned the meaning of words she shouldn't have to know yet.

"Emily, Mom's sad about Zack's death. But there's more to her gloomy mood than that. She's not happy I'm pregnant."

"You're happy, aren't you?" Emily asked.

"I'm trying to be. It's a little scary."

"Because you don't have a husband or a job?"

"Yes. And it bothers me that my son won't know his father."

Emily folded her arms across her chest. "Well, I'm glad you didn't get an abortion."

"Do you know what that is?"

"Not exactly. But when someone gets one, the baby dies, and people carry signs to protest because they're really upset."

Was she actually having this conversation with her ten-year-old sister? "Why don't we finish talking about Mom? I promise you she's going to get over being sad because she has Dad to help her."

"Yes, she does." Kurt stood in the doorway. "Are you girls worried about your mother?"

"I am," Emily said.

"Well, she just called my cell phone, and she's on her way home."

Vanessa studied her dad's face. "How was the funeral?"

"Very moving. Your mother sounded tired, but she said Zack would have been humbled to see how many officers turned out."

"Then the killer didn't show up?" Emily said.

"No, sweetie. Security was tight. They made sure he couldn't get near her or District Attorney Cromwell. We already talked about that."

"Will security be tight when she gets home?"

Kurt sat at the table and took Emily's hands in his. "I promise you her officers are doing everything possible to keep her safe. We have to trust God with the rest."

After dinner, Vanessa sat in the glider on the back porch, the evening air thick with humidity and the scent of something earthy. Her mother's words played in her mind …

Come up with a plan, Vanessa. If you want to raise your son, fight for him. You're not going to get very far if you keep thinking of yourself as a victim.

She jumped when her cell phone rang. She picked it up off the cushion and didn't recognize the number on the screen.

"Hello."

"Hi. It's Ethan."

Her heart sank. For a split second she'd thought it might be Ty.

"I didn't recognize your number."

"I forgot my cell phone. I borrowed one from one of the other roofers."

"So how was your first day on the job?"

"All right." His tone belied his answer.

"That bad, eh?"

"Oh, I'll get used to it. The other guys hardly speak English, and my Spanish is pathetic. At least it pays well. I need the tuition money. Maybe the time will go fast. So how are *you* doing?"

"Not much to tell you," Vanessa said. "My mom went to Memphis for her ex-partner's funeral. And the rest of us are under police protection here at the house. I feel like I'm under house arrest."

"Are you not allowed to go out alone?"

"That's not it. I don't have anywhere to go."

"You need to find an obstetrician."

"I will. But I'm depressed. It's all I can do to get out of bed. I don't want to drop out of college. I don't want to give up the baby. I don't want to live in Sophie Trace. I don't want my son to grow up without his father …" Her voice cracked.

"That's a lot of *don't wants*, Vanessa. You can only deal with one at a time. Which is most important?"

"That's easy." She wiped a tear off her cheek. "Decide what to do about the baby. It's hard to consider keeping him when my parents are so unenthused."

"Give them time. You just dropped a bomb out of the blue. It'll take a while for them to come around."

"Well, I don't have a while."

Ethan was silent for a moment, and then said, "Then make the decision that's right for the baby and you. You're the parent now."

"Why do I get the feeling you think I should keep the baby?"

"I've never said that. I just think you have to be at peace with the decision and not let anyone else make it for you."

"Sounds personal."

There was a moment of dead air, and Vanessa thought the connection had been broken. "Ethan?"

"I've got to go. My dinner break is over, and the other guys are already back on the roof."

"You're still working?"

"Yeah, we work till the sun goes down. I'll call you again when I'm not on the clock and not using someone else's minutes."

"Okay."

"Take care."

"You, too."

Vanessa sat in the quiet for a moment, and then realized a grandmotherly woman in a purple housedress had opened the gate.

The woman waved and then came over and stood at the bottom of the steps, and Vanessa recognized her as the next-door neighbor she had met at Thanksgiving.

"Hello, hello," Tessa Masino said. She held up a loaf of something wrapped in cellophane. "I brought you some of my fresh apricot bread. It's quite delicious toasted and buttered."

Tessa climbed the steps, opened the door, and handed the loaf to Vanessa.

"I hope you don't mind me dropping in like this," Tessa said. "But I called the house, and your dad said you were sitting out here and it would be fine if I came on back. Those nice police officers gave me the green light. Of course, I gave them a loaf too."

Tessa was short and round, no waistline, silver curls framing her face. Her smile was infectious.

"Uh, thanks," Vanessa said. "Would you like to come in and sit down?"

"Well, isn't that nice of you. Thank you, I would."

Tessa sat in the wicker chair, folding her hands in her lap. "How're you feeling, dear?"

"Good. My baby is due July twenty-eighth, in case my parents haven't told you."

"They did. How wonderful."

"It's a boy."

"Oh, my, isn't it marvelous that nowadays they can tell the gender of the child in the womb?" Tessa fiddled with the zipper on her housedress. "So, you just finished your sophomore year at the University of Memphis?"

"Yes, I'm working toward a degree in elementary educa—"

The back door opened, and Emily skipped out onto the porch and threw her arms around Tessa as if she were family.

"Dad said you were coming over," Emily said. "Did you know I'm going to be an aunt?" She pointed to Vanessa's abdomen. "There's a real baby in there."

Tessa laughed. "Indeed."

"I'm going to be Auntie Em, like on the *Wizard of Oz*."

"I never thought of that." Tessa put her hand over her smile. "You look younger than Dorothy."

Vanessa watched the interaction between the two and felt lonely again, the way she had at the Whistlin' Dixie when her dad and Ethan were talking about the stock market and she felt like an outsider.

She waited a few minutes, then got up and went into the house, wondering how long it would be before Emily and Tessa even noticed she was gone.

CHAPTER 12

BRILL got out of Rachel Howell's squad car, her overnight bag strapped to her shoulder, and trudged toward the cottage-style house she and Kurt had bought the day it went on the market. She lifted her hand in acknowledgment of the two officers in a plain DB car parked across the street.

She unlocked the door, pushed it with her shoulder, and stepped inside. In the next second she found herself enveloped in Kurt's embrace. She rested there, a wilted flower wearing a badge.

"I'm so glad you're home," Kurt finally said. "I wanted to be with you."

"It's probably better you weren't. If you'd have shown me an ounce of tenderness, I'd have broken down."

"It's allowed."

"Not when you're wearing this uniform, it isn't. Not in public anyway. Somehow I managed to hold it together. And I need to do it again tomorrow."

"Well, Sean O'Toole's funeral won't be as personal," he said.

"Are you kidding? Sean wouldn't be dead if Merrick hadn't used him to try to intimidate me."

"That's not *your* fault."

"It's still hard enough to live with."

She walked down the hall and into their bedroom, Kurt on her heels, and set the bag on the bed and unzipped it.

"Are the girls in bed?" she said.

"Yeah, they stayed up until the news was over. They worried about you all day like a couple of mother hens."

"I was never in danger. John made sure of that."

"Well, Emily's not convinced."

Brill sighed. "Poor thing. How's Vanessa feeling?"

"Good. Tessa came over to see her."

"At least we told her first so she didn't find out like the people at church."

Brill hated the sarcasm in her voice. She pulled her dirty clothes out of the bag, carried them to the bathroom, and stuffed them in the laundry hamper.

"Honey, would you slow down?" Kurt said. "Give your feelings a chance to catch up. You've been through the mill."

She came back and sat on the bed. "I can't afford to let my feelings catch up. I need to be strong for my department."

"Not tonight you don't." He stroked her cheek. "Why don't you take a hot shower and I'll massage your shoulders. You always sleep better when I do. Take a few minutes and be good to yourself. You'll hold up better tomorrow."

"You're right."

Brill got up and pulled her pajamas out of the dresser drawer, walked into the bathroom, and closed the door.

She stood at the sink, taken aback by her reflection in the mirror. Fatigue had darkened the area under her eyes. Her cheeks were colorless, her frown lines pronounced. Repressed emotion was no more attractive than a red nose and swollen eyes, just more acceptable.

She would have to allow time to make herself presentable in the morning. The media would want a statement, and the mayor and city council would not appreciate their police chief looking ghastly.

Not that she could count on keeping her job after all this. But as long as she held the authority, she would stay focused on keeping the department together—and nailing the guy who killed Sean and Zack.

Vanessa heard her mother come in. She lay in bed wide awake but didn't have the motivation or energy to get up and read or do something else. Her mind raced with tender memories of Ty and questions for which she had no answers.

She knew from the start he was not looking for a permanent relationship. Why had she ever entertained the idea that he would make theirs the exception?

He seemed so matter-of-fact when suggesting she should get an abortion that she suspected it wasn't the first time he'd been faced with the issue. She shuddered to think of how many children never took a breath so Professor Nicholson could keep his image untainted and avoid making a long-term commitment.

Vanessa was torn between anger and fear. She could deal with his unwillingness to raise their child easier than his leaving her to face labor and delivery alone. She blinked away her preconceived ideas about all that. Why worry until she took the childbirth classes and knew for sure what awaited her?

It pierced her to the heart that she was a disappointment to her parents *again,* but what else should they expect from the child who'd been sandwiched between their only son and their baby daughter—and who possessed inferior intelligence and none of the charm?

The only asset Vanessa had was her beauty. Big deal. She got wolf whistles and double takes while Ryan received a scholarship to Vanderbilt and Emily was voted math whiz of the gifted-and-talented program. Whoever said beauty was skin deep must have lived with the emptiness.

The baby kicked harder than usual, almost as if to shame her for wallowing in self-pity. The hearty thud was a tangible reminder that July twenty-eighth wasn't far off, and she still didn't know what to do.

Was it fair to saddle this little boy with a single-parent home when there were umpteen couples eagerly waiting for an infant to adopt? Couples who had reliable incomes, a solid spiritual foundation, and college funds? How could she compete with that? How was she supposed to know which decision was the right one?

Maybe all your options are right, and it's just a matter of picking the one that works best for you.

Ethan's words rang with hope. At least if she could believe all her options were good ones, she wouldn't have to feel guilty, regardless of what she decided. Why did it have to be so overwhelming?

Brill crawled under the covers, her muscles relaxed after Kurt's hands had kneaded away the stress that seemed to have settled in her neck and shoulders.

She turned on her side, facing him. "Thanks. I feel much better."

"It's the least I can do to help you through this mess. Am I going to have to worry about you tomorrow?"

"No, Trent's worked out the details with Sam Parker's deputies. Between our two departments and all the help pouring in from other departments in the region, Merrick would have to be a fool to try anything."

"Well …?"

She traced Kurt's eyebrow with her finger. "He's a lot of things, but he's no fool. He's had fifteen years to think about how to get even. He's not going to throw away his chance."

"That's reassuring."

"Not to worry. I'm just as determined as he is. He stabbed three cops, and I'm going to get him. It's just a matter of when."

"So now it's a game?"

"No." She put her finger on his lips to silence him. "It's serious business. I want Merrick put away where he'll never see the light of day. Every cop in the state does."

"He's probably thriving on the attention."

"Not for long."

"Honey, you're talking like you have the time and manpower to go after him. With the cutbacks the city council's imposed, you can barely keep the department running efficiently."

"You'd be surprised how much help we'll get. Every branch of law enforcement wants a cop killer behind bars. They make sacrifices to help us get the perp and bring him to justice."

"Well, I'll never rest while the threat's hanging over you."

She brushed the hair off his forehead. "You can't worry about it, Kurt. *I'm* not. We've got to go on with our lives. I've got the right protections in place. It's in God's hands, anyway."

"It's just hard for me to leave it there. I can't stand being out of control. Maybe it's a guy thing."

"I'm not helpless."

"But you're still my wife. My natural instinct is to protect you."

"I know. And believe it or not, that's a great feeling—even for a police chief."

He pressed his lips to hers and then pulled the covers up to her shoulder. "Get some sleep. Tomorrow's going to be rough."

CHAPTER 13

TESSA Masino eased her way down the wooden staircase and entered the living room, which was flooded with morning sun and where Antonio sat on the couch, reading the newspaper.

"You've been spying on the Jessups all morning," Antonio said. "Why don't you just call Emily and ask her whatever it is you want to know?"

Tessa felt her cheeks burning. "Antonio, I don't spy. I *observe*."

"I see. And what did you observe, my love?"

"Well, I just saw Brill leave, wearing her dress uniform. Presumably for the funeral this afternoon."

He turned the page. "Not terribly newsy, Columbo. Is that it?"

"There's a black Chevrolet Impala parked across the street. But the officers inside are different than the ones who were there last night."

"How can you tell from this far away?" He peeked over the top of his reading glasses, the corners of his mouth twitching. "Oh, that's right. You have binoculars."

"They're *opera* glasses. But they come in handy for other things." She flashed him an impish smile. "You call it spying, but I'd like to think I'm just a concerned neighbor who wants to be sure the Jessups are safe."

"Looks to me like Brill has it covered. So what's got your curiosity on tilt?"

"Frankly, I'm concerned about Vanessa. She's got a huge decision to make. And then to have all this on top of it."

"You're meddling."

"Of course I'm meddling, Antonio. That's what I do." She glanced over at the Jessups' house again. "But not just for the sake of being nosy. From the first time we met them, the Lord's put this family on my heart. You know that."

"Yes, you have the *gift* of meddling."

"Vanessa looks so lost."

"The girl's in trouble, love. How would you expect her to look?"

"It's not about what I would expect. She needs something. I don't know what it is yet."

"A husband?"

Tessa exhaled and folded her arms across her chest. "Be kind, Antonio. She's barely more than a teenager."

"Old enough to know better."

"Yet naive enough to trust her heart"—Tessa lifted one eyebrow—"*and* the professor she no doubt admired and respected."

"Women were much better off when they drew the line."

"I can't disagree with that. But how did a whole generation of girls get brainwashed into thinking that casual sex would be fulfilling? Instead, it's made them slaves, not only to passion, but also to their yearning for acceptance and affirmation. Poor things won't find shallow relationships satisfying for long."

"Men don't either, but they're not always looking for *relationship*."

Tessa sighed. "Isn't it sad that what God ordained for marriage has been taken outside and reduced to mere entertainment? These kids don't even know what they're missing."

"Well, with one out of two marriages failing, maybe they don't think commitment means much."

"It certainly does to the one out of two that *isn't* failing. I sense that Brill and Kurt worked through a rough spot right after they moved here, but they seem devoted to each other."

Antonio took off his reading glasses and put them on the end table. "Which just goes to show you that kids make their own choices, and it's sometimes the opposite of what they were taught."

"I know one thing," Tessa said. "They don't come home to deal with a predicament like Vanessa's unless they know there's a solid foundation there."

Antonio held open the glass door at Nick's Grill, and Tessa stepped inside and was hit with the aroma of garlic and herbs.

Nick walked over to them. "Well, there you are. Gus and I weren't sure if you'd make it today. We think it's great that people from your church are going to honor Sean O'Toole by holding up flags along the street while the funeral procession goes by."

"It's the least we can do." Tessa hugged him. "I can't imagine being Mrs. O'Toole today."

"What smells so good?" Antonio said.

"Grilled chicken spinach salad." Nick moved his eyebrows up and down. "I let the chicken marinate overnight in a special blend of olive oil, garlic, and spices I got from an Italian chef my folks know. It's out of this world. Comes tossed with my sweet basil dressing."

"Sounds great," Antonio said.

Tessa headed for the counter and sat in her usual place.

Antonio slid onto the stool next to her and slapped Gus on the back. "How's it going, friend?"

"Really can't complain, but I always do." Gus chuckled. "I'll cut to the chase: Get the grilled chicken spinach salad. You'll think you died and went to heaven."

"You've already eaten?" Antonio said.

"Nah, Maggie let me sample it, didn't you, doll?"

Maggie Cummings stood behind the counter, her green pad and pencil in hand. "A good marketing ploy. Did I mention there's an entire chicken breast in each salad?"

"Okay, that's what I'm having," Antonio said.

"*What* are you having?" Clint Ames took his seat at the counter.

"Grilled chicken spinach salad."

"It's amazing." Maggie looked over at Gus and winked. "Have I ever led you astray, Clint?"

"Never. Bring it on."

"Tessa?"

Tessa folded her hands on the counter, curious about the twinkle she saw in Maggie's eyes. After all these years, was she finally sweet on Gus? "Yes, it sounds delicious."

Maggie scribbled on her green pad and then headed for the kitchen, a noticeable spring in her step.

"I heard WSTN is televising the funeral." Gus took a sip of Coke. "I don't wanna see it. Too sad—what with the widow and kids and all."

"Well," Tessa said, "let's hope they use the camera to honor the life of the fallen officer and not to exploit his grieving family."

"I saw on the news that our police chief was in Memphis yesterday for her ex-partner's funeral." Clint laid his sunglasses on the counter. "She sure got a double whammy."

Tessa nodded. "I'll say." *Actually a triple whammy, if you count Vanessa.*

"It's all how you look at it." Gus rubbed his white mustache. "We've had nothin' but trouble in this town since Brill Jessup came here. And whose money do you think is payin' for all the trouble?"

"How can you reduce it to dollars and cents?" Tessa shook her head and exhaled loudly enough to show her disgust. "You really don't know the half of what that woman has been through."

"What I *do* know is we're payin' her to protect the community. Havin' a detective stabbed and then poisoned to death doesn't exactly make *me* feel safe."

"Oh, stop your bellyaching." Tessa realized she had blurted out what she was thinking and felt her cheeks burn. "Imagine how Brill feels, since *she's* the one who's been threatened."

"You're always defendin'—"

"Here we go." Maggie shot Gus a why-don't-you-change-the-subject look and set two mugs on the table. She filled them with coffee, then reached in her pocket and pulled out several tiny tubs of creamer. "I'll bring your orders in just a few minutes. And for the record, I agree with Tessa. We can't blame the police chief because a criminal she put away wants to get even."

"But the chief's a crime magnet," Gus insisted. "She hadn't been here a month when the disappearances started. She's like a bad-luck charm."

Tessa rolled her eyes. "From day one, you've blamed the disappearances on the spirits of the departed Cherokee. So which is it, Gus? You can't have it both ways."

"All I'm sayin' is trouble seems to follow her. And when it finds her, it's our tax money that's bein' used to pay for it."

Tessa took a sip of coffee. She should stop sparring with him. This was not the way to let her light shine.

"Actually," she said, softening her tone, "there's money in the police department's budget to cover it, so we don't even need to concern ourselves with it."

Antonio nudged Gus with his elbow. "What my sweetheart's trying to say is we're going to pay the same taxes whether the chief gets into hot water or not. It's a nonissue."

"Aw, I didn't mean to ruffle any feathers, y'all. I was just pointin' out the obvious. I'll tell you one thing, I wouldn't want her job."

"*Especially* today," Tessa said.

Tessa, holding an American flag, stood with Antonio in the shade of a giant oak tree as Sean O'Toole's funeral procession moved down First Street. All whispering ceased as the hearse went by, followed by the family limousines. She wondered if Mrs. O'Toole and the children were comforted at all by the impressive turnout of ordinary citizens along the funeral route. It seemed as though the entire town had come out.

A seemingly endless caravan of police cars, motorcycles, and fire trucks moved slowly toward the cemetery, with some members of law enforcement walking alongside.

Security was high—and not because the governor and both state senators were in attendance. She wondered if Brill was being kept out of sight and out of harm's way. She hoped Emily was feeling safe in the shadow of the two officers assigned to protect her family.

Tessa felt Antonio squeeze her hand, and for a split second, she imagined herself as the grieving widow and wondered how she could ever bear to lose him.

The vehicles continued to move slowly down First, and she craned but couldn't see the end.

Chimes from the bell tower of First Christian Church filled the abnormal hush with "Faith of Our Fathers." She felt a chill as she hummed the last words of the chorus: *We will be true to Thee till death.*

Death. What a cruel robber it was. Something the Creator had never intended for the people He made. She hoped that Sean O'Toole had come to know the Savior and that he hadn't felt the sting of death. Certainly his family had.

How difficult it must be for Brill to accept that this fine officer was used as a pawn—murdered to intimidate her. And how unsettling it must be for her to live day to day, knowing the murderer was still out there, stalking her.

The vehicles continued to pass for several more minutes, and finally she could see a horse at the very end of the procession, led by an officer who was on foot.

As the horse without a rider passed by, she noticed that boots had been placed backward in the stirrups. Tears blinded her, and she held tightly to Antonio's hand, saying a prayer for Sean O'Toole's widow and her children.

Brill stood in Jessica O'Toole's living room, sipping a plastic cup of 7UP and watching her officers offer their condolences to the family. The two officers assigned to protect her were just feet away.

She wondered if the dining-room table could hold any more food and assumed that someone from Jessica's church would coordinate the bringing of meals in the long, empty, difficult weeks ahead.

How could this have happened? Five days ago Sean was alive and breathing in this very house. He roughhoused with his kids. Took out the trash. Kissed his wife. Read the newspaper. Petted the dog. Watched TV. Life was normal, and he was greatly blessed.

Brill sighed. Despite the dangers police officers are taught to live with, there is no one to teach them how to die—except those who have fallen. She had learned it twice this week. She didn't want another lesson anytime soon, nor did she want to *be* the lesson.

She wondered how Emily was doing. She motioned to the two officers assigned to watch her back and walked down the hallway and into the bathroom. She took out her cell phone, hit the auto dial, and let it ring.

"Hi, Mom."

"Hi, sweetie. Did you and Dad and Vanessa watch the funeral on TV?"

"Yes, it was sad. But we think Mrs. O'Toole should be proud of the way everyone came from all over Tennessee to show they care."

Brill leaned against the sink. "She's very proud. I'm at her house right now, and lots of officers are here to pay their respects."

"Were his kids sad?"

"I'm sure they were. The oldest read a poem during the funeral service. It wouldn't surprise me if everyone got a little emotional—or felt like it. I sure did."

"Did you have bodyguards?"

"Two officers were assigned to be my shadows. They're just outside the door."

"Good."

Brill fiddled with a button on her uniform. "When we drove to the cemetery, I saw Tessa and Antonio with their church group, standing along First Street, holding American flags."

"Cool. Did you wave?"

"The limousine windows were tinted, and they wouldn't have seen me. Why don't you call and tell Tessa?"

"I will. Are you coming home for dinner?"

"I'm planning to. I need to go back to the station and make sure my people are all right. This took a lot out of them."

"Because it could've been *them* who got killed?"

"Partly. But mostly because they feel bad for Sean's wife and kids."

Emily exhaled into the receiver. "Mom, I don't think I could stand it if you got killed. I already tried to imagine it, but it really made my stomach hurt."

"I'm not going to let anything happen to me."

"Are you *sure* everyone is paying attention so that guy can't get close to you?"

"I'm sure. There's not an officer in my department or the sheriff's department that isn't determined, not just to get Merrick, but to keep him from hurting anyone else."

"But what if he dresses up like a police officer and sneaks inside the detective bureau?"

"We changed the code, sweetie. He won't have any way of finding out what it is. And no one's going to give any unauthorized person access to the DB."

There was a long moment of dead air and then Emily's voice: "I asked God to send a guarding angel to watch over you because you need *lots* of guarding."

Brill smiled at her baby girl's sincerity. "Actually, sweetie, they're called *guardian* angels. But you're right, I need lots of guarding. And I'll take all the help I can get."

Another pause told Brill that her ever-inquisitive child wasn't finished asking questions.

"Mom," Emily finally said, "did Detective O'Toole get killed because of you? That's what they said on the news."

Emily's words pierced her heart. "Merrick Fountain wanted to scare me, so he hurt Detective O'Toole. The same way he hurt another detective to scare Zack."

"Yeah, and Zack died."

"Two days later of a heart attack. He might have had the heart attack even if he hadn't been stabbed. Emily, we already talked about this … I'm not going to die."

"Promise?"

"I promise. I've got a guardian angel with me, right?"

"Right."

"Go tell Dad I'll be home early."

CHAPTER 14

BRILL hung her dress uniform in the closet just as her cell phone vibrated. She hurried over to the nightstand and saw that Dexter Babbitt was the caller. She wondered if he'd found Vanessa's deadbeat boyfriend.

"Hi, Dexter. What'd you find out?"

"I'm fine, thanks. And how are you?"

She flopped on the bed. "Sorry. It's been a long day. I forgot my manners. How are things going?"

"I've hit a brick wall. No one Nicholson worked with knows anything about his background or has a clue where he might have gone. The HR director at the university said he didn't even call to inquire about his last check. What did Vanessa tell you about him?"

"Just that he was an only child, and his parents are deceased. But the university should have his résumé and personal information on file."

"They do. He previously taught at Chambers College near Knoxville, so I drove over there, hoping to talk to some faculty members who knew him. No one remembered him. Even the chancellor didn't recognize his name or his photograph. So I dug deeper, and there's no record he ever taught there. So now I've got red flags going up right and left. I drove down to Nicholson's alma mater,

Barsfield University in Chattanooga. Long story short, they have no record that a Tyson Frederick Nicholson ever attended Barsfield University or their graduate school."

"Come on, Dexter. How can that be? He couldn't have gotten hired as a professor without teaching credentials."

"Exactly. The University of Memphis verified that he taught at Chambers College for six years and got his master's from Barsfield."

Brill ran her hand through her hair. "Then how can Barsfield not have a record of it?"

"Everyone here is clueless, and I'm burned out. I'm heading to Nashville tomorrow to see if his high school still has his records. Maybe I can work this thing forward from there. I'll tell you what: My curiosity's off the charts. I couldn't stop now, even if you weren't paying me. I'll be in touch."

"All right, Dexter. Keep me posted."

Brill set her phone on the nightstand and realized Kurt had come into the bedroom.

"Something bad happen at work?" he said.

"No, that was Dexter."

"Did he find Nicholson?"

"Not even close." Brill relayed to Kurt everything Dexter had said. "This just makes me more determined. I want to know what he's trying to pull."

"Honey, are you sure you want to know? I don't have a good feeling about this."

"What do we have to lose? Vanessa doesn't need to know what Dexter's doing unless he uncovers something useful. It just frosts me that Nicholson could get away without taking any of the responsibility."

Kurt sat next to her on the bed. "I don't like it either. But he did tell Vanessa from day one he wasn't interested in anything permanent."

"I guess he should've thought it through before he slept with her."

"He probably did. Vanessa said they were careful."

"Not careful enough."

"The guy probably thought abortion was his safety net."

"Well, he thought wrong. Whose side are you on?"

Kurt took her hand. "Vanessa's, all the way. My point in all this is that even if we find him, forcing him to take a paternity test and pay child support won't turn him into a dad. Even Vanessa understands that much."

"Vanessa doesn't understand *anything*. For heaven's sake, Kurt, it's possible he's lied to her about who he is."

"Honey, calm down. That's all the more reason why I'm not so sure I want us to find him. Maybe we're better off leaving well enough alone."

"Then Vanessa needs to take a realistic look at her options. If she's not willing to put the baby up for adoption, she'd better get in gear and figure out how to take care of him. The clock is ticking."

Kurt chewed his lip the way he did when he was deep in thought.

Finally he said, "If she's determined to keep the baby, are you totally opposed to the idea of them living with us for a while?"

Brill looked into his deep brown eyes. It hadn't taken Vanessa long to win him over.

"Kurt, there's something going on you need to know about."

"What?"

"Remember my run-in with Mayor Roswell? It ended on a shaky note."

"What do you mean by shaky?"

She told him every detail she could recall of the unpleasant confrontation.

"I essentially countered his threat with a threat. I told him to stay out of my way until we get O'Toole's killer caught and convicted. And that if the city council wants me out after that, they won't have to ask twice. When he left he told me to watch my step, that I wouldn't be hard to replace."

"For crying out loud, Brill. Why are you just now telling me this?"

"I don't know. It happened Monday when you and the girls went to see Ryan. I was asleep when you got home, and I've been burying cops ever since."

Kurt leaned forward, his elbows on his knees, and raked his hands through his hair. "I had second thoughts when we signed the mortgage papers on the house, but I was counting on you keeping this job for a long time."

"So was I. But I refuse to perform like some circus lion that sits every time the city council cracks the whip. Either I'm empowered to do my job or I'm not. If they're planning to fire me, I'm almost certain they won't do it until Fountain is locked up and convicted."

Kurt put his arm around her. "No wonder you're pushing Vanessa to make a decision. Without your salary, we'd barely be able to make ends meet, let alone foot the bill for diapers and formula."

"And I'll never find a job in law enforcement here. We could be looking at another move while she's still learning to cope with being a single mom." Brill sighed. "What I don't want is for her to feel pressured to put the baby up for adoption, based solely on a short-term cash flow problem."

Brill approached the door to Vanessa's room and overheard her two daughters talking.

"There … he kicked again." Emily giggled. "Does it feel all tickly?"

"Hardly," Vanessa said. "It feels like he's wearing boxing gloves."

"What're you going to name him?"

"I don't know. There're other things I need to figure out first."

"You can use my old baby bed. It'll fit right there against the wall. You have lots of room, and I—"

"Listen, Shortcake. I'm not sure that I'll be bringing the baby here. He might be better off if I let some nice married couple adopt him."

"If I were him, I would want *you* to be the mom."

Brill knocked on the open door. "Anybody home?"

"Come in," Vanessa said.

Brill looked at Emily. "Sweetie, would you let me have a few minutes alone with your sister?"

"Why does everybody treat me like I'm a big baby?"

"You're not a baby," Vanessa said. "You're Auntie Em, remember?"

"That's right." Emily skipped past Brill and out the door, singing "Over the Rainbow."

"Your dad said you found an obstetrician."

"I did. Doctor Shea Zimmer. I like her. She said the baby sounds strong and healthy. And judging from the size he is now, she thinks he's going to weigh around seven pounds when he's born."

A long moment of dead air followed, and Brill could hear the ticking of the clock on the nightstand.

"I guess you came in here to tell me I need to make a decision," Vanessa said.

"Actually, I was just eager to hear about your appointment with Doctor Zimmer. But since you brought it up—yes, you need to make a decision so you can start preparing yourself."

"I can't think right now." Vanessa put her hands to her temples. "I'm on overload."

"We're all on overload. That doesn't make time stand still." Brill gently grasped Vanessa's arm. "I think you know what you want. Maybe you just need to be honest with yourself."

"But how do I know it's the right decision?"

"I think you should start by praying about it. Like your dad said, God wasn't caught off guard by this child, even if the rest of us were. He has a plan for him."

Vanessa's eyes were suddenly blue pools. "But how do *I* know what that is?"

"You don't. But whatever the plan is, God will accomplish it, regardless of what you decide. But that doesn't mean the decision isn't important. It'll impact both of you for the rest of your lives."

"Are you trying to encourage me or scare me to death?"

"That's just reality, honey. Children are for keeps. If things don't turn out the way you hoped, you can't give them back."

Vanessa shot her a thanks-for-stating-the-obvious look. "I'm just not ready to decide anything yet. At least our insurance will pay for the doctor and hospital expenses."

"Don't forget there'll be a hefty deductible."

"I *know*, Mom. Stop pushing me! I'm not like you. I can't just take charge and make things happen. I need time to think."

Brill brushed the hair out of her daughter's eyes. "You've had seven months. There are only so many options."

"I can't handle this right now."

"You keep telling me what you can't handle. When are you going to decide what you *can* handle?"

"Well, not tonight."

"Fair enough." Brill took her thumb and wiped a tear off Vanessa's cheek. "You have to reach a decision your own way, but you can't keep putting it off."

"I know."

Brill put her arms around Vanessa and gently rocked her from side to side. "It's going to be all right, honey."

"Are you sure? Because I'm really scared."

Brill sat in the living room, Pouncer purring in her lap, and looked outside. The foothills had disappeared, and the silhouette of the Great Smoky Mountains looked surreal against the blazing pink sky. She sat without moving a muscle and soaked in the quiet, her mind jumping from one thought to another.

She hated that Vanessa was afraid, but she understood it on a different level. She remembered being afraid when she found out she was pregnant with Emily. It had been overwhelming to think about trying to juggle her life with a husband, a career, two school-age children, and an infant. And yet hadn't Emily turned out to be a gift in every way?

She was an easy child. Bright. Intuitive. An interesting mix of Brill's fierce independence and Kurt's sensitivity. And ultimately, wasn't it their mutual love for Emily that fueled their desire to save their marriage after his affair? The child she thought was going to spoil her life had instead given it back.

"So what did you talk to Vanessa about?" Emily flopped on the couch next to her and rubbed Pouncer's back.

"It was a private conversation, thank you."

"How come nobody tells me anything?"

"There's very little about this family you don't know."

"So tell me what I *don't* know."

"As the saying goes"—Brill tilted Emily's chin—"'what you don't know won't hurt you.'"

"Did you tell Vanessa to let someone adopt the baby?"

"That's her decision, sweetie."

"But you don't want her to keep him, right?"

"I never said that."

"But I can tell."

Emily's gaze seemed to glide past her defenses, and Brill felt her cheeks flush.

"Listen, you. You're not a mind reader."

Emily pressed her lips together, that if-you-say-so expression taking over her face. Finally she said, "I think it's so cool you're going to be a grandma."

"I'm glad you think so." *I haven't even gone through menopause yet.*

"Well, you and Dad aren't all wrinkly like some grandparents, but you're nice like Grammy and Poppy were. And it's cool that you're the police chief. When the baby gets bigger, you can take him for a drive and turn on the siren. And Dad can give him one of his wild piggyback rides."

"Hmm …"

"And you know what? Since my baby bed was yellow, Vanessa can use it. Yellow is okay for boys, too."

"Emily, Vanessa might not decide to keep the baby. I think it's best if we don't speculate."

"What does speculate mean?"

"It means we need to not guess what she's thinking. Just let her decide."

"But she *would* make a good mom. When I was little, she used to read me stories and play with me. She made me say my prayers. And she even let me sleep with her when I got scared."

"Where was I?"

Emily shrugged. "I don't remember. Working, maybe. So can you feel the guardian angel with you since I prayed?"

"I feel very safe."

Emily put her arms around Brill and squeezed her tightly. "I'm not going to let anything happen to you."

Brill waited a few moments, then pushed back and met her daughter's gaze. "It's not your responsibility to keep me safe."

"Well, I'm not taking any chances."

"Neither am I. I really don't want you worrying about me."

"But I can't help it."

Through the window, Brill spotted the plain DB car parked across the street.

"Well, try. I've got police officers and a guardian angel keeping an eye on me. What more do I need?"

Emily put her finger to her chin and looked up, her eyes moving one direction and then the other. "Let's see ... how about ice cream?"

"I need ice cream, do I?"

Emily gave a nod. "I never worry when I'm eating ice cream. I want to try that place Ethan told me about. It's called The Scoop."

"Where is it?"

Emily couldn't hold back the smile that twitched the corners of her mouth. "I just happened to see it in the phone book. It's on Second Street, next door to Beanie's Coffee Shop. Pleeease can we go?"

The only place she wanted to go was to the bathtub for a long, relaxing bubble bath. But Emily's pleading eyes tugged at her heartstrings.

"Okay. Why don't you see if Dad and Vanessa want to go too?"

"Can't you and I go by ourselves?"

"Why?"

"Because I'm only going to be the baby for a little while longer. Dad takes me on ice-cream dates. Can't we go on a mother-daughter date?"

"Sure we can." Brill tugged Emily's ponytail. "Come on, my turn to spoil you."

CHAPTER 15

BRILL sat in a red vinyl booth at The Scoop, sipping an old-fashioned chocolate malt and listening to Emily's chatter—a welcome reprieve from the sadness.

"I love the black-and-white checkered floor," Emily said, her mouth chock-full of banana. "I wish we had this in our kitchen."

Brill waited until Emily looked down before reaching across the booth and helping herself to a spoonful of her banana split, then gigged like a schoolgirl.

"Hey, police chiefs aren't supposed to steal!" Emily clamped her lips together to stop her smile from expelling the contents of her mouth.

"Here, take a bite of mine." Brill pushed her spoon into the thickest part of the malt and handed it to Emily. "It's runny. Don't drip it down the front of you."

Emily put the spoon in her mouth, her eyes wide and the same bright blue as her tank top. "Yum. It tastes like those malted milk balls I get at the movies."

"Your dad and I used to get chocolate malts when we were in college. There was a place called Al's just down the street from my dorm."

"I remember we drove by there once." Emily took the cherry from the mound of whipped cream, held it up, and ate it off the stem. "Do you ever miss living in Memphis?"

"Once in a while, but not often."

"*I* do. I liked it better."

"You still miss your friends?"

"Kind of. But mostly I miss not being afraid."

"It's going to take time, sweetie."

Emily pushed a slice of banana with her spoon. "But I can't get over being afraid because now I have something *new* to be afraid of."

"You prayed for a guardian angel, remember? We don't have to be afraid."

"Dad is."

"Says who?"

Emily shrugged. "I can just tell."

"It's dangerous trying to read someone's mind, little lady."

"Don't worry. I'm good at it."

"Oh, really?"

"I know what Vanessa's thinking."

"Then I suggest you ask her permission before you go telling the rest of us."

Emily stuffed a strawberry slice into her mouth. "Don't you want me to tell you what you're thinking?"

"I already know what I'm thinking."

"You"—Emily used her spoon as a pointer—"are afraid that if Vanessa keeps the baby, she's going to live with us—and the house will be messy and the baby will cry a lot."

"Emily, stop this nonsense. If you could read my mind, you'd know that I'm just eager for Vanessa to make a decision so we can start making plans." *Like how to feed and clothe two more people on half the income.*

"If she keeps the baby, I want him to sleep upstairs so I can rock him when he cries."

"Right. Until he cries when you want to sleep."

"I can make him stop. Babies like me—just like cats."

"Yes, but you can't let a baby outside."

Emily stuck her spoon in the mound of ice cream, seemingly lost in thought, and then said, "Vanessa cries at night. She's really sad Ty went away."

"I know, sweetie. I think her heart is broken."

"She talks to the baby and tells him she loves him. I think she doesn't want him to forget her voice"—Emily lifted her gaze—"in case he gets adopted. But if he does get adopted, does that mean he can't be hers anymore?"

"He would always be Vanessa's biological son. But his adoptive parents would love and care for him just the same as they would if he'd been born to them."

"Would Vanessa get to visit him?"

"I'm not sure. He might be confused, having two moms. But the adoptive parents could let Vanessa know how he was doing."

A row of ridges formed on Emily's forehead. "I don't want him to be adopted. I want him to be in *our* family. How come nobody cares how I feel? I promise I'll pick up his toys and rock him when he cries. He won't be that much trouble."

Brill's heart sank. Emily seemed as attached to this baby as Vanessa was.

She reached across the table and gently took Emily's hand. "Sweetie, there's so much more to this decision than I can possibly explain to you. I think your willingness to help will mean a lot to Vanessa. But she has to make up her own mind."

Tessa looked out the kitchen window and saw Brill and Emily get out of Kurt's van and walk to the front door.

"You being nosy again?" Antonio took a bite of raisin bran.

"Is it being nosy to care about my neighbors? I'm glad to see the black Impala is still parked across the street. Where do you suppose Brill and Emily went at this hour?"

"They probably went to the drugstore or something."

"I don't see any bags."

Antonio stopped chewing. "Okay, now you're being nosy. Emily called you once this evening and told you she was fine. Since when do you need a blow-by-blow?"

Tessa let the curtain fall and walked over to the kitchen table and sat across from him.

"You're never going to sleep with a full stomach," she said.

"You've been saying that for fifty-three years, my love. And one of these days you're going to be right." He chuckled and patted her hand. "You're cute."

Tessa swatted the air. "Cute like a shar-pei. I'm nothing but ripples, Antonio."

"You're still cute."

"And you're still full of poppycock."

Antonio smiled with his eyes.

Tessa sat in comfortable silence, reveling in her husband's playful compliment. What must Mrs. O'Toole be feeling tonight? How sad that she'd been denied the blessing of growing old with her husband.

There was no point questioning God's wisdom for having allowed this senseless murder. But would she ever understand it? Even if He took what was intended for evil and used it for good, it had been costly by every measurable human standard.

"Where'd you go?" Antonio waved his hand in front of her face.

"Oh, sorry. I was just wondering how Mrs. O'Toole is doing tonight. I cringe to think of what this Merrick Fountain character might be planning next."

"Brill's prepared to deal with him."

"But is Emily?"

"I'm sure Brill and Kurt have told her whatever she needs to know." Antonio pushed his bowl to the side. "That little girl is made of the same stuff as her mother. She showed remarkable presence of mind while staring down the barrel of a gun."

Tessa felt a chill crawl up her spine. "Well, I haven't been able to put it behind me, and I doubt she has either."

Nick Phillips draped a bar towel over his shoulder and sprayed booth one with Clorox water and wiped it down. No way was he going to complain that business was *too* good. But if the summer volume continued to hold at this level, he'd have to hire another waitress.

"Wouldn't *that* be a good problem to have?" he mumbled.

He could tell by the grin on the young man in booth two that his talking to himself hadn't fallen on deaf ears.

Nick smiled sheepishly. "You doing all right tonight?"

"Great," the man said. "Sure do love this grilled salmon."

"Thanks. It seems to be a favorite."

"I can see why. By the way, I'm Rob Smith."

"Nick Phillips." He reached over and shook Rob's hand.

"Nick as in Nick's Grill?"

"That's me."

"So, Nick … tell me what would be a *good* problem to have. All my problems are a real pain."

"Well, growing pains are good. A much better problem than the alternative, no?"

"I see what you mean."

"You live in Sophie Trace?"

Rob took his napkin and wiped his mouth. "Yeah. I work at the hospital."

"Is this your first time to eat here?"

"Yes, but it won't be the last."

"That's what I like to hear. If you're thinking of having dessert, the lemon meringue pie is to die for. It's my grandmother's recipe."

Rob took a sip of iced tea. "Thanks."

Nick walked to the counter and put his hand on Gus Williams's shoulder.

"Whew! Things have finally calmed down. So how was the chocolate lava cake?"

"Hit the spot."

Nick sat on the stool next to Gus. "I can't remember the last time you came in for dessert at ten o'clock at night. Something on your mind?"

Gus rubbed his white mustache. "Yeah. Maggie."

"So there *is* something going on with you two besides joking around."

"Not yet, but I'm hopin' that'll change. I can't get her out of my head."

"Ever ask her out?"

Gus's face turned crimson, and he shook his head.

"Why not?"

Gus started cracking his knuckles. "I feel silly even thinkin' about datin' at my age. Maggie and I have fun jokin' around with y'all. But I'm not sure I'd even know what to say if we were by ourselves."

"What kinds of things did you say to your wife when she was alive?"

"Reba did most of the talkin'. I did the listenin'."

"How long's she been gone?"

"Five years. Took me three to get over it. But the last two have been downright miserable. I'd like to find a woman who—"

Nick heard some commotion and spun around. A familiar figure staggered across the empty waiting area. His legs seemed to give way, and he collapsed on the floor.

Nick rolled his eyes. "Wonderful. Looks like Rusk is back on the sauce. How many times has he flushed the whiskey and then gone right out and bought some more?"

"I lost count."

"I'll tell you one thing, I'm getting tired of picking him up off my floor."

Nick got up and crossed the room. He needed to handle this with finesse. Many of the locals knew Rusk had a weakness for whiskey, but the tourists didn't and surely wouldn't appreciate the sight of him being dragged into the back room.

"This guy needs a doctor!" a man shouted.

Nick gently elbowed his way past several onlookers. "Don't be alarmed, folks. It's just—"

Nick froze. Blood was everywhere. A man lay on his back, his midsection a pool of red.

"That's … not Rusk." Nick felt as if he'd swallowed his tongue.

Someone was standing next to him, peeling off his sport coat. It was Rob Smith.

"I'm a doctor. Everybody stand back."

Rob dropped to his knees and straddled the man, his palms pressed against the bleeding wound.

"He's a cop. Detective Rousseaux." Nick saw a bloody trail that went from the entrance to where the detective lay. "Rob, what can I do to help?"

"Call 911 and get an ambulance over here—and make it quick. This man could bleed to death."

Brill turned on the bathwater and poured two capfuls of bubble bath under the flow. She'd been waiting all day for this—time to relax her mind and muscles and let her thoughts escape to wherever she decided to take them.

Bubbles formed on the top of the water, and the sweet scent of honeysuckle permeated the bathroom. Soon she would be immersed in peace, and no one would interrupt her until she emerged again, renewed.

The sound of her cell phone ringing caused her neck muscles to tighten. She went out to her nightstand and picked up the phone. Trent's name was on the display screen. This couldn't be good.

"What's up?"

"Beau Jack's in an ambulance on his way to St. Luke's. Stabbed in the midsection. It happened in the parking lot at Nick's Grill around ten. His wife was with him."

"Was he wearing his ballistic vest?"

"No, ma'am. He was off duty."

"But this is precisely why we agreed to wear the vests until we get Merrick Fountain locked up."

"I'm not sure it would've made any difference, Chief. Our vests don't protect against knife attacks."

"They're better than nothing." Brill bit her lip. Her officers would have gotten stab-resistant inserts for their ballistic vests if the city council hadn't cut her budget proposal. "Trent, what kind of shape is he in?"

"Don't know yet. He hasn't regained consciousness. The EMTs said he lost a lot of blood. He looks awful."

"Is his wife riding to the hospital with him?"

"Yeah. They had to sedate her. She was pretty shaken."

"All right. I'll be there in twenty minutes."

CHAPTER 16

BRILL marched down the long, shiny corridor at St. Luke's Hospital, Trent Norris keeping perfect stride beside her.

"The ER doctor didn't sound convincing," she said. "Grave condition is life threatening, no matter how positive he tries to spin it."

"I hate it that Beau Jack's unconscious and couldn't give us his take on what happened."

Brill couldn't believe she was about to lose a second officer in less than a week. She slowed her pace and stopped in front of the room where Jeanette Rousseaux awaited them.

"Let's make this as quick and painless as possible. She's been through enough."

Brill knocked on the door and went inside where Jeanette Rousseaux sat on the examining table, her feet dangling, her eyes glazed.

"I appreciate your willingness to talk to us," Brill said. "I wish the timing were better, but we need you to tell us everything you remember."

Jeanette nodded, her eyelids heavy from the medication she'd been given. "Merrick Fountain stabbed my husband."

"You're sure?"

"Positive."

"All right. Start at the beginning."

Jeanette laced her fingers. "Beau Jack called me from the DB just before his shift ended. Said he was starved and told me to meet him at Nick's. I got there before he did—about five after ten—and waited in the car."

Jeanette paused, her eyes closed. Brill thought she had fallen asleep, but then she started talking again.

"I was listening to talk radio when Beau Jack pulled up. I could see him in my rearview mirror. He parked his car. Got out. And started walking toward me." Jeanette stopped, her lips quivering. "Fountain grabbed him from behind and put him in a choke hold …" She put her hand to her mouth and whimpered.

Brill reached over and held her other hand. "It's okay, Jeanette, take your time."

There was a long pause, and Brill wasn't sure if Jeanette would be able to go on. It had to have been traumatic, watching her husband's brutal attack.

"Fountain raised his free hand and then jabbed Beau Jack in the stomach. I-I thought he just hit him until I saw the knife blade dripping with blood. I must've passed out after that. When I came to, I was slumped over the steering wheel."

"Did you remember what happened?"

"I was disoriented at first, but then I did. Beau Jack's car was still there, so I ran into Nick's looking for him." She closed her eyes and shook her head. "He was lying on the floor in front of the cash register. A man knelt over him, pressing his palms on the wound. There was so much blood …"

"Jeanette, what makes you sure the assailant was Fountain?"

She wiped a tear off her cheek. "The parking lot was light enough for me to see his face. He wore a ball cap, but it was the man in the mug shot you gave all the officers."

"Do you remember what else he was wearing?"

"No. The ball cap was dark—navy or black. I think it had a logo on it, but I didn't pay attention."

"Did Fountain see you?"

"I don't know."

"Do you remember anything else?"

Jeanette stared at her hands and was silent for half a minute, then looked up.

"The ghoulish grin on his face. It was chilling."

Brill's skin turned to gooseflesh. Would she ever forget the manic, almost euphoric expression on Fountain's face as his wife testified about the torturous abuse he had systematically inflicted on her? Could there be any doubt that he hated women? Brill shuddered at the idea of being stalked by him and wondered if he was saving the best for last.

She put her hand on Jeanette's shoulder. "I know it's little consolation at the moment, but we're going to get him. He's never going to see the light of day again."

A tear trailed down her cheek. "If Beau Jack doesn't make it, it won't matter what sentence this madman gets. My life will be ruined."

"Beau Jack's going to make it. He's too competitive to let Fountain win."

Jeanette hugged herself, laughing and crying at the same time. "You're right."

There was a knock, and the door opened. The ER doctor stood in the doorway, his green scrubs disheveled, the dark shadow on his face and chin adding to his weary look.

"Mrs. Rousseaux, your husband just went into surgery. He's in good hands. The nurse will call you in the waiting room with updates."

Kurt Jessup sat at the kitchen table and pushed away a half-eaten smoked turkey sandwich. He glanced at the clock and wondered if Beau Jack was out of surgery yet.

"Dad, what are you doing up so late?"

He turned and saw Vanessa clad in her yellow nightgown, her hands resting on her protruded belly.

"I should ask you the same question. Is something wrong?"

She came over and sat next to him. "Not really. The baby is just kicking like crazy. What's going on? I heard Mom leave."

He hated to worry her, but she would find out soon enough. "One of her detectives is in surgery, honey. He was stabbed tonight while off duty."

"Where'd it happen?" Vanessa's eyes belied her calm response.

"In the parking lot at Nick's Grill. He was meeting his wife for a late dinner. He should have been wearing his ballistic vest."

"Why wasn't he?"

"Good question."

"Is he going to be okay?"

Kurt looked out the window at the DB car parked across the street. "I don't know. It doesn't sound good."

"This is scary, Dad. Why can't they catch the guy who's doing this?"

What could he say to her when the same question was eating at him? "Fountain's been elusive. At least they're sure of his identity. He didn't bother wearing a disguise this time."

"Well, if I were police chief, I'd tear this town apart till I found him."

"She is. Officers and deputies are checking every motel, motor inn, campsite, RV park, and B and B in the area. But I doubt the guy was dumb enough to use his real name."

"This is so ridiculous." Vanessa seemed to study Kurt's face. "How many cops can this guy get to before he's caught? I don't know why Mom thinks she's safe. She's being naive."

"Hey, how come everybody's up?" Emily came through the doorway barefoot and dressed in pink baby-doll pajamas, her hair falling in soft curls over her shoulders. "Is Mom okay?"

"She's fine." Kurt held out his arms and motioned for Emily to sit on his knee.

"Another officer was stabbed," Vanessa said. "Beau Jack something."

"Oh, no. Not Detective Rousseaux," Emily said. "He's really nice. He saves all the red Tootsie Pops just for me. Is he dead?"

Kurt shook his head. "He's in surgery, sweetie."

"Did Merrick Fountain do it?"

"Yes, Beau Jack's wife identified him. They've got everybody in law enforcement looking for him."

The phone rang, and Emily sprang to her feet and grabbed it. "Hello."

"Baby sister? Why aren't you asleep?"

"No one's asleep. Detective Rousseaux got stabbed."

"That's what I heard. Let me talk to Dad, okay?"

"Sure." Emily handed Kurt the phone. "It's Ryan."

"Hi, Son. I could hear what you said to Emily. How'd you find out about the stabbing?"

"The band just took a break, and this place is buzzing with the news. Dad, what's going on? It's like this thing's spiraling out of control."

"Fountain didn't waste any time striking again. But your mom's right on it."

"But how could this happen? I thought the whole department had stepped up security."

"Beau Jack was off duty. He let his guard down."

"Is Mom being careful?"

"Extremely. She's got officers watching her back. Officers watching the house. And she's wearing her ballistic vest, in spite of the heat."

Emily shook her head. "Not when we went out for ice cream, she didn't."

"I heard that," Ryan said.

"I'll talk to her, son. But I don't think it'll be an option after tonight. This creep is working his way up the chain of command. Your mom can't take any chances."

Kurt felt a sinking feeling in his stomach and wished Brill were home behind locked doors.

❖ ❖ ❖

Brill sat in the waiting room, her face in her hands, and let the surgeon's words sink in.

The blade missed all his vital organs, and he should make a full recovery.

She exhaled and looked over at Trent.

"Detective Rousseaux is in serious but stable condition," the surgeon said. "We're keeping him in ICU tonight, and I would prefer he not have visitors, other than Mrs. Rousseaux. I doubt he'll be lucid anyway."

"All right," Brill said. "We're going to post two officers outside his door twenty-four/seven. Only immediate family and authorized hospital personnel will be allowed in his room."

The surgeon nodded knowingly and left.

Brill rested in the silence for a long time, and then looked over at Trent, who seemed to be lost in thought.

"We need to make sure Fountain doesn't get past security this time," she said.

"Absolutely."

"And we need to stay alert. Fountain has nothing to lose. He's not going to stop until he gets to me or until we stop him."

"He's *not* getting to you," Trent said. "I'm tightening security another notch."

"And you're probably next in his sights, Trent. You can't afford to blink."

"I know. I won't."

Brill tucked her hair behind her ear. "He may go after DA Cromwell first. I'm sure half the fun is keeping us guessing. I always knew he was dangerous, but I never thought he'd go to this extreme to punish the people who put him away. He knew we were just doing our jobs."

Trent ran his hands over the woolly curls that covered his scalp. "It takes one sick puppy to plunge his knife into people who had nothing to do with putting him away."

"He's just plain mean." Brill lowered her voice. "I'm so disgusted the city council cut my budget proposal. If they had given me what I wanted, we would already have stab-resistant inserts for our existing ballistic vests."

"Maybe you should go back and ask for more. Under the circumstances, they might agree to it."

"Yes, they hold me in such high regard," she said sarcastically. "The only way I'm going to get a nickel from those tightwads is to beg."

Kurt heard a key in the front door and opened his eyes. He got up from the couch, met Brill in the entry hall, and put his arms around her.

"I'm glad you're home."

She nodded, resting in his embrace. "It's almost a miracle that Beau Jack is going to recover."

"How's Jeanette?"

"Wiped out. Grateful. Scared. Mad. A little of everything. She's staying at the hospital tonight. Beau Jack's in ICU, but they hope to have him in a regular room sometime tomorrow."

Kurt held her tighter. "I just kept thinking that it could've been you."

"It *should* have been. I feel so guilty that Sean and Beau Jack got pulled into this."

"You can't control a nutcase like Merrick Fountain. No one blames you for his actions."

"No, but if it weren't for my baggage, Sean would be alive, and Beau Jack wouldn't be in ICU. Their poor wives. I can only imagine what they're feeling."

Kurt leaned back and looked her in the eyes. "Uh, how about your husband? Have you got a little sympathy for what I'm going through?"

"Of course I do." Brill cupped her hand around his cheek. "I hate putting you through this."

"What about me?"

Emily stood in the hallway, pajama-clad, her arms crossed.

"I thought we had an understanding that you were going to stop eavesdropping," Brill said.

"But no one can have an expectation of privacy in the *entry hall*."

Kurt bowed his head to hide his smile. "I wonder where she learned to talk like that?"

Brill punched him on the arm. "Emily, come here and let me hug you. You don't need to worry about me. I'm fine."

Emily ran to her mother's embrace.

Kurt noticed that Vanessa was sitting on the bottom step of the staircase. "Honey, come over here and get in on this hug fest."

Vanessa struggled to her feet and ambled over to her mother. "You had us worried. I'm glad you're okay."

"Then why such a solemn face?"

"I just don't understand why you can't get this guy."

"You and Mayor Roswell. Maybe you ought to run for the city council."

"Mom, you're smarter than he is. Can't you set a trap or something?"

Brill brushed the hair out of Vanessa's eyes. "I appreciate the vote of confidence, but the fact is, Merrick Fountain is both smart *and* motivated. He's a man on a mission. My officers can't protect themselves if they don't use common sense. Beau Jack knew he was at high risk. He shouldn't have been out alone, and certainly not without wearing his ballistic vest."

"How come you didn't wear yours when we went out for ice cream?" Emily asked.

"Because your mom wanted some normal mother-daughter time." Kurt shot Brill a knowing look. "She thought wearing the vest might make you afraid. But until they arrest Merrick Fountain, she has to start thinking about her safety every minute."

"Okay, okay, I hear you guys loud and clear," Brill said. "There will be no chances taken in my department. The place will be like a fortress. Trent's already working on it."

Vanessa put her arm around Brill's shoulder. "Why couldn't you have been a lawyer or something?"

"Oh, honey, I don't know. Law enforcement's in my blood. It's what I was born to do." Brill yawned and captured it with her hand. "I'm really sorry you've all been up worrying about me. I'm exhausted, and I know you must be too. Come on, let's go to bed."

❖ ❖ ❖

Kurt was floating in the gray fog somewhere between sleep and wakefulness when he heard something scrape the window. His eyes flew open, his heart nearly pounding out of his chest. Fear paralyzed him for a moment, and then he groped the nightstand for Brill's Glock and held it tightly.

Finally he threw back the covers and crept over to the window. He stood to one side and peeked out behind the drapes, half expecting Merrick Fountain's face to pop up in the window like a jack-in-the-box.

Seconds passed without a sound. He tightened his grip on the Glock. Had he imagined the noise? Was he imagining the dark shadow next to the fence? Could he afford to take a chance?

"Honey, wake up." The sound of his hammering heart filled his ears.

Brill sat up in bed and reached for her gun. "Kurt, what are you doing? Have you got my gun?"

"I heard something outside. I think someone's out there."

She slid out of bed and hurried over and stood next to him. She pulled back the corner of the drapes and peeked out into the darkness.

Silence.

"I don't see anyone," she said. "What exactly did you hear?"

"A scraping sound. I think." Kurt sighed. "Maybe I overreacted. Maybe my protective instincts kicked in too soon."

"Well, there's one way to find out. I'll have the officers check."

Brill went over to the nightstand and turned on the lamp. She picked up her cell phone and put it to her ear.

"Yes, Sergeant. It's Chief Jessup. I need you to check the side yard outside our bedroom window. My husband thought he heard something outside … yes, just to be sure … no need to call back unless you discover something … thank you. Good night."

Kurt walked over to the nightstand and set the gun down. He sat on the side of the bed next to Brill and put his arm around her.

"You've got to catch this guy before I start shooting at shadows."

"I have more faith in your judgment than that," she said. "You're a better shot than some of my officers. I think it's honorable you wanted to protect me."

"Of course I wanted to protect you. In case you haven't noticed, there's a maniac who's vowed to kill you, even if you think you're invincible."

"I don't think that at all. Why would you say that?"

Kurt looked into her eyes. "You're so good at hiding your emotions that I really never know for sure what you're feeling. You just keep pressing on, no matter what obstacles come your way."

"That's what I've been conditioned to do, Kurt. It doesn't mean I don't feel. I've just trained myself to hold it in."

He brushed the back of his hand against her cheek. "I know. But sometimes I wish I knew what it was you were holding back."

"You're better off not knowing."

"I doubt that. I'm your other half. Whether you tell me or not, it affects me."

She exhaled and seemed to look beyond him as if she were deep in thought. "Okay, the truth is I'm scared. I don't want to be one of Fountain's victims, and I sure don't want to die at forty-five and leave you and the kids to fend for yourselves. And I don't want anyone else in my department to get hurt because of me. But I can't allow myself to dwell on what *could* happen. My officers take their cues from me. I need to stay focused on keeping my people safe and getting Merrick Fountain behind bars."

"I can deal with that. Why was it so hard to say it?"

"I don't deliberately hide my feelings from you, Kurt. But I can't shift emotional gears just because I walk through the front door."

"I understand. But you don't have to be the strong one when you're here. Lean on me."

A comfortable silence passed, and then Kurt stroked her hair. "We're in this together, for better or for worse. I can't pray as effectively if I don't know what's going on inside you."

"Sometimes even I don't know. I've learned to shut it off. Law enforcement is a male-dominated profession, and any show of weakness would undermine my leadership."

"Honey, you're not the leader in this relationship. You're my *partner.*"

Her eyes glistened, and a tear fell on her cheek. "You're right. It's been a really tough day. Would you just hold me?"

Kurt gently pulled her into his arms, his lips pressing to her warm, soft cheek, and inhaled the sweet scent of her skin. He relished the moments she let herself need him. As tough as she was, there was a side of her that seemed as childlike and vulnerable as Emily. And if he had his way, he wouldn't let her go until Merrick Fountain was locked up in a maximum-security penitentiary with no chance for parole.

CHAPTER 17

THE next morning, Brill was going through the stack of papers in her in-box and stopped for a moment to drink in the glorious view outside her office window. The Great Smoky Mountains, shrouded in haze, stood as a majestic dividing line between Tennessee and North Carolina. White puffy clouds, like balls of cotton, dotted the summer sky and cast shadows on the foothills.

She sensed someone standing in the doorway and looked up, and then did a double take as FBI Special Agent David Riley came over and stood in front of her desk. He was outfitted in khaki shorts and a kelly green polo shirt—and a grin that turned his eyes to slits.

"David, what a surprise!"

She walked around the side of her desk and held his hand with both of hers.

"It's great to see you. Are you working on a case?"

"Technically, I'm on vacation for two weeks."

"I could use a little vacation myself." She raised an eyebrow. "I suppose you've been following the Merrick Fountain saga."

"I have. With great interest." An awkward silence followed, and then David finally said, "Actually, I'm here to offer my help."

"Thanks, but I can't justify involving the FBI."

He rubbed his shaved head, which had the same dark shadow as his face. "I'm not talking about involving the FBI. Can't a friend—who just happens to be a profiler—use his vacation time to help you get inside the head of this cop killer?"

"You would do that?"

"Sure. I've never been good at taking personal time. Let me help nail this guy—unofficially, of course."

"You wouldn't last twenty-four hours not being in charge."

David laughed with his eyes. "How do you know? Try me."

For heaven's sake, he's serious. She studied his face and considered the implications of his offer. "I don't need a bodyguard, if that's what you think."

David's head and face suddenly looked scalded. "Think of it as a friend watching out for a friend."

"I can't let you do it."

"Sure you can."

"My officers are capable of watching my back. What would it say about my level of confidence in them if I turn to the FBI for help?"

"You didn't turn to the FBI. I came to you as a friend. Zack was my friend too, and I don't want this creep taking you both out."

For a split second she pictured Kurt placing a rose on her coffin.

"Brill, you're being stalked by an ex-con who wants revenge, and who also happens to be a misogynist. You can't tell me you're not concerned."

"Of course I'm concerned."

"How does Kurt feel about it?"

"He's a nervous wreck."

She leaned against her desk, her arms folded, and told David about the incident the night before when Kurt heard a noise and grabbed her gun.

"There's a reason his instincts are on overload," David said. "Fountain keeps finding a way to get to whoever he wants. I have every confidence in you to get Fountain. But how are you going to focus when you're worried every second that this psycho is going to jump out from behind your shower curtain?"

She smiled wryly but didn't admit that, in her mind, she had replayed that scene from *Psycho* more than once.

"Look, Brill, you can't be mad at me for caring. Fountain's taken out two-thirds of your detective division in less than a week. The other third is at the top of his hit list. Any department would be demoralized."

"Yes, but my officers are all the more committed to keeping me safe and finding this worthless piece of garbage. And we're getting a lot of help from Sam's deputies and other police departments in the region, so we're keeping up with normal duties."

"That's great. It'll make it easier for me just to blend into the woodwork. Don't change anything you're doing. No one except Kurt has to know I'm watching your back. You can honestly tell everyone else that I'm on vacation and I'm taking my own time to help you understand the profile of a guy like Fountain. Wouldn't it feel good not to have to worry about your personal safety and just go after this cop killer with both barrels?"

Brill pushed open the arched door and went in the house, David right behind her, a delicious aroma emanating from sacks he was carrying.

Kurt came out of the kitchen and shook David's free hand. "Hey, it's good to see you. Brill called and said to set the table for lunch, that you were coming over to talk to me about something." He smiled. "I did as I was instructed."

"Come on." Brill headed for the kitchen. "We brought muffulettas and broccoli cheese soup."

Kurt and David sat at the table, and Brill took everything out of the sacks and served it, then took her seat.

Kurt said the blessing, rubbed his hands together, and picked up his soupspoon. "Boy, does this look good. David, you should come to town more often. So what's on your mind?"

"The same thing that's on yours," David said. "Keeping Brill safe."

Kurt looked at Brill and then at David. "I didn't know you were working this case."

"I'm not—officially anyway. I'm on vacation."

Brill ate her soup and just listened as David explained his plan to Kurt, as concisely as he had discussed with her earlier.

"So that's what I've got on my mind. I think this situation calls for special measures. But I wanted to get your input."

Kurt nodded. "I'm a hundred percent for it. When can you move in?"

"What?"

"I just assumed you were going to move into Ryan's room."

"Actually, I reserved a cabin at Hazy View. I brought my dog with me."

"We like dogs." Brill held up her palm. "Why should you spend money on a cabin when we've got room?"

"Besides," Kurt said, "Emily will be thrilled. She's still suffering from Post Traumatic Stress Disorder. Having you here might go a long way in calming her fears until Fountain is back in prison."

Brill cut her muffuletta in two. "She's very fond of you, David. I think she considers you her hero."

"But she had more impact on the hostage negotiation than I did."

Brill was filled with dread just remembering that icy night last fall and how afraid she was that she was going to lose her daughter. "I'm sure Emily doesn't see it that way."

"So you're staying with us, right?" Kurt said.

"What about my German shepherd?"

"Is he housebroken?"

"She. And yes, Rinnie is well behaved in the house, but she's fine being outside. She's a pussycat with people she knows. Barks at strangers." David paused for a few moments and seemed to be thinking. Finally he said, "I guess staying here does make the most sense."

Tessa Masino, Antonio on her heels, pushed open the glass door at Nick's Grill and spotted Nick at the counter. He waved, his sandy brown hair being whipped about by the ceiling fan, the extra pounds he was carrying forming a belly bulge under his blue and white Nick's Grill T-shirt.

He walked briskly over to them and shook Antonio's hand and put his other hand on Tessa's shoulder. "Welcome, friends."

"We weren't sure you'd be here," Tessa said. "We saw on the news that you had quite an upset last night."

"Boy, that's the truth. Something I don't care to repeat."

"Tell us everything," Tessa said. "It gives me chills to know that one of Brill's detectives was stabbed in your parking lot."

"Come over to the counter. Gus is waiting for you."

Antonio waited until she sat in her usual spot, then slapped Gus on the back and straddled the seat next to him.

"How's it going, friend?"

"Really can't complain, but I always do." Gus poked his ice cubes with his straw. "Well, not today. After what happened last night, I'm just glad I wasn't in the parking lot when everything went down. I was sittin' right here when that detective staggered in here. At first, Nick thought ol' Rusk was into the hooch again. But I'll let him tell it."

Tessa listened intently as Nick told them every detail of what happened from the time Beau Jack Rousseaux came in the door and collapsed until the paramedics took him away in the ambulance.

"It all happened so fast that it didn't seem real," Nick said. "That is, till Mrs. Rousseaux came in and saw her husband on the floor and started screaming. I had to hold on to her till she calmed down. Poor woman was shaking like she'd been out in the rain. Apparently, she saw the whole thing and passed out. When she came to, she saw his car and came inside looking for him. It wasn't pretty."

Tessa shook her head. "Terrible. Just terrible. This crazy man has to be stopped."

"Tell that to your neighbor, the police chief," Gus said. "It's her job to stop him. I don't think she knows what she's doin'."

"That's just because *you* don't know what she's doing," Antonio said. "We've seen her up close and personal in the midst of a hostage crisis. Trust me, the woman knows her stuff."

Tessa bit her lip, content to let Antonio defend Brill.

Gus waved his hand. "Guess I'll have to take your word for it."

"Hi, all." Clint slid onto the stool next to Tessa and set his sunglasses on the counter. "I just heard on the radio that the detective who got stabbed is out of ICU."

"Wonderful," Tessa said. "Then he's out of danger."

Gus arched his eyebrows. "That's what Mrs. O'Toole thought."

Maggie Cummings stood behind the counter, holding a fresh pot of coffee. "Gus, why do you have to be so negative?" She set three mugs on the counter and filled them with coffee. "Under that tough exterior, you're really a pussycat."

No one said anything as Maggie distributed the mugs of coffee to Antonio, Clint, and Tessa. But Tessa noticed Gus's face was almost as red as his shirt.

Brill stood with David outside Beau Jack's hospital room and greeted both of Sam's deputies posted at the door.

The older deputy nodded in recognition and shook David's hand. "It's good to see you, Special Agent Riley. I wasn't advised that you'd been called in."

"I wasn't. I'm on vacation. Just here as a friend."

"Detective Rousseaux is awake, but the doctor said no visitors except family. I'm sure he'd make an exception for you two."

"We won't be long," Brill said. "We just wanted to encourage him and Jeanette."

"Yes, ma'am. And don't worry. When he can finally have visitors, nobody's getting in there who isn't on this list."

Brill knocked on the door and slowly pushed it open. "Beau Jack, it's Chief Jessup and Special Agent Riley."

Jeanette Rousseaux rose from her chair. "He's still a little groggy, but he's awake. Honey, look who's here to see you."

Brill walked over to the bed, glad to let David introduce himself to Jeanette, and picked up Beau Jack's hand. She looked past the whiskers and the mop of unruly hair into the heart of this young detective. He resembled the homeless men she'd encountered under the bridges of Memphis, though his eyes didn't have a vacant look but rather a glimmer of rugged determination. How could she reconcile that he'd been victimized for the sole purpose of terrorizing her?

She squeezed his hand harder than she intended. "I know you enjoy being the center of attention, Beau Jack. But this is a little extreme, even for you."

Beau Jack held her gaze, his mouth twitching. "I don't remember taking center stage, but I hear I had the *floor* all to myself."

"If it wasn't so awful, it might be funny," Brill said. "At least you haven't lost your sense of humor."

David stood next to her, his fingers holding the bedrail. "We meet again, Detective."

"The FBI's involved in this?"

"I'm on vacation," David said. "But you guys can't seem to stay out of the news, and I'm hanging out with my friend here, trying to be supportive."

"I never saw it coming."

Brill nodded. "I read your statement. We're fortunate that Jeanette could ID your attacker."

Beau Jack reached up and took his wife's hand. "She knows what Merrick Fountain looks like. She studied his mug shot. He grabbed me from behind, so I never saw him. But I remember exactly what he said to me: 'Tell Chief Jessup this is what she has to look forward to.' He laughed this sinister laugh and then thrust the knife into me."

A cold chill crept up Brill's spine. "Well, I know one thing: Fountain won't get past our security this time. You're safe here."

CHAPTER 18

VANESSA sat at the kitchen table. She picked up the bowl of broccoli and emptied the last of it onto her plate, hoping no one noticed. Why was she craving vegetables? At the moment, she would have chosen a bunch of carrots, a stalk of celery, or a juicy tomato over a box of chocolates. Maybe it was just the baby's need for certain vitamins that had altered her preferences.

She glanced across the table at Special Agent Riley, surprisingly comfortable that he was staying with them. It was obvious her parents were relieved. And Emily seemed her old self—affectionate, giggly, inquisitive, not jumpy and clingy.

Hopefully, he wouldn't ask questions about her predicament. At least everyone could relax and stop worrying about the freak that was out to get her mother. Worrying took a lot of energy, and she already felt drained by her own quandary.

How was she going to deal with never seeing Ty again? The longing seemed more intense with each new day and consumed her thoughts.

She folded her napkin and laid it on the table. "If you all will excuse me, I think I'll go out on the back porch for a while. Call me when you start cleaning up, and I'll come help."

"You don't have to help." Emily looked up at Special Agent Riley. "We have an extra volunteer."

David tugged her ponytail. "At your service."

"Well, thank you." Vanessa forced a smile and struggled to her feet. "I think I'll go see if it's cooled off outside."

She left the kitchen and went through the dining room to the screened-in back porch. Did Special Agent Riley think she was socially challenged? It was all she could do to muster the energy to look pleasant, much less engage in small talk.

Vanessa sat on the glider, her eyes closed, relieved that the evening breeze had dispelled the humidity that drove her indoors earlier. Why was she so listless? Was it depression or just her body's way of acknowledging that her due date was getting closer?

She started to doze off when her cell phone rang. She didn't recognize the number on the screen and put the phone to her ear, her pulse racing. "Ty?"

"Uh, no. It's just Ethan."

"Oh."

"Sorry to disappoint you."

"You didn't." *Liar.*

"How are you?"

"Okay." *Too depressed to carry on a decent conversation.* "I found a gynecologist. How was your first week on the job?"

"Miserable. I quit."

"You can't quit. What are you going to do about money for school?"

"I've already worked it out … Vanessa, hang on for just a minute, okay?"

It sounded as if Ethan put his hand over the receiver.

Vanessa heard the doorbell ring. Rinnie started barking, and she hoped it wasn't Tessa Masino bringing over more goodies. Not that this do-gooder wasn't a sweetheart. But the bond Emily had with her made Vanessa jealous—and angry with herself for feeling that way. How could she begrudge her little sister's relationship with a grandmotherly neighbor who doted on her, especially after Grammy and Poppy had been killed in a car wreck?

"You still there?" Ethan said.

"Yes. So how are you going to pay for school?"

"Look over at the gate."

"What?"

She heard someone whistle and turned just as the gate opened and Ethan came into the yard, his hand waving.

"My uncle hired me to pour concrete. Looks like I'm going to be in Sophie Trace for the summer."

Vanessa felt the heaviness lift. "Welcome back. I can't believe this."

She pushed herself up to her feet.

Ethan bounded up the steps, came in the screened-in porch, and gave her a hug. "It's great to see you."

"You just saw me Monday."

"Yeah, but it's Friday." He patted her tummy. "How's the baby hippo?"

"Fine." Vanessa giggled and pushed his hand away. "So why'd you quit?"

"I can't speak Spanish worth a hoot and felt like I was working all by myself. Couldn't see spending the summer feeling that lonely."

"Will it be hard working for your uncle?"

"No, he's great. He would've hired me before if he'd had an opening. His company just got the contract for the new mall, and one of his key men quit. He really needs me."

"Why don't we sit?" Vanessa eased herself down on the glider.

Ethan sat next to her and gave the glider a push with his legs. "So who's the guy who answered the door—with a German shepherd by his side, no less—and gave me the green light to come on back?"

"Special Agent David Riley—of the FBI."

"Whoa, a fed? Is that because another detective was stabbed?"

"Not really. He's a good friend of Mom's. He's here on vacation, and he's staying with us. I'm glad. Everyone's more relaxed, and I feel safer with him and his dog here."

"I'm sure."

"So are you staying with your aunt and uncle?"

"Yeah, it's like coming home for me to get to spend the summer in Sophie Trace. I'd forgotten how much I miss being close to the mountains."

"Remind me how long you lived here."

Ethan leaned his head back on the glider. "Till I was a senior in high school. That's when my dad went to work for the dairy and we moved to Maryville."

"So you were born and raised here?"

"Yep."

"Well, I wasn't." Vanessa wrinkled her nose. "Memphis is my hometown. I think I told you my family moved here last summer when my mom took the job as police chief. So this is my first time to actually live here. I'm not sure I like it yet. But I have to admit it's great being home with my family."

"I knew it would be."

"How could you know that?"

Ethan shrugged. "You've always talked about your parents like you respect them."

"I do. A lot. That's why I kept putting off telling them what a mess I made."

"And yet you trusted their love for you enough to face them with it. You could've had an abortion and never told them anything. Why didn't you? Or is it none of my business?"

"I can tell you." Vanessa turned and held his gaze. "Because I believe life begins at conception, and that's the point where my rights ended and his began."

"Not really. You had the right to choose. Abortion *is* legal."

"That doesn't change what it is, Ethan. It's just getting rid of a human life so you don't have to take responsibility."

"I'm glad you feel that way. That's pretty much how I look at it."

Vanessa glanced over at him, and then played with the hem on her blouse. "Ty wanted me to get an abortion." *There, I finally said it.*

"Doesn't surprise me. Is that why you broke up?"

Vanessa nodded, the remembrance of it making her feel worthless. "He's really not a terrible person. He just couldn't handle being tied down."

"I'm not willing to be that generous, but I'm glad you told me."

A half a minute passed in silence, and then Ethan smiled and said, "I just realized I'm going to be here when baby hippo is born."

Vanessa gave him a hard nudge with her elbow. "I'm sure you can hardly wait."

"Actually, it's kind of exciting. Don't I get to be a zookeeper or a step-uncle or something?"

Vanessa laughed and let her heart feel the release. It was good having Ethan back in town.

Brill picked up her cell phone, reading the name and number of the caller, then walked down the hall and into her bedroom and shut the door.

"Hi, Dexter. How are things going?"

"Either I'm a complete idiot or Professor Nicholson isn't Professor Nicholson."

"Then who is he?"

"I have no idea. I'm convinced he didn't graduate from Barsfield University and never taught at Chambers College."

"But the HR person at the University of Memphis confirmed he had a master's from Barsfield, right?"

"Right. The documentation is all there. But she didn't actually hire Nicholson. The HR person who did is now deceased."

"So where does that leave us?"

"In the twilight zone?"

"What about his high school records?"

"Not there."

"Missing?"

Dexter exhaled into the receiver. "No one by his name attended East Nashville High—ever."

Brill flopped on the bed. What had Vanessa gotten herself into?

"So who is he and how did he get a job teaching at the University of Memphis?"

"I wish I could tell you, Brill. I'm afraid I'd be robbing your pocket if I tried to take this any further. Not that I'm not willing, but I've run smack-dab into a stone wall."

I have a feeling you were supposed to. "Well, I appreciate all you've done. I'll take it from here."

"And do what?"

"I'm not sure, but now *my* curiosity's on tilt. Send me a bill for what we owe you. This isn't the answer I was looking for, but it's information I need to know. Thanks."

"All right. Good luck."

Brill ended the call and stared at the framed family portrait on the dresser. How did her sweet, innocent Vanessa end up in this dubious relationship?

She sat for a few minutes, then got up and went out to the kitchen where Kurt and David were about to dive into the leftovers.

"Where are the girls?"

"Out on the back porch with Ethan," Kurt said.

She sat at the table where she could keep an eye on the doorway. "Dexter just called. Now *I* have a bad feeling about Professor Nicholson."

She lowered her voice and gave David a quick overview of what she'd hired Dexter to do and then told Kurt and David the details of tonight's phone call.

"There's only one logical explanation," David said.

Brill nodded. "He's in the Witness Protection Program."

"What?" Kurt moved his gaze from Brill to David and back to Brill. "That doesn't sound like good news."

"No, it doesn't." Brill put her hand on Kurt's. "But I don't think we should just drop it either."

"If you'd like," David said, "I could collect on some favors and have someone dig a little deeper."

Kurt sighed. "I suppose we can't just ignore it. If you're willing to help us, I'm all for it."

"Me, too. Thanks, David." Brill shook her head. "What in the world did Vanessa stumble into?"

"*If* this is a witness protection situation," David said, "Tyson Nicholson was a new identity. The guy probably didn't want to put down roots with Vanessa and the baby and be constantly looking over his shoulder the rest of his life."

Kurt got up and paced. "I had a bad feeling about this from the beginning. I thought we should leave well enough alone."

"Yes, you did." Brill shot David a please-help-me-out-here look. "But Vanessa's never knowing could be more harmful, especially if she decided to start looking for him on her own."

David nodded. "Kurt, she's right about that. If it's better to leave well enough alone, it'd be good for Vanessa to find out now."

Kurt sat again, his fingers tapping the table. "Good grief, this baby could be the son of a gangster."

"There are so many possibilities it's best not to speculate," Brill said. "But if he's in the Witness Protection Program, that would explain why he was so adamantly opposed to permanent ties."

Kurt leaned his head back and combed his hands through his hair. "Well, so much for sleeping tonight. Just think … fifteen minutes ago my only fear was that my wife might be brutally attacked by a knife-happy ex-con looking for a payback."

Kurt glanced at his watch. Brill, David, and Emily had gone to bed an hour ago, and Ethan was still on the back porch with Vanessa.

He opened the door and stuck his head outside.

"I'm going to bed," he said. "I'm sorry I didn't get to visit with you, Ethan."

"I probably should get going and let Vanessa get some rest." Ethan rose to his feet. "The time got away from me."

"You've got a long drive back to Maryville," Kurt said.

"Oh, my summer plans have changed, Mr. Jessup. I'm back here staying with my aunt and uncle. I'm going to go to work for my uncle, starting Monday."

Kurt listened as Ethan gave him the reason for his quitting his roofing job and expressed his enthusiasm about learning to pour concrete for his uncle's company.

"It'll give me more experience," Ethan said. "I've got to work my way through two more years of college and then grad school."

"It's great that you have a goal. It's no small thing to become a psychologist."

"Yeah, but if I don't get that far, at least I can build myself a house." Ethan smiled. "Actually, I'm determined to have my own practice someday. It's something to shoot for anyway. Well, I'd better let you folks get to bed. I never seem to know when to quit talking."

Vanessa reached up and took his hand. "I'm glad you came over. And that you'll be here all summer."

"Yeah, me, too. I'll just walk around the side of the house and back to my car. On second thought, I won't get shot, will I?"

Vanessa laughed. "Trust me, every cop watching this house knows who you are."

"Yeah, but it's dark," Kurt said. "It'd be better if you came through the house and went out the front door."

"I'll walk with you." Vanessa giggled as she struggled to get up off the glider and onto her feet. "Well, I executed that maneuver like a true hippo."

"Ah, but a *lovely* hippo," Ethan added.

Vanessa nudged Ethan with her elbow as if it was some kind of private joke between them, then locked arms with him and went in the house.

Kurt slid the bolt lock on the dining room door, dreading the day he'd have to steal what laughter Vanessa had left by telling her that Professor Ty Nicholson didn't exist.

Brill lay in bed, her eyes wide open and watching the ceiling fan go round and round in the dark. How she hated being out of control. What was Tyson Nicholson's real name? Was he a dangerous man? Did she even want to know? Could she afford not to know? If Vanessa decided to keep the baby, would she and Kurt live in fear that the boy's father would eventually show up, making Vanessa vulnerable to whatever it was he was hiding?

Lord, I'm on overload. I know You don't want me to worry. Give me wisdom.

Brill sighed. She'd hardly had time to consider the threat to her own life. Merrick Fountain was a serious danger and true to his word. There was no doubt in her mind that he intended to come after her. But who was next—Trent? DA Cromwell? A former member of Cromwell's staff—perhaps the assistant DA? As long as Fountain was out there, she could not let down her guard.

The toilet flushed in the guest bathroom. Was David restless too? How strange it seemed to have her FBI friend occupying the room across the hall. Her brief attraction to David after Kurt's affair had instantly withered when buds of forgiveness and trust bloomed once more in her marriage. How different might things be if she had acted on her impulses?

Brill turned on her side and could make out the outline of her gun on the nightstand. In her almost nineteen years in law enforcement, she had never shot anyone. Was that about to change?

"Don't worry. It's there," Kurt said.

"How did you know what I was thinking?"

"I can almost hear your wheels turning." He pulled her into his embrace, her back resting against his chest. "I didn't really think you'd be able to fall asleep."

"Me, either. My mind's racing a hundred miles an hour. But I'm exhausted."

Kurt pressed his warm lips to her neck. "Well, tomorrow's Saturday. You don't have to work all day, do you?"

"I guess not."

"Why don't we drive up to Knoxville and take the girls to a movie or something?"

"Are you going to be able to relax? Or will you be thinking every minute that Merrick Fountain could be in the theater?"

"I'll never shake the fear until you get him. But I don't think we should stop living. David has offered to watch your back. Let's let him."

CHAPTER 19

VANESSA got up early on Saturday morning and decided she couldn't stand to be locked in the house for another moment. She went out in the backyard and scratched Rinnie's neck, then slipped out the back gate and down the alley.

She went around the block and came back to Azalea Lane, confident the officers watching the house couldn't recognize her that far away, then walked down to Cherokee Valley Park.

This beautiful park had caught her eye when her dad drove her to the obstetrician's office, and this morning it was calling her name. She went over and sat on a rope swing that hung from a towering shade tree and looked out across the rolling green terrain, lush with countless varieties of flowers, trees, and shrubs.

Beyond the boundary of the park, the foothills wore the morning sun and streaks of white haze that looked to her like angel's hair. In the distance, the Etch-a-Sketch colored silhouette of the Smokies formed a formidable backdrop.

Lord, it's so good to feel Your presence. It's been such a long time.

She held on to the swing with both hands, her head leaned back, her hair loose and dangling, and pumped her legs until the swing became a pendulum. She closed her eyes and inhaled the rich, earthy scent of wet ground and listened to the clear, sweet song of a lone cardinal. The cool breeze that brushed her cheeks would soon feel like the blast of a blow dryer, but for the moment, this soft Tennessee morning was hers to—

"Makes you feel like a kid, doesn't it?" said an elderly sounding man.

Vanessa's eyes flew open. She dragged her feet on the ground and came to a stop, her pulse racing, and saw a bearded, gray-haired man on a nearby park bench. How long had he been sitting there?

"Name's Micah Harvey. You live around here?"

Should she be talking to a stranger right now? This old guy looked harmless.

"Not far," she said.

"I've lived in Sophie Trace for the past fifty-seven years, and I've never seen you in Cherokee Valley Park before. You new here?"

"Sort of. My parents live here. My name's Vanessa."

He moved his eyes down to her bulging middle and then held her gaze. "So when's your baby due?"

Was this guy ever nosy! Then again, had she ever met a small-town southerner who wasn't?

"July twenty-eighth."

Micah hooked his thumbs on the straps of his overalls. "I'm all for havin' kids. My sweet Eleanor and I had just one—a son, Charles. He gave us three grandsons. The youngest is thirty-five now. They all live somewhere else and are busy with their own lives."

"So do you live around here?" Vanessa said.

Micah took a handkerchief out of his pocket and dabbed his forehead. "I have a room at the Carter House."

"That the big blue Victorian house with the front porch that wraps all around?"

Micah nodded. "That's the one. I walk over here a couple times a day for the exercise. I can only handle so much TV and so many board games, if you know what I mean. My favorite place to be is right here. It's mighty pretty. And peaceful."

Vanessa looked out beyond the rolling green to the layers of foothills and mountains, shrouded in a milky haze. "It really is."

"So which is it—a boy or a girl?"

Vanessa smiled and the answer was out even before she meant to say it. "A boy."

"Picked out a name?"

"Not yet. *"I can't even decide whether it's right for me to keep him.*

"Names are important. Somethin' you carry with you all your life. Defines you, in a way. I always liked the name Micah. It was my grandfather's name."

"That's nice. I like family names. I wasn't named after anyone."

"Maybe your folks thought you deserved a name all your own," Micah said. "Vanessa's a right pretty name."

"Thanks. I like it now, but when I was little, it was a pain. No one ever spelled it right."

He chuckled. "Try Micah sometime. You can't believe how many ways they try to spell that one."

Vanessa relaxed the grip she had on the swing. She liked this old guy. "So you sit on that bench every time you come here?"

Micah nodded. "Unless it's taken. But it's usually free just after dawn and just before dusk. It's like an ol' friend that waits for me.

Probably sounds kinda silly, but when you don't have anybody, you start thinkin' that way."

"Your wife isn't living?"

Micah stretched out his legs and crossed them at the ankles. "Nah. Eleanor passed on twenty years ago. She was the glue of the family. Charles and my grandsons pretty much do their own thing."

"I'm sorry."

"It's okay. I've learned to be content with what I've got. Not every man my age can get around as well as I do. And Sophie Trace is a nice place to hang your hat." Micah seemed to study her for a moment. "So … you a single mom?"

Vanessa felt her face burning. Was there no end to his nosiness? "Why would you assume that?"

"I didn't see a wedding ring, that's all." Micah looked out toward the mountains. "Sorry if my curiosity seems intrusive. I just have an insatiable interest in people. It's really none of my business, eh?"

He had that right. On the other hand, what difference did it make if she told her story to a lonely old man?

"I didn't mean to snap at you," Vanessa said. "I'm still a little guarded about it, especially with older people. I don't find it helpful to hear how different things were in your generation."

Micah rubbed his beard. "Well, you won't get that from me. I like to know people, not judge 'em."

Silence nestled between them. She held on to the swing with both hands and looked down at the ground. She probably should just say a polite good-bye and head back to the house, but Micah seemed like such a nice man, and it bothered her to think about how lonely he must be.

She glanced at her watch. Emily wouldn't be up for at least another hour, and no one even knew she had left the house. What was the hurry?

Brill walked to the end of the driveway and picked up Saturday's issue of *The Gateway Gazette*. She nodded at two officers in the plain DB car she was sure all her neighbors knew was parked there.

She took in a breath of fresh morning air and stood for a moment drinking in the soft beauty of the misty foothills visible through the trees on the other side of the street.

She got in her squad car and handed the newspaper to David. "There. You can read the headlines while I drive to the station."

David slid off the rubber band, unfolded the newspaper, and held it out in front of him. "Let's see … today's lead story is …"

Ex-Con Continues Stabbing Spree

Sophie Trace police are still looking for fifty-six-year-old Merrick Fountain, who was released from Holbrook State Penitentiary three weeks ago after serving a fifteen-year sentence for second-degree murder. Fountain is believed to be responsible for four stabbings, which have resulted in the deaths of two law enforcement officers, Detective Zachary Rogers of Memphis, and Detective Sean O'Toole of Sophie Trace.

The latest victim, Detective Beau Jack Rousseaux of the Sophie Trace Police Department, sustained a stab wound to the abdomen around ten o'clock Thursday night in the parking lot of Nick's Grill at Third and Main. Rousseaux is in stable condition at St. Luke's Hospital.

Sophie Trace Police Chief Brill Jessup said an eyewitness has positively identified Rousseaux's assailant as Merrick Fountain.

Chief Jessup is involved in a state-wide manhunt to capture Fountain, whom Tennessee law enforcement officials agree is making good on a courtroom threat he made against those responsible for putting him in prison, including Chief Jessup, her former partner Zachary Rogers, and the former Memphis DA, Jason Cromwell—"

"That's enough." Brill held her palm up. "It's the same old. I was just curious if the paper had come up with a new spin."

"Looks like there's a zinger."

"What zinger?"

David shook the paper, held it taut, and continued.

An anonymous source inside the Sophie Trace Police Department told Mayor Lewis Roswell that, while everyone is sympathetic to the threat on Chief Jessup's life, a number of officers have expressed serious doubts that the chief can effectively lead in the wake of Detective Sean O'Toole's murder and the questions surrounding it.

The firestorm of controversy has continued to build since Fountain, posing as a nurse, was able to breach police security outside O'Toole's hospital room and successfully poison the recovering detective with a capsule of peanut oil, to which he was highly allergic.

The city council has called a special meeting to discuss the growing fear among police officers that Chief Jessup is not able to handle police business while these relentless attacks continue to threaten her and her officers—

"Stop!" Brill could almost hear her collar sizzling. "I don't want to hear any more."

"Okay. That's essentially the end of it."

"How *dare* he!" She gripped the wheel and squeezed it. "The mayor is lying about this anonymous source in my department because he wants to *create* doubt about my ability to lead. He's too big a coward to tell my officers and the people of this community that the city council wants me out."

"Are you sure? It wouldn't be the first time there was mutiny within the ranks of a police department."

Brill turned and glared at David. "There's no mutiny! We are as rock solid as we were during the disappearances—even more so. We're handling the day-to-day business just fine. The mayor's a liar."

"Or a puppet. Doesn't he answer to the city council?"

Brill nodded. "I guess I shouldn't be surprised. The mayor and I already had a run in over what happened to O'Toole."

Brill told David about her unpleasant encounter with Mayor Roswell on Memorial Day and her concerns about her job.

"I'm really sorry, Brill. If you think it's a gender issue, you should file a claim—"

"I'm not filing a claim! This isn't about gender. Or if it is, it's not coming from the people in my department. I'm telling you, there's no mutiny here. I read people better than that. This is nothing more than a cheap ploy to make the public question my ability to lead under fire. It's the only way the city council can get rid of me without half the department quitting in protest."

David folded the newspaper. "Why do they want to get rid of you? For crying out loud, a few months ago, you cracked the biggest case in the town's history."

"Yes, but I also drew a lot of very bad press. Most of what people associate with Police Chief Jessup is negative, and it started with the disappearances. Thanks to the cable networks, the entire world sat back and misjudged this community and my department because of the red shadows legend. Face it, outsiders tend to remember rumors, not resolution."

"Unfortunately."

"And now my name's being plastered all over the news again. It's a colossal media circus—the very kind of press this town doesn't need."

David picked up the newspaper and tapped her on the shoulder with it. "You're not responsible for Merrick Fountain's actions. You did your job by putting him away."

"Of course I did. But that's not the point, David. The city council's primary focus is to grow this town. And when that's not happening, they have to blame someone. Looks like I'm the scapegoat. Get rid of Chief Jessup. Get rid of the problem."

"It doesn't work that way."

"Maybe it does."

"Listen, you. Sophie Trace is what it is. Let the CEOs come and take a look. This town's got a whole list of things going for it, and the view of the Smokies is unsurpassed. It's a great place to raise a family."

Brill sighed. "That's going to be a hard sell as long as Merrick Fountain is wielding a knife."

Vanessa sat on the park bench next to Micah Harvey, aware that it was almost nine o'clock. Emily would be up soon. If she ever wanted to get out of the house alone again, she had to sneak back in without anyone knowing she'd been gone.

"Micah, I've really enjoyed talking to you, but I need to go."

"I've enjoyed it too. It's not often that I get to visit with a pretty young woman."

"I can't imagine that you enjoyed hearing about all my woes."

He smiled. "Why? Isn't that what friends are for?"

"I guess so. I just feel a little weird about telling you my private business. The only other person I've really confided in this way is my friend Ethan."

"So he's a pretty nice fella?"

"Very."

"Has he got a crush on you?"

"Heavens, no. Look at me." She put her hands on her middle. "We're just good friends."

"Is this Ethan a friend from college?"

Vanessa nodded. "He was in my psychology class."

"With the wayward professor, eh?"

"Don't call him wayward. Ty isn't a bad person."

"He skipped out on you, young lady. What kinda guy does that?"

"I don't know—a scared one, I suppose. A scandal could've cost him his job."

"So could walkin' off the job, don't you think?"

Vanessa shrugged. "He wouldn't have done something that risky without a good reason. The hardest thing is not knowing why."

"Can't you just accept he didn't want the responsibility?"

"Not really. I mean, he *didn't* want it—but enough to abandon his teaching position and throw away everything he worked for? I just can't see it."

"Sounds like you still love him."

"I do, but I wish I could stop."

Micah patted her hand. "Well, the important thing now is makin' sure that little boy gets what he needs. You've got some decisions to make."

Vanessa suddenly felt the pressure of her circumstances bearing down on her again.

"I really do need to go."

She shifted her weight back and forth on her bottom and inched her way to the edge of the bench, then got up on her feet.

"Thanks for listening to me, Micah. Maybe I'll see you here again."

"You know when to find me—just after dawn and just before dusk."

Vanessa left the park and walked hurriedly up the sidewalk toward the alley behind her parents' house, hoping Emily hadn't awakened to find her missing.

She had found it freeing to confide in a stranger and also a bit adventuresome. Micah was a kind old man, and she planned to run into him again—if she could keep her parents from knowing she had ventured out. After all, she wasn't the one Merrick Fountain was after.

CHAPTER 20

VANESSA went up on the back porch and sat on the glider next to Rinnie and stroked her back.

"Don't you dare say a word," she whispered. "Act normal."

She heard bare feet slapping the wood floor inside and then the back door flew open.

"There you are," Emily said. "Dad wants to know if you want a waffle or eggs and bacon."

"Eggs and bacon sounds great."

"Good, that's what we're having."

Vanessa pasted on a smile and hoped Emily didn't notice she was perspiring and winded. "How long have you been up?"

"Not very long. Mom and Special Agent David went to work, but they're coming home at lunch so we can go to a movie in Knoxville. Dad wants to make a day of it and not come back till tonight."

"Sounds exhausting."

"Not to me. I love going places besides Sophie Trace."

"You could probably see the same movies here."

"Yeah, but it's not as much fun."

Rinnie let out a low growl and then barked. Vanessa grabbed her collar.

"What is it, girl?"

206

"Yoo-hoo …"

Vanessa turned and saw Tessa Masino's short portly frame waddling up the slight grade toward the porch, a rectangular plastic container in her hands.

"It's okay." Vanessa stroked the dog's back. "She's a friend."

"I just made sweet rolls and thought you might like to have some," Tessa said, sounding out of breath. "I used my homemade strawberry preserves for the centers. They're quite tasty."

"Yum." Emily pushed open the screen door and skipped down the steps, then gave Tessa a big hug. "Perfect timing. Dad's fixing breakfast."

"I made sure there were extra rolls for Special Agent Riley," Tessa said. "That *was* him I saw unpacking his truck yesterday?"

"Uh-huh. He's spending his whole vacation at our house. And this is his dog. Her name's Rinnie."

"She's very pretty. Well, tell him hello for me."

"I will. Why don't you come up on the porch and talk to Vanessa and I'll take these to Dad?" Emily gingerly climbed the steps, the container held out in front of her, a kid-at-Christmas expression on her face. She carefully opened the screen door and went in the house.

Tessa came up the steps and onto the porch, wiping her hands on her apron. "How are you feeling, Vanessa?"

"Fat and sluggish. I guess that's normal."

"I suppose. Though you're the picture of health, I must say. Too bad you can't get out and walk because of the threat to your mother."

Vanessa's gaze collided with Tessa's.

Was the woman playing with her? Had she seen her cutting through the alley? Should she ask? Should she just leave it alone?

"Mom wants us to stay inside till the guy's caught."

"Well, I suppose it's best not to take chances, though I imagine you could get *restless*. You're certainly welcome to come to our house any time. Antonio and I would love to get to know you. Emily adores you and has told us so much about you."

"Emily adores me?"

"Oh my, yes. You didn't know?"

"Not really."

"Well, I suppose sisters don't always express their feelings to each other the way they do to others."

"I honestly never gave it much thought. I always thought Emily idolized Ryan."

"Oh, she does. She thinks the sun rises and sets on *both* of you. I do hope you'll give some thought to coming over for a visit. You're probably feeling a little cabin fever, what with being watched around the clock and all."

Vanessa studied Tessa's expression. What were the odds that this nosy neighbor had looked out just as Vanessa passed by in the alley? Then again, the woman didn't seem to miss anything. If she snitched, not only would Vanessa have to endure a lecture for not heeding her mother's orders, she would be assured of never getting out of the house again by herself. Maybe it was smart to befriend Tessa.

"I'd like to come over," Vanessa said. "In some ways, I feel like I already know you."

"Antonio and I aren't doing a thing this afternoon after we have lunch at Nick's. We're usually home by one-thirty."

"Thanks, I'll call you." *There's my excuse to skip the movie.*

"I look forward to it. Tell your folks hello for me—and Special Agent Riley. He was there when Emily and I went through that awful hostage ordeal, you know. I'm very fond of him." Tessa brushed a lock of silver out of her eyes. "Well, I've got to hurry back and finish making the casserole for Mr. Quinlan. He's in Alzheimer's care. About the only thing he'll eat is my chicken divan. He took a liking to it when he started wandering and ended up in my kitchen. Junior and Mary Ann are beside themselves that he's not eating enough. That's Mr. Quinlan's son and daughter-in-law. They live in the three-story white house on the corner. Okay, dear, toodleoo. Call me."

Vanessa smiled in spite of herself as Tessa waddled briskly toward the front gate and could almost picture a whirlwind of dust trailing her blue housedress and ruffled apron. Tessa Masino might be a busybody, but she seemed extraordinarily caring and generous.

Brill followed Trent into her office and closed the door.

"You can sit there at the table, Trent. I want to update you on what's going on."

His eyes grew wide when he saw David Riley sitting at the conference table. "You called in the FBI?"

"No. David's here on vacation."

Trent paused for a few moments as if he were processing, then sat across from David, a smile tugging at his cheeks. "I see ... so, Special Agent Riley, shall I give you a list of tourist attractions you shouldn't miss while you're here?"

David, dressed in khaki shorts and a yellow golf shirt, leaned back in his chair, his hands clasped behind his head. "I think we both know how I'm going to be spending my vacation—unofficially, of course."

Trent pursed his lips, the lines on his forehead suddenly scrunched. "This isn't necessary, Chief. I've got your back covered."

"I know you do," Brill said. "But you and I are the two most likely targets at this end of the state. David's offered to use his vacation time to help cover my back, which means we can concentrate more of our manpower on keeping you safe. I'm very concerned that Fountain is planning to come after you next."

"He can't get to me, ma'am. I've got a wall of blue around me. And we're coordinating with sheriff's deputies and other police officers in the region to keep extra security at city hall and the hospital, and also surveillance teams to watch your home and mine. Our day-to-day police business is on track, even without O'Toole and Rousseaux."

"I'm proud of the way you're handling this," Brill said.

Trent looked at David and then at her. "If I have any concern, it's how long we can realistically keep this up. Manpower on loan can only last so long."

"Let's take it one day at a time," Brill said. "Right now every law enforcement person in the state is outraged and wants this cop killer off the street."

"By the way"—David reached for something on the chair next to him—"I brought some of our body armor for you and Brill to use. I don't know of anything that protects a hundred percent against knife blades, but these are made with a special weave that has stab resistance *and* ballistic protection."

"So wear it," Brill said. "That's an order."

"Yes, ma'am." Trent took the ballistic vest and looked it over. "The FBI does everything first class. If Beau Jack'd had one of these, he would've been wearing it Thursday night when Fountain came calling. Thanks."

David winked. "Any time. Your tax dollars at work."

"I see no reason to make a formal announcement about David's being here," Brill said. "I don't want his presence to suggest that I'm not the one heading up this investigation or that I've lost confidence in this department to protect me. But between you and me, I'm glad he's here and that he accepted Kurt's invitation to be our houseguest. That's helped to ease the tension at home, especially with Emily."

"What if I'm *asked* why he's here?"

"Say he's here on vacation and not in any official capacity. Let them draw their own conclusions about anything unofficial he may be doing."

Tessa got out of the car and stood on the sidewalk in front of Nick's Grill. The green and white striped awning of the Toffee Emporium next door seemed to glow in the noonday sun.

As she struggled to open the glass door at Nick's, Antonio stepped up behind her, grumbling that he'd get the door for her if she'd just slow down.

"Welcome, friends." Nick walked over and shook Antonio's hand and put his other hand on her shoulder. "Today's special is a

low-fat salmon pasta that'll knock your socks off. You get your choice
of bread and beverage. Gus is waiting for you."

Tessa walked over to the counter and sat at her usual place.

Antonio straddled the stool next to her and slapped Gus on the
back. "How's it going, friend?"

Gus smiled. "Really can't complain. But I always do."

"So what do you know?"

Gus took a sip of Coke and wiped his white mustache. "I hear
the feds are involved in the stabbing cases now."

"Says who?"

"I have a friend who works for the sheriff's department," Gus
said. "That bigwig FBI fella's back in town. You know, the one who
took over durin' the disappearances?"

"Special Agent Riley?" Tessa said. "He's just here on vacation."

"And if you believe that, I've got some beachfront property to
sell you at Cades Cove."

Tessa folded her hands on the counter. "For your information,
Gus, I was over at the Jessups' this morning and was told he's here on
vacation. In fact, he's staying with the Jessups."

"I'll just bet he is."

"Oh, wipe that smirk off your face," Tessa said. "You're trying to
make something out of nothing."

"Nothin'? Didn't you read the newspaper? It's kinda obvious
the city council doesn't trust Chief Jessup to run the case anymore,
especially after she let Detective O'Toole die right under her nose."

"That's a cruel and totally unfair accusation," Tessa said. "Nobody
in her department was expecting that awful, despicable man to attack
the detective a second time."

"Well, looks like the mayor and city council thought they should've. The buck stops with the chief. She wanted to be equal to a man. Let her take the heat like a man."

Tessa counted to ten, relieved when Maggie Cummings walked over to the counter and stood in front of Gus, her hands on her hips.

"If Chief Hennessey was still heading up the department," Maggie said, "would you have been so quick to point a finger at him?"

"Aw, don't go gettin' all ticked off," Gus said. "My opinion of Chief Jessup has nothin' to do with her bein' female."

"Oh, admit it, Gus. You never did think a woman would be an effective police chief."

"You're twistin' things. Chief Jessup has been controversial from the get-go."

Maggie shook her head. "No, *you* made her controversial because she pooh-poohed the red shadows legend during her investigation of the disappearances."

"Which just proves she's an outsider," Gus said. "She marched into town flauntin' her hotshot credentials from the Memphis police force. She didn't know the first thing about how things work here."

"And yet who cracked the big case? Maybe you should give her some credit."

"I'm not the only one who has trouble with her. Mayor Roswell isn't impressed."

"Lewis Roswell was *born* cranky," Maggie said. "I used to babysit the guy when he was still in diapers, and he hasn't changed. He still throws a fit when things don't go his way. He and the city council are miffed because the media didn't paint Sophie Trace in a good light. I can understand that. But to blame Chief Jessup is totally unfair." Maggie leaned forward on the counter, her weight resting on her palms, and looked at Gus. "The media hyped the legend for all it was worth. Chief Jessup wasn't responsible for any of that. I can't say the same for your barber friend."

"Now don't be throwin' stones at Billy Dan."

Antonio patted Gus on the back. "You have to admit he made a fool of himself on *Larry King Live*. We all know he's sane, even though he believes to the core that he spent time with the spirits of the departed Cherokee. But you know the rest of the world couldn't keep a straight face."

"None of that changes the fact that Chief Jessup is an outsider. She doesn't understand our roots, our history, or the legend. And, yes, I resent it."

Tessa shook her head. "What you resent is a woman who can actually fill Chief Hennessey's boots. You *want* her to fail."

"That's nuts."

"Yes, it is," Tessa said. "At least that's *something* we can agree on."

CHAPTER 21

NICK Phillips stood outside Nick's Grill and waved at Tessa and Antonio as they got into their car. He made small talk with a family of tourists as they strolled by on the sidewalk, and then went back inside.

He walked over to the counter where Gus Williams sat poking the ice cubes in his empty Coke glass.

"If you were trying to score points with Maggie, you blew it big-time," Nick said.

"I know. Don't rub it in."

"You've got a giant chip on your shoulder because of Chief Jessup, and I don't know what it's going to take to knock it off."

Gus sighed. "Well, it sure isn't because she's a woman."

"Then why did you make the comment that if she wanted to be *equal* to a man, let her take the heat like a man? That kind of dialogue is loaded, friend."

"Tessa'll get over it. She always does. But I didn't mean to get Maggie's nose out of joint."

"Gus, *my* nose is out of joint. Chief Jessup was tested last fall and, by anybody's standards, she passed with flying colors. I don't know how many law enforcement people, male or female, would've hung in there and stayed focused enough to break the case."

"That's what we're payin' her for."

"All right. So at what point do you stop treating her like an outsider and accept her as a legitimate member of the community? If you're holding it against her that she doesn't believe there's anything to the red shadows legend, just remember that I don't believe it either. In fact, most people in Sophie Trace don't. The difference is we accept those of you who do and don't belittle you, even though it's got outsiders laughing at us."

"Aw, don't say that."

"Why not? It's true. The whole world had a good laugh at our expense. The cable coverage of the disappearances didn't portray us in a positive light. The mayor and city council are way out of line to blame Chief Jessup for our image problem. It went south when the media got wind of the legend and ran with it."

"First time I've ever heard *you* take sides."

Nick sat on the stool next to Gus, his hands folded on the counter. "We go back a long way. I wouldn't be much of a friend if I didn't tell you how I see things. I wouldn't hurt you for the world. But you've got to change your attitude about Chief Jessup or keep your feelings to yourself."

Gus tipped his glass and crunched a mouthful of ice. "You think I *want* her to fail?"

"Sure seems that way."

"I suppose I have been pretty negative."

"Do you think?" Nick nudged Gus with his shoulder. "It was a huge shock for all of us when Chief Hennessey dropped dead and the city council chose a young female spitfire to replace him. She's a stark contrast to what we're used to. But how can anyone deny that she's done a bang-up job—and in the midst of some really tough circumstances?"

Gus didn't say anything for half a minute and then said, "I guess mentally I've refused to accept her as chief of police. I keep thinkin' Chief Hennessey oughta be in there."

"I miss him too. But he's dead and buried, and life goes on."

"Well, you're right about me needin' an attitude adjustment. I'll work on it."

Maggie whizzed past the counter, order pad in hand, and went into the kitchen without speaking.

"Looks like you've got some damage control to do with Maggie."

"Might be too late."

"I doubt that. She just needs to see more of your tame side."

Brill sat at the conference table with David, going over the facts of the case.

"I don't know what more we can do to brace ourselves for Merrick Fountain's next move," she said.

David put down his pencil. "Yeah, it's a waiting game. But there's no doubt in my mind that he's planning it."

"I can still see the meanness in his eyes. I always knew he was dangerous. I'm sure he would've killed his wife if she hadn't gone into hiding."

"You scared?"

Brill wiped a smudge off the table with her index finger. "I'd be a fool not to be."

"Kurt is. We had a long talk about it."

"Did you reassure him?"

"Tried to. He loves you a lot."

"I know."

David shifted his weight and seemed to be thinking. Finally he said, "Brill, did you ever tell him about what happened?"

"You mean the *kiss*?" She lifted her gaze. "Actually, I did. Kurt and I don't keep secrets from each other."

"I'm surprised he trusts me to stay at your house."

"He doesn't have to trust you, he trusts *me*. There's only one man in my life."

"Yeah, that's obvious."

"Has this been eating at you since October?"

"Pretty much."

"Good. Then it won't ever happen again. Now let's forget it."

"All right." David stared at his hands, the corners of his mouth twitching. "Would you believe Patricia and I are getting remarried?"

"And you're just now telling me?" She laughed, then wadded a piece of notepaper and threw it at him. "When?"

"We haven't set a date, but we're talking. Things are as good as they've ever been. I don't want to blow it this time."

"You'd better not. I'm so happy for you."

"Me, too."

"So why aren't you spending your vacation with her?"

"Patricia's still in Dallas, managing her dance studio. She's looking for a buyer and can't really take time off right now. I've got more time off than I want or need."

"I wouldn't exactly call watching my back 'time off.'"

"No, but what better way to spend it than watching out for a friend?"

"I'm touched—really." Brill studied his face. "I just hope you know what you're getting yourself into."

Vanessa stood in the doorway of the living room. She might as well get this over with.

"There you are," Kurt said. "So which movie do *you* vote for?"

"Actually … would it be okay with everyone if I stayed home?"

"Oh, honey, we were hoping this could be a family outing," Brill said. "Why don't you want to go?"

"It just sounds exhausting." Vanessa leaned against the doorway. "I'll be fine here. I can take a nap. And Tessa invited me to come over. She seems really nice."

"Tessa is *so* nice," Emily said. "And she always has something yummy to eat."

Kurt folded the newspaper. "I doubt we'll be home before eight or nine o'clock. You sure you want to stay home by yourself?"

"Absolutely. I've got Rinnie to keep me company. And those two officers are watching the house."

Brill looked over at David. "Are you comfortable with it?"

"I think so. Fountain hasn't given us any reason to think he would target a family member. Just keep the doors locked and the security alarm on. If you go to the Masinos', have them walk you back and forth."

"So I can skip the movie?"

Her parents looked at each other.

"I'm okay with it, if you are," Kurt said.

Brill sighed. "All right, Vanessa. I'm really disappointed, though. I haven't had much time with you."

Thanks for the guilt trip, Mom.

"But I'm glad you're making an effort with the Masinos. They're wonderful Christian neighbors, and Tessa is a great prayer warrior to have on your side."

"It should be nice spending a little time with them."

"You have to let them feel the baby kick," Emily said.

"Not everyone's as gung ho about it as you are." *Including Mom and Dad.*

"If Vanessa's not going to the movie, can I ask Jasmine?" Emily pleaded.

Brill shook her head. "Sweetie, with the way things are, I don't think we should involve anyone else."

"Mom's right," Kurt said. "How about a rain check?"

Emily folded her arms and stuck out her lower lip. "Oh, all right. But it's not easy being the police chief's kid."

"On the other hand," David said, "not every kid gets an FBI special agent escorting her to the movies. I'm kind of a fun date."

Emily grinned. "Is this a date? My dad takes me on dates."

"Then I'd better ask his permission to take you out."

Vanessa set the security alarm and explained to the officers watching the house that she was going to walk next door with Antonio and Tessa.

The trio strolled down the sidewalk toward the ivy-clad tan brick house and turned at the walkway leading up to the arched wood door.

Vanessa stepped up under the small burgundy awning on the stoop.

"Here, let me get the front door for you," Antonio said.

Vanessa entered a spacious foyer dominated by an elegant oak staircase and turned her gaze to the room on the right, where two walls of windows seemed to bring the outdoors in.

"Oh, I love all this light."

She moved to the doorway and let her eyes feast on the view outside. The yard was a green carpet, shaded by towering trees and bordered by neatly manicured hedges. A circular bed of pansies dressed up the ground around the stone birdbath in the center of the yard.

"I could sit here for hours and just think," Vanessa said.

Tessa nodded. "I always have my quiet time in here. It's our living room, but we think of it as our garden room. We love the light, airy atmosphere and feel blessed to have it."

Vanessa felt as if she were turning the pages of one of those house-and-garden magazines. The furniture looked invitingly comfortable, and the floral and solid fabrics were nicely coordinated in soft shades of green and yellow and white. An oriental rug covered much of the hardwood floor and tied the room together.

"I'd call this cozy elegance."

"Thanks," Tessa said. "I'll give you a tour of the rest of the house in a bit, but why don't we rest a few minutes and have some lemonade?"

"That sounds great."

"I'll bring it," Antonio said. "You girls get comfy."

"Sit anywhere," Tessa said. "And feel free to kick your sandals off."

Vanessa sat on one of the couches and looked out through the walls of glass. "I just love being able to see the green. We enjoy our bay window in the kitchen, and we can see the mountains. But this really is like a sunroom."

Tessa sat in an armchair facing Vanessa. "This is the room that compelled us to buy this house when Antonio retired. We've never been sorry."

A black-and-white cat jumped up on the couch and sniffed Vanessa's hand.

"And who are you?"

"That's our Abby," Tessa said. "She's makes herself right at home. Push her off if she gets to be a pest."

"She's fine." Vanessa rubbed her fur, and Abby started purring. "I love cats."

"So … is the baby kicking a lot these days?"

"Almost nonstop. I think he's going to be a black belt."

"Have you thought of a name?"

No. Once I name him, he'll be mine, and I'll never be able to let go. "Not really."

"I get a kick out of Emily." Tessa waved her hand. "She talks about him like he's her baby. That girl is something else."

"You two seem to have a special bond."

Tessa was quiet for a moment and seemed far away. "Well, I suppose having gone through a frightening experience together has something to do with it."

"Emily never talks about it. My parents don't either."

"I think each of us has already talked it out in his or her own way. Antonio and I finally stopped having nightmares."

Vanessa nodded. "Emily, too. But she practically broke out in a cold sweat when we were at dinner the other night and she saw some men at the bar. She kept clinging to Dad and saying she wanted to go home."

"Don't you think this threat on your mother has triggered the old fears?"

"Definitely. But I'd never seen Emily like that. I felt helpless." Vanessa continued stroking the cat, relaxed by the purring. "Do you think you ever get over something like that?"

"Not entirely, but I'd like to think there will be lengthy periods of time when we forget about it."

"Here you go," Antonio said.

He came in the living room carrying a small tray with three glasses of lemonade. He offered the first to Vanessa.

"Thanks. This looks good."

"There's just nothing like it on a hot summer day," he said.

Vanessa took a sip. "You're right."

Antonio handed Tessa a glass of lemonade. "By the way, there was a recording on the phone. Gus called to apologize for being so negative about you-know-who."

"We can talk about this later, dear," Tessa said.

"Gus just wanted you to know he's rethinking the blame game."

"I should hope. Now let's not neglect our sweet guest."

Antonio sat in the other armchair facing Vanessa. "When's that baby due?"

"July twenty-eighth."

Antonio nodded, and then an awkward silence fell over the room as if no one knew which questions were okay to ask and which were not.

"Antonio," Vanessa finally said. "What did you do before you retired?"

"I was busy saving *soles*—in the shoe business." He laughed. "I had three retail stores and a shoe repair shop."

Vanessa took a sip of lemonade and pretended to be interested. At least she didn't have to do the talking. The Masinos were nice. Maybe she could stay for an hour or two and then go back to her parents' house and have the evening free.

Free. How wonderful that sounded. Once the officers thought she was locked in for the evening, she could sneak out and do whatever she wanted.

CHAPTER 22

BRILL sat in the back row of the movie theater, Kurt holding her hand, and tried to focus on the animated film that seemed to evoke laughter from everyone but her.

"You okay, honey?" Kurt whispered.

"I'm fine. Why?"

"You seem uptight." Kurt brought her hand to his lips. "I was hoping we could all relax for a few hours and forget about everything else."

"That's why I'm here. Pay attention to the show. It's really cute." *As if I have a clue what it's about.*

Kurt offered her the bag of popcorn, and she took a handful, her thoughts flashing back to their college days when they were broke and went to dollar matinees at the old Dickinson Theatre. Fake stars twinkled on the dome ceiling and bulky red curtains parted as the lights dimmed and the projector's beam of light turned the screen into the feature presentation. She and Kurt sat next to the wall in the back row of the balcony, and whenever they had privacy, made out as if they were the only two people on earth.

Life was sweeter then. But was it easier? Balancing her desire to be with Kurt and her commitment to graduating with a bachelor's degree in criminology took fierce determination and discipline—

especially once the match of physical desire had been struck. How many times had she gone to the Lord and reaffirmed the covenant she had made to save her virginity for her husband?

And hadn't it been worth the wait? A month after graduation, she and Kurt were married. What glorious, unrestrained, almost insatiable passion was unleashed that honeymoon week in New York. The newlywed phase was a welcome reprieve from the difficult disciplines of the college years.

But had any of those disciplines prepared her for the mini-crisis that came four months later when she got a positive pregnancy test and withdrew her application to the police academy? Her disappointment was soon overshadowed by the joys of expectant motherhood. Ryan was born the morning of their first wedding anniversary, and thirteen months later, they welcomed Vanessa.

Vanessa Colleen Jessup. Could she ever forget bringing home her little china doll, terrified that she wouldn't be able to handle two babies? And weren't her fears unfounded?

Brill sighed. Were they unfounded now? Why couldn't she shake the heaviness that had weighed her down since the moment Vanessa stepped out of the car, her tummy bulging? She understood how, in a moment of weakness, her daughter could have given in to unrestrained passion. But how could Vanessa have deceived herself into thinking that being in love somehow trumped God's commands regarding sex, or that sleeping with the psych professor made her special? No doubt Ty Nicholson had capitalized on her daughter's fragile self-esteem.

The letch.

Brill reached for the cup of Coke and took a sip. Who was this mysterious man who had stolen her daughter's heart and her innocence? If only Vanessa's experience could have been as a cherished bride instead of the psychology professor's pick of the semester—

"We need to leave." David's whispering voice was urgent.

Brill turned and saw him standing in the aisle next to Kurt's seat.

"No time to explain." He summoned her with his hand. "Let's go."

Brill took Emily's arm and gently pulled her to the aisle.

David bent down and whispered something to Emily. She nodded, her eyes wide.

"Kurt, you and Emily follow us."

David took Brill's arm and quickly ushered her out of the movie theater and into the lobby.

"What's going on?" Kurt said.

"I think I spotted Merrick Fountain." David seemed to be looking over Kurt's shoulder. "Come on, let's go to the car."

David clutched even more tightly to her arm and walked as fast as anyone could until they reached the car. He covered her head with his open hand and pushed her down into the passenger seat as if she was someone he had arrested.

Kurt got in the driver's seat, his face ashen.

David crawled in back next to Emily. "Lock the doors."

Kurt started the motor and all four doors automatically locked.

"Are you sure it was Fountain?" Brill said.

"As sure as I can be at a distance, but a man his size is hard to miss. He was wearing a Yankees ball cap and appeared to be loitering in the lobby. I tried to move around and nab him from behind, but he disappeared before I could get to him. You should call Knoxville

PD and get officers over here to comb the area. He might still be here."

"I want to go home." Emily's whiny voice sounded babyish.

"That's where we're going, honey," David said. "You're perfectly safe with me."

Brill pulled down the visor and looked at David in the rearview mirror. "Why would Fountain risk being seen when he knows he can't get close enough to attack me?"

"Good question."

Vanessa set the security alarm and went out the back door.

Free at last.

Not that her time with the Masinos had been unpleasant. They were sweethearts. But getting out of the house alone had felt so good before that she was eager to do it again.

She scratched Rinnie's chin, then opened the back gate and slipped into the alley. But this time she walked in the opposite direction, taking no chances that Tessa could see her.

She walked to the end of the alley and turned left, then squared back to Azalea Lane and headed for Cherokee Valley Park. It was packed with people, and cars were parallel parked all around the perimeter.

Vanessa strolled the grounds and people-watched, envying the young couples with children. The smell of something delicious cooking on the barbecue grills made her mouth water. What she wouldn't give for a fat, juicy hot dog with relish. Or a piece of grilled chicken. Or a cheeseburger with onion, lettuce, and tomato. Was there a food stand anywhere in the park? She couldn't remember seeing one.

The June breeze was warm and muggy and the evening sky clear except for a swirl of clouds that was a sure promise of a beautiful sunset.

She glanced at her watch and decided she needed to be home in an hour. Too bad. It would be fun to see Micah again, but she couldn't stay until dusk.

She stopped and leaned against a tree and watched a mother nursing a baby on a nearby park bench. She could almost feel her own baby in her arms and wondered all over again how she would gather the courage to give him up.

"It's quite a picture, isn't it? Motherhood, I mean."

Vanessa jumped, her hand over her heart. She turned around, more angry than scared, and looked up into Micah's face.

"Why do you do that?"

"Do what?"

"That's the second time you've startled me. Can't you cough or something? Sheesh."

"Sorry, young lady. I spotted you over here and wanted to say hey."

"I thought you didn't come to the park until dusk."

Micah shrugged. "I make it a point to be here at dusk. But sometimes I come early and just roam around, takin' it all in. Weekends are the most fun. I didn't expect to see you again today."

"It's a beautiful day—too nice to spend indoors."

"Yep, it is. Why don't you come over here and sit a spell. It's warm this evenin'. Kinda taxin' on someone carryin' a baby."

Vanessa didn't argue and went over to an empty bench and sat. Micah flopped down next to her.

"Whew." He wiped his forehead with a handkerchief. "I don't handle the heat like I used to. Guess I'm just gettin' old."

"How old are you?" Vanessa smiled and pushed a rock with her sandal. "No one said it's impolite for a woman to ask a man's age."

"Doesn't matter. I'm eighty-six and proud of it."

"You should be, especially since you're in such great shape."

"I have my aches and pains, but I'm more fortunate than most, that's for sure."

Vanessa started to ask him something, then changed her mind, and then decided to go ahead. "You said you've lived here more than fifty years, right?"

"Sure have."

"Then can I ask you a personal question that's been bugging me?"

Micah lifted an eyebrow. "More personal than my age?"

"What's your take on the legend of the red shadows?"

"Now why would you up and ask me somethin' like that?"

"Because I'm a newcomer to the area. My parents were here last fall when the disappearances happened, and it was their experience that lots of older people believe the legend. Do you?"

Micah rubbed his beard. "Does it matter?"

"Not at all. I'm more interested in your point of view. I think legends are fascinating, and this one certainly put Sophie Trace on the map. My folks don't think there's any truth to it. But I've never had anyone who's lived here a long time explain it to me so I can make up my own mind."

"And you think *I'm* the right person to do that?"

"Well, sure. Why not? You've probably heard it hundreds of times."

Micah hooked his thumbs on the straps of his overalls. "Not really."

"But you've lived here half a century."

"Well, to be honest, I don't go for superstition, so I don't listen to all the talk about the legend."

"But it's been front page news. You must have some feeling about it."

"I just told you my feelin' about superstition. There's really nothin' I can tell you about the legend. Never cared to know the details. Sorry."

"That's okay."

Micah leaned back on the bench, his eyes closed, his face reddish as the evening sun warmed it.

"So how's that little boy been today?"

"Kicking like there's no tomorrow. Honestly, I have no idea why I'm not bruised."

Micah chuckled. "I saw the way you were eyein' that mama nursin' her little one. You've got what it takes to be a single mom."

Vanessa turned to him. "You think so?"

"Sure do."

"I wish I were as certain."

"You can do it. You've just got to believe in yourself. Check out your options for financial help. You might even be able to go back to college."

"I really want to get my degree in elementary education. I love working with children."

"There you go then. That's what you ought to be doin'." Micah tugged at his mustache and seemed to be thinking. "As long as we're askin' personal questions, is there any chance the father's gonna kick in on this deal?"

"It's not likely. He has no interest in raising a child. Or taking on any permanent responsibility. He's too busy looking out for number one. Could we not talk about him? It's depressing."

"I'm sorry. Didn't mean to be nosin' where I'm not welcome. Bad habit. It gets boring over at the Carter House, and we've got nothin' better to do than to pry into each other's business … you like hot dogs?"

Vanessa smiled. "As a matter of fact, I do."

"So do I. The doc says they'll kill me, but I'm willin' to go happy. How about if I treat? There's a vendor that works the northeast corner of the park. Think you can walk that far?"

Vanessa got up and stretched her back. "Sure. I need the exercise. But you don't need to treat me. I've got money."

"That's not the point. Can't an old gentleman buy a new friend a hot dog?"

Vanessa glanced at her watch. Did she have time to walk that far and back and then to her home in just fifty minutes? Then again, why did seven-thirty have to be the magic number for her to be back? Her dad said they wouldn't be home until eight or nine o'clock. And her parents would probably stretch out the evening and spoil Emily rotten.

CHAPTER 23

VANESSA listened to the laughter of energetic children gathered around the duck pond at Cherokee Valley Park. She felt six years old again. She popped the last bite of her second hot dog into her mouth and smiled as she swallowed it.

"That tasted sooooo good, Micah. I don't know why I've been craving hot dogs, but that really hit the spot. Thanks."

"You're welcome. Few things in life are better than a good hot dog. I promise you, if there was a God, He would've made them grow on trees."

Vanessa laughed. "I'm all for that … I'm surprised you don't believe in God, though. You don't strike me as agnostic."

"Yep. All the talk about a Higher Power rates right up there with that legend in my book."

"Oh." Should she just leave it at that?

"If you're thinkin' of tryin' to convince me there's a God, don't bother. It hasn't worked in eighty-two years."

"I thought you were eighty-six."

Micah's face was suddenly expressionless. "I *am* eighty-six. What'd I say?"

"Eighty-two."

"Shoot, I'm liable to say anything when we get on the subject of religion. It's confusing and confrontational."

Vanessa gently gripped his arm. "Don't worry, I would never try to shove my Christian beliefs down anyone's throat. It doesn't work anyway. I'm fine with changing the subject."

Micah held her gaze and seemed to study her. "Just like that? You're not gonna try to lay a guilt trip on me like all the Bible thumpers I've talked to?"

"Why would I do that?"

"All right. Now I'm curious. Let's go over there and sit on the bench, and you can tell me why it should even matter to me if there's a God."

Was he looking for answers or an outlet for his cynicism? Vanessa followed him to an empty park bench. How was she supposed to convince a skeptic that he needed Jesus? Witnessing had never been easy for her.

Micah sat next to her, his hands clasped behind his head. "Go on. I'm listenin', though I've probably heard it all before."

"I really don't have a need to get into this."

"I'm askin'. I'd like to hear what you have to say—assuming you have somethin' to say."

"Actually, I rarely talk about my beliefs. But as long as you asked, have you seriously thought about what's at stake? I mean, are you so sure God doesn't exist that you're willing to gamble your eternal future on it?"

"I don't see it as gamblin'," Micah said. "I'm a good person. Why do I need to worry about threats of judgment and hell? That kind of talk turns me off."

"Well, maybe the hell part turned you off before you heard the grace part."

"Where's the grace in a God who would throw someone like me into hell?"

Vanessa cringed at Micah's defensive tone. Why get enmeshed

in this age-old argument that never seemed to go anywhere? She wanted to drop it, but this man was old and his days numbered. Didn't he deserve an honest response?

"It's not just you, Micah. We're *all* sinners."

"Bad enough to deserve hell?"

"Or not good enough to deserve heaven—depending on your perspective. God's standard is perfection. And no one's perfect."

Micah's eyebrows came together. "Then He's sending us *all* to hell?"

"Actually, He provided the one way to avoid it. He sent His Son Jesus to pay the price for our sins. It's only because of Jesus' death and resurrection that we can be forgiven and made perfect in His sight. It's a gift. We can't earn it. We can only choose it."

Why did I allow myself to get roped into this? This stuff never sounds credible when I say it out loud.

Micah stared at the ground. "Yeah, well, that's a whole lot to swallow."

"God never forces anyone. He's given us the truth in the Bible. Each person has to come to the realization that he's a sinner and needs to repent and put his faith in Jesus as his Lord and Savior."

"Every religion claims to have the truth. Why should I believe yours?"

"I don't expect you just to take my word for it. But you owe it to yourself to read the New Testament, or at least the gospel of John, and see what was written about the greatest man who ever lived. You're eighty-six, which is a lot closer to the end of your life than the beginning. Doesn't it make sense to find out what could be waiting for you when you die?"

Micah studied her, seemingly amused. "You say that with some measure of authority, missy."

Good thing you can't hear my knees knocking.

"You said I don't strike you as agnostic. Well, you don't strike me as Christian."

His words pierced her. "That's because I'm not a very good one. I've been doing my own thing since I went off to college, and you can see where it's gotten me. But I grew up in a home where we read the Bible and talked about it. Accepting Jesus Christ is a lot more than getting saved from hell. It's the beginning of a relationship with God that starts now and lasts forever. Every person should intelligently consider what the Bible says about Jesus instead of just blowing it off."

Micah's eyes narrowed. "Give me the bottom line."

"Okay. If what the Bible says is true, all of us are going to be around for eternity. The only question is *where*—with God in heaven, or without Him in hell. We choose."

"Hmm …" Micah hooked his thumbs on his overalls and seemed to stare at nothing, his scowl reminiscent of Ty's every time she tried to talk to him about her faith. He didn't believe her either.

Why didn't I just keep my mouth shut? I'm sure I said everything wrong. He probably thinks I'm a fanatic.

"Vanessa!"

She turned to the voice and saw a young man running along the duck pond in her direction. As he got closer she spotted his dark curly hair and glasses.

"It's Ethan Langley." She stood and waved. "He's a friend of mine from college."

"Yes, you mentioned him this morning. I didn't realize he lived in Sophie Trace."

"Just for the summer. He's working for his uncle."

Ethan came to a stop in front of Vanessa, his hair windblown and his face flushed. "Whew! I was afraid I'd miss you." He paused to catch his breath. "I was driving past the park on my way to your house when I spotted you. Where's your family?"

"At the movies. This is Micah Harvey. We met in the park, and we've enjoyed some time getting to know each other."

Ethan extended his hand. "Ethan Langley. Nice to meet you."

"Same here."

Ethan put his lips to her ear. "Why are you out here alone? You're supposed to have police protection."

Vanessa smiled at Micah. "I need to get going. Maybe I'll see you here again sometime."

"I sure hope so, young lady."

"Thanks again for the hot dogs"

"My pleasure."

Vanessa started walking across the park in the direction of her house. "Listen, my parents don't know about this. I sort of took some time by myself. No one knows. The police think I'm in the house with the security alarm set. As you can see, I'm perfectly safe. This nut is after my mother, not me."

"Why would you even chance it, Vanessa?"

She stopped and threw her hands in the air. "Because I'm feeling smothered. Try having cops following you everywhere."

"I'd think you'd consider it a blessing."

"Well, I don't. I mean I do, but I don't. It's just getting old."

"When are your folks coming home?"

"Any minute. I need to go." She started walking again.

"I'll drive you. It'll save time. My uncle's Mustang is parked just across the street, down by that red van."

"Okay, thanks. But you have to leave me off in the alley and drive around front, ring the bell, and let me answer it. That way the officers won't suspect a thing."

Ethan stepped off the curb, took her arm, and led the way to his uncle's car. "I don't like being deceitful."

"It's not as though I'm out raising Cain like a rebellious teenager. I'm just trying to find a little space so I can breathe. I'm an adult. I should be able to make some decisions without my parents' permission. Please tell me you're not going to feel compelled to tell them."

Ethan sighed and opened the passenger door. "Get in."

"If you blow the whistle, it'll ruin everything."

Ethan shut the door, then walked around the car and slid in behind the wheel. "You're putting me in a very awkward position, Vanessa. I'm a truthful guy."

"I'm not putting you in any position. You're the one who came running up to me."

"What if you're wrong about this freak that's stalking your mother? What if he'll take whatever he can get of the Jessups?"

Vanessa rolled her eyes. "If that were true, the guy's had two chances to get me."

"Two—you've done this before?"

"Yes, early this morning. It was glorious. I'm not hurting anybody, but if my parents find out, that'll be the end of it. I feel like I'm locked in a dungeon. Promise me you won't say anything."

Vanessa heard the front door open and then voices and shuffling feet.

"We're out here," she hollered.

Her mother walked through the kitchen doorway, Emily and David Riley on her heels, and set her purse on the countertop.

"Ethan and I are enjoying your peanut butter cookies," Vanessa said. "How was the movie?"

"We had to cut it short. David thought he spotted Merrick Fountain and decided it best if we didn't stay."

"More like we panicked and left." Emily sat in a kitchen chair next to Ethan, her arms folded across her chest. "The first movie was sold out, so we waited and waited till the next one started, and then we still didn't get to see it all." Emily pushed out her bottom lip. "Be glad your last name isn't Jessup. It's no fun."

"So everything was fine here?" Brill said, obviously wanting to redirect the conversation.

"Great." Vanessa took a sip of ice water and looked at Ethan over the top of her glass.

"Did you go to the Masinos'?"

"I did. They are the nicest people. And I *love* their living room with all the windows."

"Did you meet Abby?" Emily said.

"Yes, and after my visit, I came home and took a long nap, and the next thing I knew Ethan was at the front door. I'm sorry your movie got cut short."

"Just playing it safe," David said. "I can't be sure the man I saw was Fountain, but I'd rather err on the side of caution."

Kurt came into the kitchen and put his arm around Brill. "Since our outing got cut short, how about we order pizza?"

"Yay!" Emily clapped her hands. "Can Ethan stay?"

"He's certainly welcome." Kurt went over to a stack of papers by the phone. "I've got some coupons for Luigi's. I heard their pizza's the best."

"So are you staying?" Emily batted her round blue eyes at Ethan.

"Uh, thanks for the invite. But I don't want to overstay my welcome."

Brill smiled. "You're not. And I'm sure Emily will talk you into playing Monopoly before the evening's over. So Vanessa, what did you and the Masinos talk about?"

"Oh, a lot of chitchat about this and that. Antonio told me about the shoe business he had. They seemed shy about asking me many questions, though."

Kurt chortled. "Are you telling me that Tessa Masino didn't pry? That's a first."

"Well," Brill said, "I'd like to think she's sensitive enough to realize that Vanessa's not sure what she wants to do. Anybody else want a salad with their pizza?"

"I'll tell you what"—Kurt waved a coupon—"the Luigi Supreme seems hard to beat. Has sausage, pepperoni, ham, cheese, onions, peppers, mushrooms, black *and* green olives—and you get two for the price of one. Any takers?"

"Me!" Emily said.

"Sold—to the bottomless pit in the pink T-shirt." Kurt tickled Emily till she squealed. "Is everybody okay with the ingredients—other than I already know Vanessa will pick off the green olives?"

Everyone nodded.

"Why don't I order their giant salad bowl and we'll divvy it up? We've got plenty of soft drinks in the fridge. I'll call it in and go pick it up. Emily, you want to ride with me?"

"Is Agent David going?"

"Of course." David winked, and then bowed, his hands clasped behind his back. "I am your slave."

Emily giggled. "Then you can clean my room, too."

Brill's cell phone rang, and she put it to her ear. "Yes, Trent … Good grief … Where is he now …? What's his condition …? Any witnesses …? Did the investigating officers get his statement …? All right. Call if you get an update. Keep that vest on and don't go anywhere without someone watching your back … Thanks. I definitely will."

Vanessa couldn't believe how white her mother's faced looked. "Mom, what happened?"

"Jason Cromwell was stabbed at the country club where he plays golf."

David shook his head. "Here we go again. It had to be Fountain. Anybody see him?"

"No one's come forward. It happened in the men's room at the clubhouse. Cromwell lost consciousness before police could question him, but apparently he told the paramedics that a man in a ski mask came at him, they struggled, and when Cromwell broke free and started to run away, he was stabbed in the back."

"How serious is it?" David said.

"Very. He's going to lose a kidney, and he lost an awful lot of blood. We'll know more when he gets out of surgery. His family's at the hospital."

The lines on David's forehead deepened. "If Fountain's in Memphis, then I was wrong about the man I saw at the theater."

"Oh, brother," Emily said. "You mean we left the movie for *nothing*?"

Kurt put his finger to his lips and scolded Emily with his gaze.

"Well," Brill said, "at least Fountain's doing what he said he was going to do. This is no surprise."

"Am I supposed to find that comforting?" Kurt arched his eyebrows. "Do the math, Chief. Two down, one to go."

"This didn't have to happen, Kurt. The old goat refused police protection."

"I'm scared." Emily's eyes were wide.

"It's all right, sweetie. Come here."

Emily ran over to her mother and wrapped her arms tightly around her waist. "I don't want you to die."

"Shhh." Brill gently rocked from side to side and stroked Emily's hair. "No one said anything about dying. I'm doing everything I possibly can to stay safe."

"That's right." David knelt down beside Emily. "And I'm here to watch out for all of you. You trust me, don't you, honey?"

"I guess so."

Vanessa ached with the same emotions as Emily but with none of the openness. Why was it so hard to let down her guard with her mother?

Lord, please don't let Mom die. I need her so much right now. I have a million things to say to her. I just don't know how.

CHAPTER 24

VANESSA sat between her mother and Emily in the third row at Cross Way Bible Fellowship as Pastor Gavin Bonner gave the Sunday sermon. But all she could think about was Micah's brutally honest words that had pierced her to the heart and kept her up most of the night.

You don't strike me as Christian.

Could there be any statement more convicting? More devastating? More humiliating? Nothing like a godless man to point out the obvious.

Two years ago she was totally involved in her youth group, Bible study, mission trips, teaching Sunday school to five-year-olds, volunteering at the church's thrift store. All that ended when she started college, but she never filled the void. Somehow she had convinced herself that studying would require all her concentration; she made no effort to get involved in any of the Christian groups on campus—and she misled her parents into thinking she had.

How could she have been so foolish? The lack of fellowship and accountability made it easy to say yes when the worldly Professor Nicholson asked her out, asked her to keep their relationship secret, and finally invited her into his bed.

She hadn't seen her sexual encounters with Ty as sinful, even though she couldn't silence the still small voice of her conscience. Once she fell in love with him, it all seemed right.

Vanessa sighed. How could she have put her promise ring in a drawer and given herself to Ty with little regard for the vow she had made—or the Savior whose trust she had betrayed?

She brushed a tear off her cheek and hoped her mother didn't notice. How could she explain what she was feeling? Conviction was breaking her heart, but differently than condemnation. It was as though her eyes had been opened and she was clearly seeing what she had tried so hard to deny. And it wasn't beautiful.

Vanessa took in a slow, deep breath and let it out. She did not want to cry. Not here. Not until she could find privacy and grieve through her sin.

The baby kicked, and she rested her arms on her belly. This little boy was the one beautiful thing that had come from her relationship with Ty. She wondered what their baby would look like. Would he ever know his father? Did she even want him to?

Emily tapped her arm. "Time to sing the last song. Your nose is red. Are you crying?"

"My allergies are acting up," Vanessa said, satisfied that it was partially true. She shifted her weight from one hip to the other and then rose to her feet just as the congregation began singing:

What a friend we have in Jesus,
all our sins and griefs to bear!
What a privilege to carry
everything to God in prayer!

Jesus. How had she come so close to Him and then strayed so far? She wondered what Micah was doing this morning and if he had any idea how much pain his simple assessment of her had caused.

"You have *too* been crying." Emily pushed the other half of the hymnal into Vanessa's hands.

"Pregnant women cry a lot, Shortcake. It doesn't mean anything. Just sing."

Vanessa blinked to clear her eyes and then willed away the tears as she joined the congregation in singing the remainder of the final hymn:

> *Have you trials and temptations?*
> *Is there trouble anywhere?*
> *We should never be discouraged;*
> *take it to the Lord in prayer.*

Vanessa looked out the huge cross-shaped window above the pulpit to the bluebird sky. If only she'd taken it to the Lord in prayer before she had an affair with a man she knew had no intention of committing himself to her.

And now she had to decide whether or not she was going to give their baby to someone else to love and nurture. The thought of parting with him was agonizing.

The baby delivered a series of whopping thumps, and Vanessa held her breath, bracing herself for the bigger blows that always followed. He was going to be a handful. Micah said she had what it takes to be a single mom, but did she? She'd done a lot of babysitting and had interacted with the five-year-old boys in her Sunday school class. Was that enough experience? Then again, most new parents didn't have much experience.

Vanessa felt something tapping her head and realized it was Emily's knuckles.

"Hello, is anybody home? Church is over."

Vanessa felt the blood rush to her face and looked around, hoping nobody saw Emily knocking on her head. Her parents were visiting with some people in the row behind them.

"You know, you can be a real pain," Vanessa said.

"Well, how come you're being so weird? You act like you're in a spell or something."

"I'm just deep in thought. I have a lot on my mind."

"Like where Ty went?"

"I'll probably never know that."

"Then whether you're going to keep the baby?"

Vanessa put her hands on her sister's shoulders and squeezed. "Emily, stop it. You're butting in where you don't belong."

"Tessa does that too."

"Stop it."

Emily's face fell, her big blue eyes suddenly solemn. "Nobody cares how I feel about anything."

"I never said I don't care how you feel. I just want you to respect how I feel."

"I *do*. But I have feelings, too." Emily lowered her voice. "I want you to keep the baby. When you have a lot on your mind and act weird, I get scared because I think you've decided to let someone adopt him."

Vanessa stroked Emily's ponytail. "I haven't decided anything.

But you have to let *me* make the decision. This isn't like getting a pet. Raising a child is serious business."

Vanessa felt a hand on her shoulder.

"You girls ready?" Brill said. "Your dad went to get the car."

"We're coming." Vanessa put her lips to Emily's ear. "When I've finally decided what I'm going to do, I'll come tell you first. Okay?"

"Okay." Emily's eyes grew wide and she put her arms around Vanessa. "I hope it's *yes.*"

Tessa went inside Nick's Grill, Antonio holding open the glass door. The place was bustling. She spotted Nick and waved.

Nick moved briskly toward them, a full head of sandy brown hair and twenty extra pounds hanging over his belt. He put his arm around her and shook Antonio's hand.

"Welcome, friends."

"What is that heavenly aroma?" Tessa said.

"That's my cheese bread baking." Nick closed his eyes and inhaled slowly. "It goes great with today's veggie pasta special. Penne pasta tossed with grilled red, green, and yellow bell peppers, onions, mushrooms, celery, artichokes, and a light creamy sauce that's heart healthy. It'll knock your socks off."

"Sounds great to me," Tessa said.

"Ditto."

Tessa headed for the counter and noticed that Gus Williams was already there. Was he still pouting over their tiff yesterday?

"Hello, Gus."

"Hey, Tessa."

Antonio patted Gus on the back and slid onto the stool next to him.

"How's it going, friend?"

"Really can't complain. But I always do." Gus chuckled. "How was church?"

"Excellent," Antonio said. "Yours?"

"Good." Gus poked at the ice cubes in his glass, seemingly avoiding eye contact. "Uh, I'd like to apologize for bein' a jerk. I *haven't* been fair to Chief Jessup. I'll try to do better."

Tessa studied Gus, taken aback by his sudden willingness to apologize. "Well, of course I accept your apology, Gus. I do get my hackles up sometimes. Perhaps I could have reacted better."

"So we can put it behind us?" Gus looked down the counter at her.

"Yes, I'd like to."

Maggie Cummings seemed to come out of nowhere and set a Coke refill in front of Gus, then stood behind the counter, her green pad in hand. "What can I get for the Masinos today?"

"The special for my sweetheart and for me," Antonio said. "Heavy on the cheese bread for this half."

"Okay, I'll be right back with your coffee, folks." She winked at Gus.

So that's what precipitated his apology. Tessa elbowed Antonio, hoping he'd seen it. At least those two were talking again.

"Tessa and I saw on the news that the former DA who helped put away Merrick Fountain was stabbed yesterday."

Gus nodded. "I saw that. Fountain isn't wastin' any time followin' through on his threats. If I was Chief Jessup, I think I'd lock myself belowdecks till they net this guy."

"Has to be frightening for the family," Tessa said. "Antonio and I had Vanessa Jessup over for a visit yesterday afternoon."

"She the pregnant one?" Gus lifted an eyebrow.

"She's the oldest daughter who happens to be pregnant," Antonio said. "A very nice girl."

Gus took a sip of Coke. "So is she gonna get married?"

"We don't ask personal questions like that." Antonio nudged Gus with his shoulder. "Kids today have their own agenda. We just go with the flow."

"Hi, everybody." Clint Ames slid onto the stool next to Tessa. "Don't let me interrupt. Go with what flow?"

"Oh," Gus said, "we were just sayin' that goin' with the flow is the only way to deal with the different moral code young people have today."

"How did y'all get on that subject?" Clint set his sunglasses on the counter.

"We were just talkin' about the police chief's unmarried daughter bein' pregnant."

Tessa glared at Gus. *You stinker.*

"Yeah, I heard about that down at the barbershop," Clint said. "Unfortunately, it's not that uncommon anymore. Plenty of good kids make mistakes."

"The difference between our generation and theirs is we *knew* it was a mistake." Gus raised his eyebrows. "Lots of them don't even believe it's wrong."

Maggie came over to the counter and filled two mugs with coffee and set them in front of the Masinos, then reached in her smock and took out several tiny tubs of cream and gave them to Antonio.

"I'll throw in my two cents," she said. "Every generation of kids has faced temptations. They're just packaged differently. But kids today have it worse than we did because evil is so easy to *access*. It's everywhere—music, TV, movies, video games, the Internet. Kids are exposed to drugs, alcohol, and every kind of debauchery at a very young age. I don't envy anybody raising children today. We ought to be praying for them, not criticizing them."

A long, uncomfortable moment of dead air followed.

Finally Gus said, "I think we've been properly chastised."

Brill looked down from the window in her office and admired the shady, well-kept grounds around city hall and the colorful awnings of the quaint shops that lined the other side of Main Street.

The historic city hall and brick buildings, the brick streets of downtown, and the gazebo in Shady Park were as big a tourist draw as the Civil War museum and the antebellum homes. Thanks to her department, downtown was a safe place for people to walk around.

Brill looked out through the trees and drank in the postcard-perfect view of the Great Smoky Mountains. How could Sophie Trace be such a wonderful place to live, and yet her family cowered in fear of some lunatic who blamed Zack Rogers, DA Cromwell, and her for a sentence he knew he deserved?

"A penny for your thoughts," David said.

Brill turned around and leaned against the window. "I doubt they're worth that much. What's up?"

"I need to talk to you about a phone call I just got from the field office." David closed the door and nodded toward the conference table. "Why don't we sit?"

"Now I'm getting nervous."

Brill sat across from David, her hands folded on the table.

"A friend of mine in the bureau did some nosing around on his own time, trying to find out what he could about Ty Nicholson. He was told in no uncertain terms to back off."

"What exactly does 'back off' mean?"

"No one's going to come right out and say it, but I interpret it to mean you and I were right, that Nicholson is in witness protection."

"They can't tell me *anything*?"

David shook his head. "It's a stone wall. End of story."

"I'm not sure what I hoped to hear, but that wasn't it."

"Has to be disappointing not knowing where he is—or even who he is. But you're going to have to live with it. Are you going to tell Vanessa?"

Brill blew out a breath and combed her fingers through her hair. "I don't know. What do you think?"

"Hey, you're the parent. I bow to you on that one."

"Is it legal to name Ty Nicholson as the father on the birth certificate when we know the name is made up? And would this complicate an adoption?"

David shrugged. "You're getting into an area I know zero about, but my guess is Vanessa can list the name he went by. Paternity isn't proved by the name anyway."

"My guess is she's going to keep the baby. Not that we talk about it."

"I haven't felt like it's my place to ask questions, so I haven't. But I've wondered."

Brill picked up a pencil and bounced the eraser on the table. "Vanessa came home from college at the end of May. Kurt and I didn't know she was pregnant until she got out of the car. How's that for having a close relationship with your daughter?"

David sat back in his chair. "What a shocker. Did she say why she waited so long to tell you?"

"Said she loved us and dreaded disappointing us again. She feels as if that's all she does, that she's somehow in competition with Ryan and Emily when it comes to producing good grades. It's a long story, and I won't bore you with it. Suffice it to say her perspective is off."

David shook his head. "Poor kid. I can't imagine the agony she must've felt, keeping it from you all that time."

"Poor *kid?* How about poor mom and dad?" Brill's eyes clouded over, and she blinked to clear them, hoping David hadn't noticed.

"Hey, come on, I didn't mean to be insensitive. I just can't imagine a young girl in trouble, especially one with two parents who love her, suffering in silence that long."

"Me either. Frankly, it's still a bit overwhelming."

"Are you about finished here? You've still got a fair amount of Sunday afternoon to enjoy."

"I'm not sure I'm capable of enjoying anything at the moment."

"You've got a full plate, that's for sure. But Cromwell is going to pull through, so you can put that to bed. I have a feeling your family would love to spend some quality time with you."

Brill tucked her hair behind her ear. "Any suggestions? Don't tell Emily, but I couldn't focus on the movie at all."

"Why don't you pop popcorn and play a game of Monopoly? Emily seems to like that."

"Do you like Monopoly?"

David smiled sheepishly, his face and shaved head suddenly flushed. "Yeah, I do."

"Good, then you can play with us. The more the merrier."

"Don't worry. I always go easy on kids and give them a few breaks. Most kids aren't good losers."

Brill chuckled. "Emily doesn't understand the word *lose*. Trust me, she'll take every dollar you've got and think nothing of it. Sell her Boardwalk and Park Place and prepare to go bankrupt."

CHAPTER 25

KURT picked up one of the game pieces that had fallen on the kitchen floor and put it back in the Monopoly game box, wondering how long it had been since he'd had that much fun.

"Here's the last of the snack bowls." Brill put them in the dishwasher and brushed her hands together. "Done."

Kurt pulled her into his arms and held her gaze. "I love you. I wish I had the afternoon on tape so I could replay it when things get too intense. When's the last time we were all this relaxed?"

"I don't know, but I had fun too. Did you see David's face when Emily finally put hotels on the entire left side of the board?"

Kurt chuckled. "She's *brill*iant. Like her mother."

"I think Vanessa was enjoying herself, though she didn't seem focused."

"I noticed that too."

Brill glanced up at the clock. "I'd better go get ready for bed if I don't want to be a zombie in the morning."

"I'm not far behind you. I need to email my Maryville manager. I'd planned to drive over there and meet with him tomorrow, but David thinks I should stay close to home. I can always meet with him online for now."

"Thanks. I'd feel better if you kept a low profile."

Kurt drew her close, held her face in his hands, and let his lips melt into hers. They had worked so hard to put the pieces back together after his foolish affair. He just wanted this Fountain character in jail so they could find peace again.

"Let me go send my email," Kurt said. "I won't be long."

"Good. I have something I need to talk to you about."

"Anything wrong?"

She looked at him, seemingly amused. "Kurt, *everything's* wrong. But I promise this won't throw you over the edge."

He kissed the top of her head. "See you in a few minutes."

Kurt went down the hall and into his office, flipped on the light, and sat at his computer. After he typed out an email to his Maryville manager and sent it, he cleared his in-box, marveling that he could operate a chain of quick-copy stores from a bedroom-turned-office that didn't even have respectable furniture or a rug on the floor. Brill had been after him to pick out a desk and credenza. He finally found something online that appealed to him, but it was extremely pricey. How could he justify the cost when most of his office hours were spent in the car? On the other hand, working off a cafeteria table and a folding chair wasn't very professional.

Kurt heard the crackling of a piece of paper under his shoe. He reached down and picked it up and realized it was the receipt from Valentine's Day for the deluxe suite at the White Mountain Inn. His mind flashed back to his lifting Brill into his arms and carrying her across the threshold just hours after they had renewed their wedding vows during the Sunday service at Cross Way Bible Fellowship.

He remembered the two of them relaxing in front of a crackling fire … watching the snow come down … making love like a couple of newlyweds. Wouldn't it have been enough just to receive Brill's forgiveness for his fling with Victoria? But after Emily's brush with death, Brill no longer seemed consumed with bitterness. She began to soften toward him and eventually wanted to work things out. God had answered his prayers beyond anything he could have imagined.

An image of Merrick Fountain barged into his thoughts. No way was he letting this creep take his wife from him. But how could he ignore the terrifying truth that Fountain seemed to know how to get to whoever he wanted?

David had reminded him that not a single victim who was stabbed had anyone watching his back. Still, the ease with which Fountain conned his way into O'Toole's hospital room was unsettling. What scheme had he devised to get to Brill? No one could watch her every second of every day.

Kurt set the receipt on his desk and bowed his head. *Lord, put a hedge around Brill and keep her safe from harm. Empower her people and David to do everything they know how to keep her safe. And Father, send Your angels to do what no man can do.*

He got up and straightened his desk, then turned off the light, curious about what Brill wanted to talk to him about.

Kurt sat on the side of the bed and set his alarm for seven, aware that a dog was barking and the shower was on in David's bathroom.

"Did you get your email sent?" Brill closed a dresser drawer and walked to the other side of the bed, dressed in her ivory silk pajamas.

Kurt swung his legs into the bed and turned on his side facing her. "Yes, I'm all set for an online meeting at ten. So what is it you want to talk to me about?"

"Ty Nicholson." Brill climbed into bed and hugged a pillow. "The guy David had looking into Nicholson's background was told in no uncertain terms to back off."

"By whom?"

"Had to be another fed, and David thinks this is a strong indicator that Nicholson is in witness protection—which means case closed, end of story."

"So we'll never know who this con man really is?"

Brill fluffed the pillow and turned facing him. "I guess not. When the feds say back off, it's no small matter."

"Well, if you'll recall, I wasn't wild about finding Nicholson in the first place. But the more mysterious this thing got, the more I wanted answers. I'm disappointed that we'll never know who he is." He brushed her hair out of her eyes. "Do we tell Vanessa?"

"I think we have to. It's important that she let go of him and any hope that he might come back. Once that's taken off the table, maybe she'll be motivated to move forward."

"And do what, honey? You're the one who's convinced that Vanessa's already chosen to keep the baby."

"She's got to start facing reality, and so do we. I may be without a job. If that happens, I'm not sure we can cover our own expenses, much less a baby's." Brill's eyes glistened. "I can't believe my job's on the line at such a critical time."

"Hey, do you really think God is going to let us go hungry? We need to make decisions that are right for our family—and trust that He'll provide what we need. And that includes Vanessa and the baby."

"You're right, Kurt. What was I thinking?"

"One of these days Vanessa is bound to regret that she missed the excitement of being engaged, the magic of being a bride, and the miracle of sharing childbirth with her husband. But I'm like you—I don't want her to regret the decision she makes about her son."

"I've never heard you refer to the baby as her son before."

Kurt brought Brill's hand to his cheek. "If Vanessa's determined to keep him, they're both going to need all the love and support they can get. You and I are not the only ones whose lives would be affected. Emily's life would change dramatically."

"Emily wants this baby more than Vanessa does."

Kurt took his thumb and stopped a tear trickling down Brill's cheek. "I wish we could turn back the clock so Vanessa could finish college and fall in love and get married *before* she had to deal with all this. But we can at least be proud of her for choosing life. She needs our love and support as she's about to make a pivotal decision that affects all of us." He pulled her into his arms and stroked her hair.

"Kurt, you know I'm with you a hundred percent. The two of us speak with one voice."

He pushed back and looked into her eyes. "Yes, but are we speaking to God with one voice? We've each been praying individually. I'd like us to start praying together every day about Vanessa's decision."

Vanessa lay in bed watching the ceiling fan go round and round, unable to get comfortable in any position, the baby kicking her bladder. At this rate, it was going to be a long night.

The deep conviction that she had experienced in church that morning was still with her. It was a good kind of hurt, void of condemnation, a feeling that she had never experienced before.

For the first time, her love affair with Ty didn't seem beautiful. Wasn't she just one of many young women Ty had seduced and led to believe was special? How could she have abandoned her vow so readily?

You don't strike me as Christian.

Micah's words still stung. Did she really know what it was to be a Christian? What a sorry representation she was of all she had been taught, all her parents had instilled in her. If she let some wonderful Christian couple adopt her baby, people would eventually forget this chapter of her life. But would *she*? Was she supposed to? Her son's steps had already been ordered by the Lord. What part, if any, was she to play in his future?

A tear rolled down the side of her face.

Lord, I'm so sorry I deceived myself. I knew my relationship with Ty was wrong. You've promised that if we confess our sins, You'll forgive us and cleanse us. I need that, Lord. I need to start fresh. I need to feel close to You again. I need to know You forgive me for breaking my vow.

"Are you crying?" someone whispered.

Vanessa's eyes flew open, and she saw Emily standing by her bed, clutching what appeared to be one of her American Girl dolls.

"What do you want, Emily?"

"Can I sleep with you?"

"Why?"

"I had a nightmare, and my heart's thumping. I'm scared to close my eyes because it might come back."

She heard the fear in Emily's voice and patted the empty side of the bed. "Okay, come on."

Emily climbed up into the bed and nestled next to her.

She pulled her baby sister into her arms and held her close. "Do you want to talk about the nightmare?"

Emily shook her head.

"Don't worry, Shortcake. You're safe with me. But you know dreams aren't real."

"They feel like it."

"I know."

"I just want them to stop."

"Do they happen every night?"

"Not anymore." Emily looked up, her blue eyes wide and so much like their mother's. "Could I just lay here and not talk about it?"

"Sure."

Vanessa suddenly felt maternal. She rested in the quiet, the herbal scent of Emily's hair sending her thoughts back to when Emily was toddler. How many times had Vanessa awakened to find her baby sister sound asleep, nestled next to her like a kitten?

Emily giggled. "Hey, the baby kicked. I felt him. There! He did it again. Could you tell?"

Vanessa nodded. "Oh, yeah. He's liable to be at it all night."

"That's okay. I like it." Emily put her hand on Vanessa's tummy. "I think he knows my voice now."

"Good. Then would you tell him Mommy's tired and it's time to go to sleep?"

The silence lasted several seconds, and then Emily said, "You called yourself Mommy."

"Go to sleep, Emily."

"You'd make a *good* mommy. Really."

Vanessa took her thumb and index finger and gently clamped Emily's lips together, unable to keep her own from smiling.

"I am Queen Vanessa, and I hereby decree eight hours of silence throughout the kingdom. Anyone defying my decree will be banished to her own room. Got it?"

Emily giggled and nodded.

Silence once again filled the room.

Lord, are You speaking to me through Emily, or is she just a sweet ten-year-old who wants a baby to play with? I need Your wisdom. I need You to make it clear to me what I need to do about this baby's future.

CHAPTER 26

BRILL, Trent, and David walked down the long, shiny corridor at St. Luke's Hospital and stopped in front of Beau Jack Rousseaux's hospital room. She greeted one of Sam Parker's deputies and then rapped on the door.

"Beau Jack, it's Chief Jessup. I've got Captain Norris and Special Agent Riley with me. May we come in?"

"Yeah, come in."

Brill went in, pleased to see the drapes open and the windowsill overflowing with flowers, plants, and cards. She went over to the bed and squeezed Beau Jack's hand.

"How're you feeling?"

"Sore. But bored out of my skull and anxious to get back to work."

"Well," Trent said, "everyone on the force misses you, you crazy Cajun. But I don't want you back till the doctor says it's okay."

David reached down and shook Beau Jack's hand. "It's good to see you're on the mend, Detective."

"Thanks. At least I've still got both kidneys. I hear that former DA in Memphis wasn't so lucky."

"DA Cromwell's going to be all right," Brill said. "But none of us can afford to refuse protection anymore."

Beau Jack's gaze moved to David. "So I hear you're here on *vacation*."

"That's right. The chief and her husband are great tour guides, and it's amazing what there is to see and do in this area."

Beau Jack smiled knowingly.

"So when do you get out of here?" Trent said.

"Probably this afternoon if my discharge papers are ready. The doc wants me home for a couple weeks, and then I can ease back into the job. Might be stuck at a desk for a while."

"That'll work," Trent said. "There's plenty to keep you busy. We need to get you a new partner."

Beau Jack's cheerful expression faded. "I'm not sure I'll ever get used to Sean being gone. I still see him on the floor in the chief's office, covered in blood. That image wakes me up at night. I just want to get this guy."

"There's not a law enforcement officer in this county who doesn't," Brill said. "He's been elusive, but we're going to nail him." Her confident tone concealed her growing fear that Fountain was unstoppable.

Trent eyed a bag of Tootsie Pops on the rolling table. "Mind if I bum one of those? I finally quit smoking, but it's still a battle."

"Help yourself. Which reminds me, Chief … open that top drawer. I saved the red ones for Emily."

Brill opened the drawer and took out a bouquet of red Tootsie Pops, held together by a rubber band. "Thanks. She'll be thrilled. She was pretty upset when she heard about the stabbing."

"Well, tell her I'm only temporarily out of commission. Can't keep a good Cajun down." He looked at Trent. "Somebody watching *your* back?"

"Yep. Don't worry about me."

Brill started to say that David lent them ballistic vests that were stab resistant, then decided Beau Jack didn't need to hear that while he was nursing a hole in his gut.

"We're not going to stay," Brill said. "We've got a meeting with Sheriff Parker this morning. We just wanted to come by and let you know we're thinking of you."

"Thanks. That means a lot."

Trent unwrapped the Tootsie Pop and stuck it in his mouth. "I'll check in when you're settled at home. I want you to take it easy and do whatever the doctor tells you."

"He's right," Brill said. "We've got more volunteer cops right now than we have places to put them. The important thing is that you heal so you can get back on your feet."

"Yes, ma'am." A grin spread slowly across Beau Jack's face. "Maybe I'll watch Oprah and Doctor Phil. I think I'm the only one who hasn't."

Brill laughed. "Just don't get hooked. We want you back."

Brill heard footsteps and looked up in time to see Sam Parker's brawny frame fill the doorway. Why was he so intimidating?

"Come in, Sheriff. I'm glad you could make it." Brill walked over and shook his hand. "Trent and David are waiting for you at the conference table. Can I get you something to drink: coffee, Coke, water?"

"I believe I'll have a Coke, Chief Jessup." He smiled, his gold tooth seeming almost as glaring as his ego. "Awful kind of you to wait on me."

Only you would think of it that way. "Have a seat, Sheriff. I'll be right there."

Brill reached inside her small refrigerator and took out two cans of Coke, then walked over to the conference table.

"If you'd prefer to have a cup and ice, feel free to go down to the officer's lounge and help yourself. I'm sure you remember where that is."

"This is just fine."

Brill popped the top on her Coke and took a sip, then folded her hands on the table. "All right, then. I called this meeting specifically to give Sam the latest on Detective Rousseaux and DA Cromwell, and to lay out the steps we're taking to keep Trent and me and our families safe." She looked at Sam. "I would like to start by saying how much I've appreciated the work of your deputies. They've been invaluable."

Sam gave a nod. "I'm always happy to step in. Mayor Roswell and the city council have also expressed their gratitude."

I'll just bet they have.

Brill took the next several minutes and told Sam everything she knew about Cromwell's condition and prognosis, and also about Beau Jack Rousseaux's going home.

"We're all grateful that these two are going to recover," Brill said.

"Well, of course we are." Sam leaned forward on his elbows. "But Detective O'Toole was not so fortunate, now, was he? Could you fill me in on how the DA's investigation of Officer Ulman is goin'?"

He already knew. Did he find this entertaining? "The DA's office is ready to begin its questioning. They've requested Ulman to report to their office tomorrow morning at nine."

Sam knitted his fingers together. "Since his negligence resulted in Detective O'Toole's death, I don't see this goin' well for him."

Like you even want it to. "Sam, the only real question concerning Ulman is whether he was negligent in his screening of the people admitted to O'Toole's hospital room. I think we should refrain from offering our opinions and let the DA's office do its job."

Sam held up his palm. "Okay. I didn't mean to ruffle your feathers, Chief Jessup. If you'll indulge me, I have a question." He looked over at David. "Since I have not been advised that the FBI is now involved in this case, I'm curious why Special Agent Riley is sittin' in on this meeting."

You know exactly why, you troublemaker.

Brill forced a pleasant expression. "It's no secret that David is spending two weeks of his vacation in Sophie Trace with my family. He's offered to use his *personal* time to watch my back—unofficially, of course."

"Am I to assume, then, that you don't trust your department or mine to do it?"

"Not at all, Sheriff. It's just one more layer of protection. This is a team effort, and your deputies are playing a vital role, especially in securing city hall. And though Special Agent Riley's offer to help was completely unsolicited, I didn't hesitate to accept. Emily is still suffering Post Traumatic Stress Disorder, and his staying in our home has eased the stress tremendously."

"I'd like to say something." David wiped his upper lip. "Merrick Fountain went to prison for the stabbing death of his brother-in-law. Since his release, he's killed two cops, stabbed two others and the former DA, and has threatened several times to come after Chief

Jessup. This man is worse than a cop killer. He's also a marital sex offender who perpetrated unspeakable acts on his wife before she finally got the courage to go into hiding. He's evil. He's dangerous. He has nothing to lose. I don't want him anywhere near Chief Jessup. Those of us who have the power to stop him, *must*."

"I assure you, that's what my deputies are doing."

Brill nodded. "Yes, they're doing everything they know to do. But if you were in my situation, with a young daughter suffering from PTSD, would you refuse an FBI friend's help—especially one who's a top profiler and the most proficient shot in the field office?"

"Well, y'all seem to have everything figured out," Sam said. "Far be it from me to second-guess you."

Since when?

Sam looked at David and then at her. "So, am I to believe that you, Chief Jessup, are runnin' this investigation?"

"Absolutely. David is my shadow, that's it. This is not the FBI's case."

Sam pursed his lips. "All right. But surely you can see why I was befuddled to see Special Agent Riley here."

Baloney. I'm sure you knew all about his being here long before this meeting. "It was not my intention to exclude you, Sam. But since David's here on his own time and not acting in an official capacity, I haven't made any kind of announcement."

There was that annoying gold-tooth grin again. "Well, you know how news zips around town."

Tessa walked in the front door of Nick's Grill, Antonio on her heels.

"Oh, my," she said. "I smell something chocolate baking. I feel my willpower fading already."

Nick waved. He finished saying something to a couple seated in a booth by the windows, then walked over and shook Antonio's hand.

"Welcome, friends." He squeezed Tessa's shoulder. "I've got a surprise dessert today—a low-sugar, low-fat, devil's food cake that's so moist you could ring it out like a sponge."

Tessa raised an eyebrow. "Really?"

"Okay, that may be a *slight* exaggeration." Nick laughed. "But it'll stick to your fork, and you won't miss the sugar or the fat."

"Hmm … I just might have to splurge and try it."

"The special is grilled veggies and Swiss cheese on your choice of rye, sourdough, or whole wheat. Comes with a cup of tomato basil soup."

"I'm in," Antonio said.

"Definitely." Tessa headed for her usual seat at the counter, not surprised to see that Gus had already arrived.

"Hey, Tessa."

"Hey, yourself."

Antonio slid onto the stool next to her and slapped Gus on the back. "How's it going, friend?"

"Really can't complain. But I always do."

"What do you know?"

Gus stuck a straw in his Coke. "Well, a friend of mine in the sheriff's department says they've got deputies watching Chief Jessup's place—and two detectives' homes. No disrespect intended, but I'm wonderin' why Chief Jessup needs to borrow the sheriff's deputies when she's got an entire police department."

"They're shorthanded, for one thing," Antonio said. "Remember two of her three detectives are victims. Someone's got to investigate those cases."

"And don't forget there are three eight-hour shifts in a twenty-four-hour period." Tessa looked down the counter at him. "We have a good view of the Jessups' house from ours, and I've been paying close attention. Now times that by three households. That's eighteen different officers every day."

Gus wiped the Coke off his mustache and displayed a wide grin. "Well, aren't you the informed one?"

"My sweetheart doesn't miss a beat." Antonio patted her knee. "She doesn't spy, she *observes*."

Tessa felt her face get hot. "I admit I have shown more interest than most people, but it's because I care so much about the Jessups and all they've gone through. Each of them is a prayer concern of mine."

Nick winked at her. "Well, Tessa just confirms how extensive the operation is to protect the chief and her key people."

"And they're using plain cars," Tessa said. "So it's impossible to tell which are police and which are deputies. But I heard on the news that Chief Jessup has gotten volunteer help from other police departments in the region. So I doubt it's just sheriff's deputies doing the watching."

Gus shrugged. "Hey, I'm just reportin' what my friend said."

Intending to stir the pot, if you ask me.

Maggie stood behind the counter, her green pad in hand. "So what are the Masinos having today?"

"The special on rye," Antonio said.

"I'll have the same." Tessa covered her smile with her hand. "Better save me a piece of that chocolate cake."

"Antonio?"

"You betcha."

"I'll be right back with your coffee."

Tessa heard footsteps behind her, and then Clint Ames took his seat next to her without even greeting the group.

Everyone at the counter stopped talking and turned their attention to him.

"Something wrong?" Nick said.

Clint put his sunglasses on the counter and let out a loud sigh. "Yeah, I just heard on the radio that DA Cromwell died."

CHAPTER 27

VANESSA waited until her dad and Emily left the house to go to the dentist, then slipped out the back gate and walked to Cherokee Valley Park.

The June sun was hot but the shade abundant. Considerably fewer people were in the park than on Saturday, and the swing that hung from the giant oak tree was unoccupied. She sat on it, her hands gripping the ropes, her eyes drinking in the lush green of the park and misty mountains in the distance. She decided she could stay for an hour and easily be home before her dad and Emily.

She pushed with her feet and got the swing in motion, and then pumped with her legs until it was a pendulum. She closed her eyes, free as the wind, hoping to avoid another encounter with Micah. She really hadn't wanted to discuss her beliefs in the first place, and she had neither inclination nor confidence to pick up the conversation where they left off. What more could she tell him?

She believed every word she had told Micah, so why was it so difficult for her to live the Christian life? The heaviness in her heart had not let up since the church service on Sunday. How she regretted having distanced herself from the faith. Hadn't the lack of fellowship during her first two years of college removed all accountability and made it easy for her to justify her relationship with Ty? If only she'd stuck by the principles she'd been taught, maybe she'd be a happy coed instead of a scared single mother-to-be.

She opened her eyes at the sound of a child's playful shrieking and smiled at a handful of children pushing the merry-go-round. How was she ever going to part with this child she was carrying?

She heard deep voices and spotted a man standing at the curb, talking to someone in a black sedan. She studied him for a moment. Was that Micah? Why was he here so early? She let the swing lose its momentum, then dragged her feet and slowly came to a stop.

She got up and leaned on the backside of the oak tree, hoping he hadn't seen her. She hardly breathed for half a minute. The voices got louder—angry—then tires screeched, and the black sedan sped up to the corner and turned left. Micah shot past her in the direction of the duck pond—and with the agility of a man half his age.

Was he all right?

"Micah! Wait up!"

He slowed to a stop and turned around, seemingly annoyed.

Vanessa walked briskly to where he was standing, "Is everything all right? I saw that car speed away."

"I'm fine."

One of his eyes was blue, the other brown. He wore contacts?

"Okay," she said. "I wanted to be sure before I left."

"That was just my wayward grandson."

"I thought your grandsons didn't live here."

"They don't. This one comes through every so often askin' for drug money."

"I've never seen a man your age run that fast."

Micah smiled. "I ran my share of marathons in my younger days. Guess my grandson made me mad enough for this ol' body to kick into gear."

And not be winded? She spotted the missing contact on the front of his shirt. Who was this guy? He certainly wasn't eighty-six. Why would he lie to her?

"Okay, I'm going now," she said.

Micah hooked his thumbs on his suspenders. His hands didn't have any age spots. Why hadn't she noticed that before?

"Have a nice afternoon, young lady. See you around."

Not anymore, you won't. Vanessa walked swiftly across the park toward Azalea Lane, trying to remember whether she had told him where she lived.

Brill sat at a booth next to the windows at Nick's Grill, David and Trent sitting across from her. She stuffed a sweet potato fry into her mouth.

"I hate it that Sam's so patronizing," she said. "I know he's talking behind my back to Mayor Roswell and the city council—no doubt undermining everything I'm trying to do."

Trent arched his eyebrows. "You think they don't know what a weasel he is?"

"I'm sure they're willing to overlook that fact if it serves their purposes. And getting rid of me seems to be high on their list."

"Don't assume the worst." David snitched one of her sweet potato fries. "You're right, these *are* good."

"Told you. Nick makes the best."

"I hate to see you adopt a defeatist attitude," David said. "I still say the mayor and city council are too smart to lose a good thing. When things calm down and they get their senses about them, they're going to realize what you've brought to the plate."

"Yes, but unfortunately Merrick Fountain came with it."

Trent lifted his gaze. "Just one of the hazards of being a cop, Chief. No one blames you for what that scumbag's doing."

"Why not? I blame me."

David's eyebrows came together. "Come on, Brill. You're a professional. You know better than that."

She looked across the street at the man and little girl standing under the Pastry Parlor's pink awning. "In my head I do."

She was glad neither of them tried to talk her out of her feelings.

Trent turned to David. "Have you ever had to deal with someone dying and felt like it should've been you?"

"A couple of times. You just can't lose your perspective. No one ever said law enforcement was safe. We all know the risks going in."

Brill nodded. "I just wish it didn't have to affect my family."

Vanessa set the bolt lock on the back door and then keyed in the security code.

Was she reading too much into the incident with Micah? Was it implausible that an old guy could sprint like that? Or that he would wear colored contacts? Or that he might have a wayward grandson who tried to bleed him for drug money? Was she just being paranoid?

Or was the Enemy trying to drive a wedge between Micah and her so they would not have another opportunity to talk about God? Was Satan capable of such trickery?

She walked out to the living room, Rinnie on her heels. She peeked out the drapes, glad to see the unmarked car parked across the street.

Vanessa went to the kitchen and grabbed the phone book. She looked through the H's until she found the listing for Harvey. No Micah.

She went to the business pages and looked up Carter House and dialed the number. Why was she checking up on the guy as if he were a criminal? Wasn't this the lonely old man who told her the park bench was his friend?

It's like an ol' friend that waits for me. When you don't have anybody, you start thinkin' that way.

"Good afternoon, Carter House. How may I direct your call?"

"I'd like to speak with Micah Harvey, please."

"I'm sorry. No one by that name is a resident here."

"Maybe I misunderstood his last name. Do you have any Micahs?"

"I'm sorry, ma'am. Our privacy policy prohibits me from revealing the names of our guests."

"I understand. Thank you."

Vanessa hung up the phone. So did he lie about living at the Carter House or lie about his name—or both? And why?

Rinnie started barking just as Vanessa heard a loud banging on the back door. She jumped, her hand over her heart, and went through the kitchen and into the dining room. Through the sheers she saw a short, portly woman standing on the porch.

Tessa.

Vanessa turned off the security alarm and opened the door.

"Hi."

"Hello, Vanessa. I gave those nice officers out front some fresh-baked brownies and told them I was bringing some for your family. I love to bake, and there are just too many for Antonio and me."

Vanessa accepted the Tupperware container. "Thanks. These look great. Would you like to come in?"

"Maybe for a minute."

Tessa, looking adorable in an aqua shift and sandals to match, stepped inside.

"Come into the kitchen. Can I get you something cold to drink? We've got bottled water, Coke, Diet Dr Pepper, and diet green tea."

Tessa brought her hands together. "Oh, I'd love some green tea. I see it in the store but have never tried it."

"Why don't you get comfortable at the table. Would you like a brownie?"

"No, I'm afraid I've already had more than I should."

"I think I'm going to have one with my tea."

Vanessa brought the container of brownies and two glasses with green tea on ice and handed one to Tessa.

"This is very good." Tessa peered over the top of the glass, an I'm-about-to-invade-your-space gleam in her eyes. "I was washing my baking dishes a while ago and was sure I saw you running down the alley. Of course that's silly. I know you don't go out alone."

Vanessa felt her face get hot. She took a bite of brownie. "Tessa, this is incredible. How do you get your brownies so moist?"

"Butter, cocoa, eggs, sugar, flour. And a teaspoon of this and that. Nothing magical about it, but they do come out moist."

"Mmm …" Vanessa nodded and kept chewing, hoping Tessa wouldn't push her point. Why would she even care what Vanessa did?

"I heard that DA Cromwell passed away," Tessa finally said. "Do tell your mother how very sorry I am."

"I will."

"So how are you feeling, dear?"

"Good. And huge." Vanessa smiled. "In some ways I want to get it over with, but it's awesome carrying a human being inside me. I actually enjoy his kicking."

Tessa nodded. "I did too. It's amazing."

"You have children, Tessa? I never even asked." She remembered seeing pictures on the bookcase.

"One daughter, Sabrina. She and her husband, Phil, and my only granddaughter, Jessie, live in London. Phil teaches American history at Evanshire College."

"I'll bet you miss them."

Tessa's eyes glistened. "Terribly. Jessie is ten. I haven't seen her in a year and a half. Antonio and I are planning a trip there next spring."

"That should be fun." *Good. We're off the subject.*

"Vanessa … I realize this is none of my business … but do you think it's safe for you to be out alone? There's no point pretending it wasn't you I've seen twice in the alley. I'm quite concerned for you. The officers can't protect you if they don't know where you are."

What should she do now—lie? Tell the truth and risk having Tessa tell her parents?

"Uh, this is really awkward. I-I guess there's no point in denying it. But I'm not going out alone anymore," she quickly added. "I just went down to the park. It felt so good to get out by myself. I'm not used to having all these people breathing down my neck."

"You're a private person, aren't you, dear?"

"How did you know?"

"Takes one to know one. I'm a busybody, but I need my space too."

"You're not going to tell my parents, are you?"

"No. You're an adult." Tessa put her hand on Vanessa's. "But I do hope you mean what you said about not going out alone anymore."

"I do. I'm getting a little paranoid with what all's going on with Mom." *And I'm staying away from that oddball in the park.*

CHAPTER 28

EARLY that evening, Brill sat at the kitchen table with her family and David, her hunger pleasantly satisfied by a second helping of Vanessa's meatloaf and spicy rice.

"That was really good, honey."

"Mom, it's *your* recipe."

Brill smiled. "I almost forgot I used to be a good cook, way back when. I really appreciate your fixing dinner for us."

"You're welcome." Vanessa glanced at David. "I enjoy cooking."

"Did Tessa have anything to say when she brought the brownies?" Kurt asked.

"Not really. Other than she's really sorry that DA Cromwell died. She wanted to be sure I told Mom that."

Brill didn't want to talk about another victim with Emily at the table. "So, Emily … your no-cavity report is the big news of the day. You deserve a reward."

"Like what?"

"Well, how about a new dress? You've just about outgrown the ones you have. Why don't we go to the mall and shop?" *While I'm still drawing a paycheck.*

"Really?" Emily's grin stole her face. "You don't have to work tonight?"

"Absolutely not. If we leave now, we'll have more than two hours before it closes."

"Cool. I think I want a pink sundress. Or maybe a yellow one. I'm not sure."

"I'm assuming David will escort you ladies?" Kurt said. "I'll gladly clean up the dishes, and then I have some paperwork I need to do."

"I want Vanessa to come too," Emily said.

"Oh, Shortcake, I don't know if I have the energy."

"Yes, you do. Pleeeeease?" Emily assumed a pleading pose. "We never get to go shopping, and you always know if something looks really pretty or not."

"All right. But no whining if I need to find a place to sit every so often."

Brill lifted her eyes and caught David's gaze. "I think you just got roped into the night shift."

"Kurt, help me out here," David said. "Why don't you go with us?"

"I'd really love to, but I've got to read through a stack of applications. I'm trying to hire an assistant manager for my Athens store."

"Hey, the clock's ticking." Emily rose to her feet. "I'm going to change my shoes."

Brill wiped her mouth with a napkin and started stacking dishes. "Let me get the table cleared."

Kurt picked up her hand and kissed it. "Did you see Emily's face? I haven't seen her that excited in a long time. I'll do the dishes. You go have fun with the girls."

Vanessa stood outside the dressing room, several sundresses laid across her arm, and waited for her mother to bring out the rejects and take these in for Emily to try on.

David stood on the other side of the main aisle, several yards away, looking through a sale rack of men's shirts. Every few seconds he glanced over at her.

The store was surprisingly busy for a weeknight, and she wished she were a size six again so she could buy some of the cute dresses on sale. Would she *ever* be a size six again? Or at least have a decent figure after the baby was born? Dr. Zimmer had suggested she hold her weight gain to thirty pounds, but she had already gained twenty-two. Maybe she should start saying no to some of the goodies Tessa brought over.

She moved her gaze slowly across the expanse of Reagan's Department Store. Why didn't she realize until tonight that Sophie Trace had such a great mall? She wanted to look at baby clothes but resisted the urge. Her mother would lay a guilt trip on her, and why exacerbate her own maternal instinct that was getting harder and harder to suppress?

She caught a glimpse of a man leaning against a post and did a double take, her heart nearly pounding out of her chest.

Micah?

Was this guy following her? What were the odds that he just happened to be in the same store at the same time as she? Should she tell David? Tell him what—that she had met Micah at the park when she ignored her parents' wishes that she not go out alone? That he bought her hot dogs and they'd had a poignant discussion about God and Christianity? That he lied about his age and living at the Carter

House, and that he wore colored contacts? What was an FBI special agent supposed to do about that?

If Micah saw her, he didn't show any signs of it. Was he with someone? She decided she had to say something to him.

She walked across the aisle to David. "I see a friend over there. I'll be right back." She walked up to Micah, and he didn't look surprised. "I'm beginning to think you're following me."

"I'm here for the sale. I need a pair of trousers and a dress shirt."

"I tried calling you at the Carter House. The operator said you weren't a resident."

"What was it you wanted?"

"Look …" She lowered her voice. "We both know you haven't been truthful with me. I'd be surprised if your real name is Micah Harvey, and I don't believe a man of eighty-six could run the way you did. You don't have blue eyes either. Did you think I wouldn't notice when your contact fell out? Is that gray mustache and beard phony, too?"

The old man's face turned crimson, and he seemed totally flustered. "Hold on, missy. The Carter House doesn't have me listed as a resident because I'm movin' to Nashville tomorrow to live with my son. As for runnin', it's true I'm more limber that most ol' duffers. I was a marathon runner. But why would I tell you I wear blue contacts? What difference does it make?"

It doesn't. I'm an idiot. Vanessa felt as if her words were stuck to the roof of her mouth. Finally she said, "I'm just paranoid. Forget I said anything. You've been nothing but nice to me. So are you excited about the move?"

Micah seemed to look at something beyond her. "You do what you've gotta do. Truth is, I got a bad diagnosis this week. Figured I needed to be close to my son for the next three to six months. It's about time we made peace anyway."

"You're dying?" She wasn't sure if she said the words out loud or just thought them.

He squeezed her shoulder. "We're all dyin', Vanessa. I'm just closer to the end. I haven't got any complaints."

"Sorry to interrupt," David said. "Your mom said Emily's ready to try on whatever it is you've got."

Vanessa handed the dresses to David. "I'll be right there. My friend is moving tomorrow, and I'd like to finish saying good-bye."

"Sure." David seemed to study Micah, and then held out his hand. "Hi. David Riley."

"Micah Harvey. Nice to make your acquaintance."

Vanessa shifted her weight as the two men shook hands, hoping David wouldn't ask how she had come to know Micah.

Finally David left, and Vanessa stood in awkward silence. How should she say good-bye to someone who was terminally ill?

"I wish you luck with that little boy," Micah said. "I know you'll figure out what's best for the both of you."

"I hope so."

"You can handle it, young lady. Don't let anybody talk you out of what your heart knows is right for you."

"I won't." Vanessa wrung her hands. "I'm glad we met."

"So am I."

"I hope the time you have with your son is special and makes up for the time you didn't have with him."

Micah gave a nod. "We both want that … by the way, I've been readin' the gospel of John. It's startin' to make sense."

"Really?"

"Heaven or hell—I choose, right?"

"Vanessa!"

"That's my mom. I guess I need to go." Why did her shoes feel as if they were glued to the floor?

"Cherish your family, Vanessa. I'll always regret that I didn't. Go on. I'm gonna be fine."

Vanessa stood mute for a moment, then finally she heard herself say, "When you've finished reading John, read Acts."

She turned and walked toward the dressing room, blinking the stinging from her eyes. Where was the emotion coming from? It wasn't that she was going to miss Micah. She hardly knew him.

"Who was that?" Brill said.

"Just a sweet old man I met. He's moving to Nashville tomorrow to live with his son."

"Emily wants to know where you got this dress"—Brill held up the blue one—"and if they have it in other colors."

"I think I got it over by the wall. I'll go see."

Vanessa walked toward the rack where she had picked up the dress and glanced over her shoulder. Micah was gone.

Brill turned out the bedroom lamp and nestled next to Kurt.

"I'm glad I went shopping with the girls. Emily's delighted with her new dress, and it was nice to turn the spotlight on her instead of dwelling on the gloom and doom of Merrick Fountain's victims."

"I agree. And I'm relieved to have gotten through all the job applications for assistant manager at the Athens store and picked several people to interview."

"Good. I worry that you're not devoting enough time to your business."

"It's not a matter of time as much as it is concentration. There are a lot of distractions right now."

"That's an understatement." Brill cupped his cheek in her hand. "Has Vanessa talked to you any more about her plans for this baby?"

"Not a word. I hate to pressure her, but we've got to stop putting off talking about it. What about you? Have you thought any more about it?"

Brill nodded. "I think you're right. I haven't been trusting the Lord. We need to concentrate on what's best for Vanessa and the baby and not limit what God can do."

"Exactly. So what *is* best for them?"

"My first inclination is adoption. But I honestly don't think Vanessa's even considering it."

"Probably not. What about the moral issue? Is it wrong for her to choose to be a single mom when there are so many loving Christian couples that could provide a two-parent family?"

"I'm not willing to make that judgment, Kurt. Are you?" Brill looked into his eyes. "We're still a family. If Vanessa wants to raise her son, surely we can muster enough love to make a home for them?"

"What if you lose your job?"

"I'll get another one."

"Are you willing to sell the house?"

"If it comes to that, sure. We can make a home no matter what house we live in. I just don't want Vanessa to make a decision she'll regret for the rest of her life."

"That could work both ways, you know." Kurt ran his fingers through her hair. "Vanessa could decide to keep him and have second thoughts later on."

"I doubt she'll have second thoughts as long she has a support system. How can she go wrong with the entire family behind her? And Emily will be more help the older she gets. Remember how much help Vanessa was at her age?"

Kurt smiled. "I do."

"We shouldn't put off telling her what we know about Nicholson, just in case she's holding on to a thread of hope that he's going to help her."

"I agree."

Brill fiddled with the button on Kurt's pajama shirt. "To tell you the truth, I'm glad we don't have to deal with the two of them being unequally yoked. After his insistence that she get an abortion, I'm not sure I would find it easy to like him."

A loud bang shook the window. Brill sat up and threw her legs over the side of the bed, her heart pounding wildly. Before she could grab her gun, she heard giggling and the sound of bare feet running across the floor above them.

"It was just a door slamming," Kurt said. "The girls must be clowning around."

Brill exhaled, comforted by the warmth of Kurt's hand on her back. "I nearly had a stroke. I guess I'm even edgier than I thought."

"That's two of us. You've hardly said a word about Cromwell's dying. What are you doing to tighten security?"

"I don't know what else to do, Kurt. Everyone in law enforcement is on high alert. I've got a wall of blue around me—plus David. There's no way Fountain can get to me."

"Really?" He looked into her eyes with such intensity she had to look away. "Because Fountain's batting a thousand. He's threatened more than once to kill you. What if you can't stop him?"

CHAPTER 29

BRILL sat at the conference table in her office, Tuesday morning's newspaper lying to one side, and reread the lab report on the trace evidence collected in Sean O'Toole's hospital room and on Beau Jack Rousseaux's clothing after the stabbing.

So what, if no evidence was found in O'Toole's room that could link his poisoning death to Merrick Fountain? The lack of physical evidence would be offset by Brill's testimony that she recognized Fountain as O'Toole's nurse. And by Ulman's statement that the nurse was the only person alone with O'Toole just prior to his death.

At least the DNA from two hair follicles found on Rousseaux's shirt matched Fountain's. That, and Jeanette's eyewitness account of her husband's stabbing, would be enough to put Fountain away—if they could just find him.

Brill glanced out the window at the mountains. What she wouldn't give just to drive up to the White Mountain Inn and veg for a few days in one of their deluxe suites.

She took the photographs out of the case file. The stab wounds on O'Toole, Rousseaux, her ex-partner Zack Rogers, and DA Cromwell were almost identical. Probably inflicted with the same eight-inch blade. The medical examiner's report indicated the perp was left-handed and approximately five feet ten. Everything pointed to Merrick Fountain.

"A penny for your thoughts," David said.

"Oh, the evidence is so overwhelming that Fountain's our man that it'll be a slam dunk once we get him."

"I think you're right. What's eating you? It's more than just Merrick Fountain."

Brill planted her elbows on the table, her chin resting on her palms. "Two things, actually. My lack of job security and my daughter's future. Each affects the other, and I have control over neither."

"And you're terrible at not being in control."

"You're right. At least I'm getting better at accepting that God's in control."

David put up his palms. "Not me. I don't know how you and Kurt can think that way."

"How do you know we do?"

"Just because I haven't mentioned it till now doesn't mean I haven't picked up on it. You're a lot more spiritual than I ever took you for."

"My faith's been important to me since I was a little girl, but I don't wear it on my sleeve."

"You really don't. It wouldn't serve you well in this profession anyway—too much cynicism. But if you think God's in control, why aren't you furious with Him? I don't see any peace on earth and good will toward men."

"That's because you don't have His perspective. The peace He's promised isn't external."

David arched his eyebrows. "Is this where you tell me I need to be born again?"

"Let's just say if you ever get serious about wanting to know more, we'll talk."

"Thanks for letting me off the hook. Let's get back to your two concerns. I think you should erase job security from your list of worries. I'm telling you, the city council isn't going to let you go."

"David, Mayor Roswell told me to watch my step, said that I wouldn't be hard to replace."

"I think he knows better than that."

"Let's hope. I don't think the city council would do anything until we get Merrick Fountain convicted."

"Let's go on to Vanessa's future. Where are you guys in that process? Have you thought any more about telling her what you know about Nicholson?"

"Yes, Kurt and I agree we need to do it. And we're also on board with the possibility that Vanessa's going to keep the baby and live with us."

David seemed to study her. "That's pretty generous of you."

"She's our daughter. Her child is our grandson. We can make sacrifices and even tighten our belts if we have to."

"Yeah, I'm sure you can. But do you *want* to?"

"I will if it comes to that. I don't want Vanessa pressured into giving up her child and regretting it the rest of her life."

"I don't think it's nearly as traumatic these days. The birth mother can stay in touch."

"Vanessa knows that. It's her call. My gut feeling is that she had already decided to keep the baby before she came home. I think she's stalling, hoping that Kurt and I will come around."

"She doesn't know you have?"

"No, we just talked about it last night. I'm reluctant to share that with Vanessa because we really don't want to sway her decision either way. But once she knows the baby's father is completely out of the picture, I think she'll take a serious, and hopefully realistic, look at whether or not she's up to the challenge of being a single mom."

Tessa walked over to the counter at Nick's Grill and noticed that Gus had gotten a haircut and was dressed in dark trousers and a pale blue shirt—and smelled as if he'd been marinated in Old Spice.

She sat in her usual place. "My, don't you look nice."

Antonio slid onto the stool next to her and slapped Gus on the back. "How's it going, friend?"

"Really can't complain, but I always do. Well, maybe not today."

Antonio sniffed several times. "Since when do you wear cologne? What's the occasion?"

"Maggie and I have a date."

"Well, you ol' fox." Antonio nudged Gus with his elbow. "It's about time."

Maggie appeared at the counter, her gray hair newly cut and bobbed. "I'm off at two, and Gus is taking me to Sevierville to see *Arsenic and Old Lace* at the civic theater."

"Well, well, well." Antonio's voice was playful. "I had no idea Gus was into the arts."

Tessa looked down the counter, and Gus's face was redder than the ketchup bottle. "I think it's wonderful."

"So do I," Maggie said. "We also have reservations at Filbert's."

"In case you don't know," Gus added, "that's the new steak house that was written up in Sunday's newspaper. Five star. Coat and tie required."

Antonio chuckled. "You even remember how to tie a tie?"

"It's like ridin' a bicycle, my friend."

Tessa studied Maggie's glowing face. She was definitely not mad at Gus anymore.

"Today's special is oriental salad," Maggie said. "There're six grilled shrimp and a sliced chicken breast on each one. It's fabulous."

"That's what I'll have," Tessa said.

Antonio nodded. "Ditto."

"I'll bring your coffee in just a minute." Maggie winked at Gus, then turned and went through the swinging doors.

"Hi, everybody." Clint took his place at the counter. "Did anyone else notice there's a bazillion cop cars at city hall?"

"I did," Gus said. "My friend in the sheriff's department told me that law enforcement volunteers from all across the region are workin' together to keep Chief Jessup safe from that nutcase. Too bad they didn't do it for O'Toole and Rousseaux and those cops in Memphis."

"Let's be fair," Tessa said. "With the exception of Detective O'Toole, the officers who were stabbed and also the former DA were offered protection and refused it."

"Well, Chief Jessup sure didn't refuse it." Gus crunched a mouthful of ice. "I know there's money in the budget for stuff like this. But she's not gonna score points with the city council if she uses up every dollar on herself."

Tessa pressed her lips together. She didn't want to engage him in this line of conversation, but how could she just sit there and let it slide?

"What price tag would you put on *your* life, Gus?"

"Aw, don't get your feathers ruffled, Tessa. I didn't say the chief was wrong to accept it."

"Wasn't that the implication?"

"Erase that. I just meant that the city council might see her as high maintenance." Gus put his hand over his mouth. "I need to shut up before I stick my foot in my mouth."

"You mean the *other* foot?"

"Aw, come on, Tessa. I'm tryin' to do better and you know it. But there *is* friction between the chief, the city council, and Mayor Roswell. I didn't make it up, for cryin' out loud."

Tessa breathed in slowly and let it out. Gus was right about that. Why keep bickering and spoil his date?

Maggie came out of the kitchen with a coffeepot and two mugs. "So what'd I miss?"

"Absolutely nothing of consequence," Tessa said. "How could anything top the news about you and Gus?"

Kurt studied the framed wedding picture on the bedroom dresser. How could twenty-two years have passed by so quickly? Would they get another twenty-two? Would the protections Brill had put in place be good enough to keep Merrick Fountain from getting to her?

"Dad ..."

Kurt turned and saw Vanessa standing in the doorway.

"You worried about Mom?" she said.

"I'm trying not to be. What's up?"

"Could I talk to you for a few minutes?"

"Sure, come in."

Vanessa sat in the chair, and Kurt sat on the side of the bed, facing her.

"What's on your mind, honey?"

"Everything."

"Could you be more specific?"

Vanessa seemed to be staring at her hands for a long time, then lifted her gaze. "I know I have to make a decision about the baby, but I still don't know the right thing to do."

"Have you even explored your options?"

Vanessa shrugged. "When I was in Memphis. But it was depressing."

"In what way?"

"I can't imagine trusting someone else to raise my son. And I can't imagine ever making enough money to support him."

"So you're caught in a trap?"

Vanessa's eyes glistened. "Uh-huh."

"And you're running out of time?"

She nodded.

Why wasn't Brill present to hear this? Should he wait to have this discussion with Vanessa? How could he? She might never be this open again.

Kurt held out his hand. "Come here."

Vanessa came over and sat beside him on the bed.

"If money wasn't an issue, what would you do?"

"Keep him."

"You didn't hesitate for one second to answer."

"Because I know what I want." A tear spilled down Vanessa's cheek. "I just feel guilty because every child deserves to have two parents. Everyone will think I'm selfish."

"Forget everyone else, Vanessa. Do you feel you can love this child and be a strong Christian parent?"

"I really do. I mean, I might have to ask you and Mom lots of questions. I'm sure I have a lot to learn. But I already love him, Dad. I don't think I could stand to give him up." Vanessa put her face in her hands and sniffled.

Brill, why aren't you here? Lord, give me wisdom.

Kurt put his arm around Vanessa and pulled her close. "If you want this badly enough, there has to be a way."

"Mom said if I want to keep him, I have to fight for him. I've been thinking about that, and I have an idea." She pulled back and looked into his eyes. "I don't know if you and Mom will go for it, but I don't have anything to lose by asking."

CHAPTER 30

BRILL hung up her desk phone and stepped over to the window, her hands clasped behind her, and stared at the bank of dark clouds rolling in over the mountains.

"So," David said, "how did Captain Donovan react when you told him you're not going back to Memphis for Cromwell's funeral?"

"He understood. There'll be ample higher-ups from law enforcement coming. I won't be missed." Brill turned around and leaned against the glass. "Poor guy sounded demoralized. I understand how he feels. We're both weary of burying our friends and colleagues."

David closed the case file. "Well, unless you want us burying *you,* you need to stay off the radar until we can get this rodent back in the cage."

"Maybe we should set a trap and force him to make his next move."

"He'd see right through it."

"Maybe not. So far, he's been successful in surprising each of his victims. We could set up a scenario and let him think he's doing it again."

David sat back in his chair, balancing his weight on the balls of his feet. "No way am I putting you out there."

"It's not your call, David."

The room was suddenly pin-drop still.

David raised his eyebrows. "You're right. I'm just here on vacation. I take my cues from you."

"I knew you'd have trouble not being in charge."

"I just forgot my place for a moment. You're right. It's your call."

"Thank you. Actually, I'm inclined to think that Fountain is planning to go after Trent next. Why not use him for bait and speed up the process, but in an environment where we can control everything?"

"I'm listening."

"I hesitate even to ask Trent to take the risk, but he's at risk anyway as long as Fountain is out there."

Vanessa sat on the glider on the screened-in porch, basking in the warmth of the June afternoon and the relief of having finally admitted to her dad that the desire of her heart was to keep the baby. Her cell phone rang and startled her. She smiled when she saw the number on the screen, and put it to her ear.

"Hi, Ethan. How's the new job going?"

"Great," he said. "Sorry I haven't talked to you in a couple days. My aunt and uncle had some people over after church Sunday and wanted me to hang out with them. And then I started the new job on Monday."

"So you like it?"

"Yeah. My uncle's got me on a fast track. I love a challenge. At the moment, I'm taking a short break, having a Snickers, and thinking of you. So how are you feeling?"

"Good."

"And the baby hippo?"

Vanessa giggled. "He's active as ever. Kicking up a storm."

"When's your next appointment with Dr. Zimmer?"

"Next week."

"Is your mother going with you?"

"She hasn't offered, and I won't ask."

A long moment of dead air made her wonder if the connection had been lost.

"Look," Ethan finally said, "I don't have the right to tell you what to do. But I think you should consider inviting your mother to go with you to your appointments."

"She's busy. Dad's schedule is more flexible."

"You need your mother right now."

Vanessa blinked the stinging from her eyes. "She's so disappointed in me, I think she just wants to get it over with."

"Have you told her you want to keep the baby?"

"Not in so many words. But I told my dad this morning. I didn't really intend to tell him, but he drew it out of me."

"Good. Was he supportive?"

Vanessa stared at the hummingbird suspended at the feeder her dad had just hung on the eaves. "Actually he was. He told me that he and Mom talked about it last night and agreed that if I choose to keep the baby, I can live at home and they'll help me get on my feet."

"Hey, that's terrific. So you've made your decision?"

"I want to talk to my mother face-to-face first. It's important to me that she's not just agreeing to this because my dad pressured her."

"Vanessa, she'll come around the minute she holds that baby. He's her grandson."

"That's what I'm hoping. I did what she asked and came up with a plan. Dad wanted me to wait and tell them both tonight."

"Can you tell me about it?"

"Sure. I thought I'd have to quit school, and then I found out I can take college classes online. Since I won't have to live in the dorm, it'll save my parents a ton of money that we could apply toward the expenses of the baby and me living at home."

"Sounds like a great idea."

"You can't believe how much diapers and formula cost. If I nurse the baby, that'll save about a hundred dollars a month."

"I'm proud of you, Vanessa. Sounds like you've got it figured out."

"Believe it or not, if I live at home and go to school online and keep the baby, it'll be cheaper than if I go back to the University of Memphis. We would even have enough left over to hire a babysitter a few hours a day so I could study."

"I can't imagine your folks won't go for the idea. This is so great. Does Emily suspect anything?"

"No, and I promised to tell her first. I didn't intend to tell my dad as much as I did, and I need to tell Emily before my mom gets home. But once I tell her, it's like it's final."

"Isn't that what you want?"

"I think so. I mean, I definitely want to keep the baby. But everything else is overwhelming."

"Just take it a step at a time. Admitting you want to keep the baby is a huge step."

"It feels good to have it out in the open. Dad wasn't surprised. I doubt Mom will be either."

Tessa peeked out the kitchen curtain and saw that only Kurt's van was parked in the driveway at the Jessups' house.

"I wonder if Brill is coming home for dinner."

"You're meddling, love."

Tessa smiled and let the curtain fall back in place, then went over to the kitchen table and sat across from Antonio.

"I worry that Vanessa doesn't spend much time with her mother."

"How do you know what goes on in that house?" Antonio said.

"I don't. But Brill gets home late most nights, and she's being stalked by some crazy man. I doubt that's very conducive to nurturing a relationship with her pregnant daughter."

"You can't help any of that."

"I've been talking to the Lord about it every morning."

"And is He talking back?" Antonio squeezed her hand, a twinkle in his eyes.

"Not in words. But I feel as if I should invite Vanessa over more often."

"Fine with me. She's a real sweet girl. I don't approve of her getting involved with her professor, but I was wrong to judge her."

"I wonder when she's going to decide whether or not to let the baby be adopted."

"Oh, I'm sure you'll find a way to get her to tell you." Antonio chuckled. "Ever think of starting your own Dear Tessa column?"

"I wish I didn't feel drawn to people's problems. But so many times I really do believe it's the Lord's doing."

"I give you a hard time, but I can't really argue with that. I've seen you minister to lots of folks over the years."

"Speaking of folks …"—Tessa smiled without meaning to—"wouldn't you just love to be a fly on the wall tonight when Gus and Maggie go to the civic theater and then to Filbert's for dinner? Gus can get my dander up faster than anyone, but you know I'm fond of him. I really want Maggie and him to hit it off."

"Me, too. Gus has seemed lost since his wife died. Who knows? A little romance might even improve his negative view of everything."

"And every*one*, especially Brill." Tessa felt Abby rub against her leg and picked her up. "It's beyond me that Gus won't acknowledge that Brill handled the disappearances like the professional she is. Even Special Agent Riley publicly commended her."

"Well, if Gus had been here when Brill talked down the gangbanger who held us at gunpoint, he'd have respect for her."

"Yes …" Tessa shuddered at the memory. "I'm sure he would."

"Gus thinks there's one point of view: his. I hope Maggie rubs off on him, and not the other way around. But you have to admit, having lunch at Nick's every day wouldn't be half as much fun without him."

"I suppose not. As annoying as he can be, he does tend to spark stimulating conversation."

Antonio laughed. "More like *ignite*."

Vanessa stood outside Emily's bedroom and saw her baby sister sitting cross-legged on the bed, absorbed in a book. She knocked softly on the open door.

"Hey, Shortcake. Can I come in?"

Emily closed the book and looked up. "Sure. Perfect timing. I just finished the chapter."

Vanessa went in and closed the door behind her, then sat on the bed. "I've made a decision."

Emily's eyes grew wide and animated. "About the baby?"

"Uh-huh. I know I promised I'd come tell you first, and I meant to do that ... but this morning Dad sort of pulled it out of me. I haven't told Mom yet."

"Just *tell* me."

Vanessa tilted Emily's chin. "We'd better get your crib out of the attic because there's going to be a baby in the house."

Emily squealed and threw her arms around Vanessa. "I knew it. I knew you'd bring him home." She stood on the bed and started bouncing up and down as if it were a trampoline. "When can I tell Jasmine?"

"Will you settle down?" Vanessa grabbed Emily's ankles and let her fall on her bottom. "You can't tell anybody—not even Dad—that I told you before I told Mom."

"She hates being the last one to know things."

"I didn't mean for it to happen that way." Vanessa stroked Emily's ponytail. "I'll tell her as soon as she gets home. Just act surprised when Mom and Dad come tell you."

"That's the same as lying."

"No, it isn't."

"Yes, it is."

"Then don't act surprised. Get excited like you did when *I* told you. There's nothing fake about that."

"I'll probably giggle or something and spoil everything."

Vanessa sighed. "Emily, don't make this complicated. Just be yourself so Mom won't get her feelings hurt, okay?"

"All right." A grin stretched Emily's cheeks. "Auntie Em. Auntie Em," she whispered.

"You are *so* hyper." Vanessa laughed, glad that at least one person in the family was genuinely happy about the baby.

CHAPTER 31

BRILL closed the front door, the fragrance of roses reminding her of Kurt's promise of faithfulness and her promise not to revisit the dark chapter in their marriage.

Thank You, Lord, for a husband who loves me.

"Hi, you're earlier than I expected." Kurt kissed her cheek. "Where's David?"

"Talking to the officers parked across the street. Are we having dinner out or in?"

"In. Vanessa's got herb chicken in the oven. I thought after dinner we could take her aside and tell her what we've found out about Nicholson."

"Good. She should also know about our conversation last night."

Kurt's eyebrows furrowed. "About that ... there's something I need to tell you. Come in the bedroom for a minute."

Brill went down the hall and into their room and sat on the side of the bed. Kurt closed the door behind him.

"Vanessa came to me earlier," he said, "and told me how conflicted she's been about the best course of action for the baby and for her. Long story short, she wants to keep the baby. You don't know how badly I wanted you to be there to hear what she had to say. But I was afraid if I made her wait, she might shut down again."

"Go on."

"You were right about her mind being made up. She feels selfish that she doesn't want to give him up, but she's confident that with the love and support of her family, she can be a good single parent."

"So much for Mom's input." Brill unbuttoned the top button on her uniform shirt. "I can't really blame her for wanting to confide in you and not me. You have a way with her."

"Honey, it just poured out. I honestly don't think she planned it that way. In fact, she reminded me that *you* said if she wanted to keep the baby she needed to fight for him. She's come up with a plan. She wants to talk to us about it after dinner."

"Vanessa didn't tell you?"

Kurt shook his head. "No, she wanted us to hear it at the same time. Which will work out great, since we're ready to tell her what we've discovered about Nicholson."

"I wonder if that will change her decision."

"I doubt it." Kurt stroked her cheek, his dark eyes seeming to probe her thoughts. "You should've seen Vanessa's face light up. She's nuts about this baby—more than I realized."

"I wonder what kind of plan she came up with."

"I don't know, but she said it all came to her in the past few days. She seemed very eager to run it by us."

Vanessa carried the last of the dinner dishes over to the dishwasher and set them on the countertop.

"They're all yours," she said to Emily.

"Agent David and I will load the dishwasher—in case anyone needs to go do something else." Emily pressed her lips together, a grin tugging at her cheeks.

Vanessa scolded Emily with her eyes, and then went into the living room where her parents were watching TV.

"I'm ready to talk whenever you are," she said.

"Now is great with us." Kurt put down the newspaper.

Brill got up and poked her head in the kitchen. "Can you two handle kitchen duty?"

David laughed. "Blindfolded. Then I'm going to whip Emily at checkers."

"Why don't we go out on the back porch?" Vanessa said. "It's nice out."

Vanessa followed her parents outside and pulled the door shut. She sat in the wicker chair in the corner and looked over at the glider—and two pairs of questioning eyes.

"I guess Dad told you about our conversation?"

Brill nodded.

"It's important to me that you're *both* okay with the baby and me living with you. I know it's going to mean some adjustments for all of us. But I can't do it unless there's harmony at home."

"Your dad said you have a plan. We'd like to hear it."

Vanessa laid out the details of her plan to take college classes online and use the money that would have gone for the dorm to cover baby costs and living expenses.

"It'll actually be cheaper than if I went back to the University of Memphis, but you'll still be putting me through college."

Her parents looked at each other. Did they like her idea? Or was she being presumptuous?

"It's obvious you've put some thought into this," Kurt said.

"I did what Mom asked. I came up with a plan. I want to keep my son, and I'm fighting for him. But I can't do this without your help. If I get a job, most of what I make will go for childcare. This way, at least I'm still working toward getting my teaching degree. Once I do that, I can support myself and my son."

"Your father and I are already on board with you and the baby living with us," Brill said. "Your plan is certainly doable."

Kurt nodded. "There's enough in the college fund to cover it."

Only because my brainy brother got a four-year scholarship to Vanderbilt. Vanessa studied her mother's face. "I don't want to do anything that would cause friction between you two."

Kurt reached over and took Brill's hand. "Your mother and I are in agreement. But there is something we need to tell *you*. We hired a private investigator to look for Professor Nicholson."

Brill held up her palm. "We didn't find him."

"Why didn't you tell me?"

"Your dad wasn't too keen on the idea of hiring a PI. But I convinced him that we should find the baby's father, hold his feet to the fire, and get you child support. We didn't say anything because we didn't want to get your hopes up. If we had found him and he'd responded positively, we would have told you."

Vanessa folded her arms across her chest. "I'm not a child. You didn't have to keep it from me."

"You had enough to deal with," Kurt said. "But we've uncovered some things you need to know. I'll let your mother tell you since she's the one who spoke with the PI."

"What things?" Vanessa waited for her mother to respond. Why did she seem hesitant?

"Honey, there's no easy way to say this: There's no record that Professor Tyson Frederick Nicholson taught at Chambers College."

"What are you talking about? He taught there for six years."

Brill shook her head. "He didn't. And he didn't graduate from Barsfield University either."

"This has to be a mistake. He got his master's there."

"There's no record of it."

"There has to be."

"There isn't. There's no record that he ever attended East Nashville High School either."

Vanessa sighed. "That can't be right. How could he get hired to teach psychology without teaching credentials?"

"He couldn't. His personnel file at the University of Memphis contained his transcript and all the proper documentation to show that he graduated from Barsfield with a master's *and* that he taught at Chambers College. But when my PI friend dug deeper, neither of those schools had any records on him."

"Did somebody talk to the human resources person at the University of Memphis who handled all Ty's paperwork when he was hired?"

"That person is deceased." Brill looked at Kurt and then at Vanessa. "It's obvious something is terribly awry. So David asked a friend at the bureau to make some inquiries. The friend was told in no uncertain terms to back off."

"What exactly does 'back off' mean?"

"It means we've hit a brick wall, that the professor is probably in the Witness Protection Program, and that his identity was made up."

Vanessa could almost hear the door of her heart slam shut. "So Ty Nicholson isn't even his real name?"

"Looks that way."

Vanessa's mind raced in reverse as she tried to process the implications. "Then he lied to me …"

"He lied to everyone. When a person goes into witness protection, he turns his back on his past and assumes a whole new identity. He's trying to hide from someone who's threatened to kill him, possibly because he testified against the mafia or a gang. For the rest of his life, he'll be looking over his shoulder and can never have an honest long-term relationship with anyone without endangering the other person."

"So that's why he didn't want any permanent commitments." Vanessa wiped a tear off her cheek. "Poor Ty."

"Honey, before you start feeling sorry for the guy, you should know that he could also be a gangster who agreed to testify against another gangster in order to avoid doing prison time."

"You think Ty was in the mob?"

"There's no way to know. He must've had a teaching background or the feds wouldn't have carved out this identity for him. It's pointless to speculate."

"Vanessa, I know this is a shock," Kurt said. "But it's important that you face the fact that the baby's father is out of the picture, which means you're not going to get any child support or moral support from him."

"I never thought I was, Dad."

"Then if you still feel confident that you can handle single parenting, your mother and I welcome you home and will do whatever we can to help raise this child until you get your teaching degree and can afford to be out on your own."

"Thanks. I can't believe you're being so gracious about it." Vanessa dabbed her eyes. "I know it's not what you wanted."

"Ultimately, we want what you want," Brill said. "This is a huge decision that will impact the rest of your life."

Vanessa lay across her bed and heard feet running toward her and then felt a big thud as Emily landed on the bed.

"Yipee! We're going to have a baby in the house."

"Did Mom and Dad tell you?" Vanessa said.

"Uh-huh. Don't worry. I just got excited and didn't lie."

"How did they seem to you?"

"They didn't jump up and down on the bed like I did, but they weren't mad. They said they were counting on me to help. And that a baby changes everything."

"Did they say anything about Ty?"

"No, but they never do."

"They hired a private investigator to try to find Ty, and he couldn't. It's obvious that Ty doesn't want to be found. So I have to deal with the fact that I really am going to raise this baby without his father." That seemed like enough information for a ten-year-old.

"Maybe you'll get married and he'll have a new dad."

"Don't hold your breath."

Emily picked up a lock of Vanessa's hair. "You're pretty. And you're nice. I'll bet lots of guys would want to marry you."

"You're sweet to say that. But I'd like to fall in love first—*and* finish school."

"Well, Dad can be the grandpa. That's almost as good."

Vanessa smiled, remembering Poppy. "Grandpas are great. Dad seems a little young, though."

"Yeah, he's not all wrinkly like some grandpas. And he doesn't have a big belly. But he's so much fun, and he's a pushover when it comes to going out for ice cream."

"That's because you've got him wrapped around your little finger."

"I know." Emily grinned. "That's my job. I'm the baby."

"Not for long. Is it going to be hard to give up your spot?"

"Not really. I want to be an aunt. That's more grown up. Are you going to take those classes where they teach you how to change diapers, and burp the baby, and other cool stuff?"

"I'm sure I will. I'm a little rusty."

"Can I go? Are kids allowed?"

Vanessa stroked Emily's ponytail. "I don't know. I can find out."

"Well, I want to learn how to do everything so I can help you."

"You're really excited about this, aren't you?"

Emily nodded. "Big-time. Can I be in the room when the baby's born?"

"I'm not sure how comfortable I'd be with that."

"I saw a baby born on TV. I thought it was so neat."

"I have a feeling it's different when you're right there."

"I can handle it. I want to be an obstetrician when I grow up."

"I thought you wanted to be a nanny."

"That's when I was nine. Now I want to deliver babies." Emily took her index finger and traced the flower pattern on Vanessa's sundress. "I think it's awesome that when a baby comes out of the mother, all it needs is a breath of air, and then it can live out here in *this* world. It's kind of a miracle. Like when God breathed into Adam."

"It really is. Go open my top drawer. I want you to see something."

Emily slid off of the bed, went over to the dresser, and opened the top drawer. "What am I looking for?"

"Ultrasound pictures of your nephew."

"Here they are."

Emily held the stack of pictures with both hands and walked slowly toward the bed, her full attention on the picture on top. "Wow … this is awesome. You can see his face."

"Go to the next one."

Emily sat on the side of the bed and slid the top picture to the bottom of the stack. "Look at those teensy tiny feet! Have Mom and Dad seen these?"

"No, I've kept them to myself. It was too painful to share them when I didn't even know if I was going to keep him."

Emily sat quietly looking at the pictures, one at a time. And then went through the stack again. Finally she said, "Mom and Dad *have* to see these. They're amazing."

Emily put the pictures on the nightstand, then climbed up on the bed. She turned her head sideways and placed her ear on Vanessa's tummy.

"Can I hear his heartbeat this way?"

"No. But if you want to, you can go with me next week when I see Dr. Zimmer. I promise you, hearing the baby's heartbeat will blow your mind."

Emily sat up straight and then fell back on the bed, her head next to Vanessa's. "I'll tell you one thing. This is the most exciting thing that's ever happened in this family."

Vanessa closed her eyes and let her sister's words settle over her heart. Nothing about this baby's conception was as it should be. But at this moment, in the company of innocence, she was filled with wonder at the miracle of life.

CHAPTER 32

BRILL sat beside Trent at the conference table in her office, David and Sam facing them.

"I want you all to know that, yesterday Rick Ulman completed the first round of questions in the DA's investigation of Sean O'Toole's death. And he's gearing up for a second round of questioning this afternoon."

"How is he holding up?" Trent said.

"It was tough. I reminded him that all he needs to do is tell the truth. He has nothing to hide."

Sam put his fist to his mouth. "I think y'all better brace yourselves for the outcome. Officer Ulman was negligent. The DA's office can hardly conclude otherwise."

Brill bit her lip and then said, "Rick Ulman is a fine police officer, Sam. What happened was unfortunate, but there are extenuating circumstances that need to be considered. I think we should refrain from doing the DA's investigating for him." *Though I'm certain you'll make sure the city council hears your two cents' worth.*

"Now to the most pressing matter." Brill folded her hands on the table. "We all know I'm the only person on Merrick Fountain's hit list who has not yet been targeted. And since he's already taken out two of my detectives in order to intimidate me, we have to prepare for the likelihood that he's planning to go after Trent next."

"I'm ready." Trent patted his chest with both hands. "I'm wearing the ballistic vest Special Agent Riley let me borrow. And I never leave city hall without at least one police officer watching my back. In fact, I hardly go out at all. Which is a real problem since I'm all that's left of our detective division."

"My deputies are helpin' you, aren't they?" Sam said.

Trent nodded. "Yes, and I appreciate it, Sheriff. But we've got a number of ongoing investigations that I've been involved with from the get-go, and I can only stretch so far."

"Rousseaux will be back soon," Brill added, "and I'm working on getting a replacement for O'Toole. But let's get back to the immediate problem. Knowing that Merrick Fountain will likely target you next, I don't think we should wait around, I think we should set a trap and bait him. I'm open to suggestions on how we do it, but I want control." She looked squarely at Trent. "I might add that I would much prefer to *be* the bait, but I don't think Fountain would fall for it. My guess is he's well aware that David is watching my back."

Trent nodded. "I agree. So what trap did you have in mind, Chief? It's got to be something believable that makes me look vulnerable."

"I can think of one," Brill said. "You could drive out to the cemetery and visit O'Toole's gravesite. As I recall, it's just a few yards from the woods, and we could have six of our best officers hidden behind those trees before you get there—and two snipers from Sam's department positioned on high ground.

"We'll make sure the only visitor besides you is Officer Howell, who'll be standing at a grave a comfortable distance away, dabbing her eyes with a hanky to make things appear normal."

A grin slowly spread across Trent's face. "I already like the sound of it."

"Assuming that Fountain is bold enough to follow you into the cemetery," she said, "he'll probably wait a few minutes to pull in behind you. He shouldn't feel threatened since he'll see only two cars—yours, with Sergeant Chavez there, and the lady mourner's."

"Go on," Trent said.

"If he gets out of his car, no doubt he'll pretend to be visiting a gravesite in close proximity to O'Toole's. Meanwhile, you're standing at O'Toole's grave with your back to the cars and your head bowed, and Sergeant Chavez is leaning on the radio car, having a cigarette. Once Chavez senses Fountain is where he wants to be, he'll walk over to the trees and pretend to be relieving himself. With both of you distracted, Fountain would have half a minute or more to make his move." Brill took a sip of Coke. "And when he does, Sergeants Tiller and Huntman will jump out of the back of the radio car in pursuit. If Fountain fails to halt and poses a threat to them or to Trent, the snipers will take him out."

Sam's eyes narrowed. "And if he tries to escape, he'll be spinnin' his wheels because the woods'll be covered, and the entrance and exit blocked. So whether he's on foot or jumps in the car and makes a run for it, we've got him." Sam rubbed his chin. "This seems a little too obvious. Then again, would Fountain be expectin' the obvious?"

"Scenario seems real natural to me," Trent said.

Brill looked over at David. "What do you think?"

"I think Fountain's getting to your last detective would be the ultimate intimidation tactic. I doubt he could resist going for it as long as he feels sure he won't get caught before he gets his hands on *you.*"

Brill shuddered and blinked away the image that popped into her mind.

"Y'all, there's a lot of what-ifs," Sam said. "We don't even know for sure that Fountain's watchin' Trent or that he'll follow him to the cemetery. Or that any of it would go down this way."

Brill tucked a lock of hair behind her ear. "True, but I'm willing to set the bait and hope he swallows it."

Vanessa sat on the back porch, sipping a glass of lemonade and wondering about the man she knew as Ty Nicholson.

Rinnie growled and got up on all fours. "What is it, girl?"

In the next instant Ethan Langley came through the gate, a bouquet of flowers in his hand.

Rinnie's tail swished back and forth, and she whined. Finally Vanessa let go of her, and she jumped up on the screen door.

Ethan walked over to the porch and bounded up the steps. He opened the door, scratched Rinnie's ears and got her settled down, then went over to Vanessa, his smile as wide as the Grand Canyon.

"Hello, pretty lady. I got clearance from your dad and the cops out front to come say congratulations." He kissed her cheek and handed her the bouquet of pale blue daisies.

Vanessa felt almost giddy. "Thanks. It feels great. Scary, but great."

Ethan sat at the opposite end of the glider. "I'll keep my distance. I'm a sweaty mess. I can only stay a minute. I get a half hour for lunch and I've got just enough time to get back. But I really wanted to come over and congratulate you on your big decision."

"I love the flowers. Did you pick blue on purpose?"

"Of course. It's a boy, right? I'm just so happy for you, Vanessa. I know it's been difficult coming to this decision. I was so revved up after you called me last night that I hardly slept."

"Me, either. But it's more because of what my parents told me about Ty."

"Yeah, that was a shocker."

"Do you have any idea how horrible it feels to realize that I compromised everything I believe in for a man whose real name I don't even know? And that my son will have to go through life never knowing who his father really is?"

"I'm sorry. It's got to be hard. But I hope you don't let the downside ruin the upside. You've got your whole life ahead of you. You don't know what God has planned down the road."

Vanessa smiled. "Now that I've decided to do this, I just need to grab a little of Emily's excitement. She's bouncing off the walls. In fact, she wants to take parenting classes so she can learn how to take care of the baby. *And* she wants to be in the delivery room when he's born."

"Really?"

"She wants to be an obstetrician when she grows up. She's convinced she can handle it. I'm not sure *I'm* comfortable with it. We'll see."

"Did your parents seem excited?"

"Not overly. But I think they were so concerned about how I would handle the news about Ty they just wanted to tell me and get it over with."

Ethan laced his fingers. "Well at least you know why the professor lied about his identity and why he disappeared when you decided to have his baby. He was trying to protect you from any permanent connection to whatever it is he's running from. That's worth something."

"I guess I should be grateful."

"Aren't you?"

"Not really. I can't just shake off the anger I've had all these months. It's hard to be grateful for a broken heart."

Tessa sat at the counter at Nick's Grill and glanced over her shoulder for the umpteenth time. She noticed Chief Jessup and Special Agent Riley had come in and were sitting in a booth by the window.

"I wonder what's keeping Gus?" she said.

"We're early." Antonio pointed to his watch. "You're the one who insisted on getting here before noon."

"Well, Gus is always here waiting when we arrive. Wouldn't you know the one day we come early he doesn't?"

Antonio chuckled and patted her hand. "Meddling comes with a price, love."

"Aren't you curious how his date with Maggie went?"

"Of course I am. But the sun doesn't rise and set on the answer." He looked up at the chalkboard on the wall. "I'm hungrier than I am curious. What did Nick say the special was?"

"Grilled tilapia."

"What's that? It sounds too healthy."

"It's fish, Antonio. It comes with sweet potato fries and coleslaw. That's what I'm having."

"No chance I can have a cheeseburger?"

"Sure, if you don't mind celery and carrots for dinner."

"Hey, guys." Gus slid onto the stool at the end of the counter, dressed in khakis and a white polo shirt.

Antonio slapped him on the back. "So how's it going, friend?"

"Really can't complain—*not* today."

"So you had a lovely time with Maggie?" Tessa said, the smell of Gus's cologne all the confirmation she needed.

"I sure did." His toothy grin said a lot more than his three-word reply.

"No overalls," Antonio said, "two days in a row?"

"I'm tryin' to clean up my act—for my lady."

My lady? Tessa covered her smile with her hand. "Did you like the civic theater?"

"It was right nice," Gus said. "And Filbert's was out of this world. White tablecloths, those tall skinny candles, and real flowers. Violin music so you didn't have to holler to carry on a conversation. Maggie said it was the kind of place you go to dine—not just eat. We were there almost two hours."

"It was elegant." Maggie was suddenly standing behind the counter, her green order pad in hand. "Gus and I are going to Knoxville tomorrow night to see *Phantom of the Opera.*"

Gus folded his hands on the counter. "I tried to get her to go on a cruise to Alaska, but she turned me down."

"Call me old-fashioned," Maggie said, "but I think a cruise is an inappropriate *date*—even for people our age."

"Hey, you turned me down when I asked you to marry me."

Maggie gave a dismissive wave, a smile tugging at the corners of her mouth. "First things first. Any takers for the special?"

Gus raised his hand. "One."

"Two," Tessa said.

Antonio rolled his eyes. "I can't pronounce it, but I guess that's what I'm having."   .

Maggie scribbled on her pad. "It's really good. You'll like it. I'll be right back with your drinks."

Brill pushed the other half of her grilled veggie burger aside.

"Sorry you're not hungry," David said. "Stress affects me just the opposite."

Brill's phone vibrated. She glanced at the screen. "It's Captain Dickson." She put the phone to her ear. "Yes, Pate."

"Everyone's in place, ma'am. Both snipers have assumed strategic positions on high ground and six officers are hidden in the woods—none of them visible from the road. Rachel Howell changed into a sundress and sandals and is positioned at a gravesite approximately fifteen yards from where O'Toole is buried. Officers are standing by, ready to block both the entrance and the exit once the suspect has entered the cemetery."

"Good work." She looked over at David and gave a nod. "Captain Norris will call you when he and Sergeant Chavez are on the move. Let's put an end to Merrick Fountain's reign of terror."

"Yes, ma'am."

She folded her phone and held it in her hands. "They're good to go. It's hard not being out there."

"I know, but one target at the cemetery is enough. It was the right call."

Her phone buzzed again.

"It's Kurt. I'd better take it."

"Hi."

"Hi, Chief. I've got to drive over to the Pigeon Forge store and cover for my manager so he can take his son to the doctor. Emily's going to ride with me, and Vanessa's going to take a nap."

"How does she seem today?"

"Relieved, I think. I know *I* am."

"Me too. At least we're all on the same page now."

There was a long pause, but she could tell Kurt was still on the line.

"Have you decided when you're going to proceed with setting the trap?" he finally said.

"Whatever happened to 'don't ask, don't tell'?"

"Yeah, you're right. I get crazy when I know too much."

"Relax. I'm not going anywhere near the action. I love you."

"I love you, too."

Just as Brill ended the call, someone else beeped in. It was Trent.

"Are you ready to roll?" she said.

"We're ready, ma'am. Dickson and I will take it from here."

Brill felt as if her heart would pound out of her chest. *Father, be with him. Be with all of them.* "Play it safe, Trent. No heroics. I don't want to lose another officer to this piece of garbage."

"I'll call you the minute we have him."

Brill put her cell phone on the belt clip and picked up the check. "Come on. Let's get back to the station."

A blast of humid air hit Brill in the face as she pushed open the glass door and left Nick's Grill. She nodded at the two officers parked at a meter across the street, and headed for the small parking lot tucked between Nick's and the Toffee Emporium. She glanced up at the digital numbers displayed at the bank.

"It feels hotter than eighty-seven to me," she said to David.

She turned into the lot and walked to the end of the row where her squad car was parked, and reached in her pocket for the key, David waiting at the passenger door.

"Let's hope Fountain takes the bait," he said. "I can hardly wait for you to lock him up and throw away—" David let out a shriek and fell to the pavement, the unmistakable clicking of a Taser gun coming from behind her.

In the next instant, she was in a choke hold, aware of someone removing her gun from the holster and tossing it under the car— and then something sharp pressed against the side of her neck.

"I could just cut you from ear to ear and be done with it," said an all-too-familiar male voice, "but I have bigger plans for you."

Brill dug her fingernails into Merrick Fountain's flesh, her pulse racing wildly, and struggled to breathe as his bicep tightened like a vice around her throat. Where were the two officers who had watched her come out of Nick's Grill? Was Fountain working alone or did he have a partner?

He pulled her backward, his choke hold even tighter, and she heard what sounded like a van door sliding open.

"Nighty-night." He laughed derisively, and then held a wet cloth over her face. "You're about to live your worst nightmare—or should I say *die?*"

She continued to fight him but felt as if she were falling down a deep hole … falling … falling … into a dark abyss.

CHAPTER 33

BRILL was aware of a damp, musty smell—and a headache so intense that it seemed to immobilize her. She had no recollection of how she came to be sitting on a cold floor, her back flush against a hard surface, her feet and hands bound. She felt sick to her stomach and dreaded the thought that she might vomit.

She was startled by the sound of footsteps coming down stairs.

"Time to wake up, Chief!"

The voice jolted her memory, and Brill opened her eyes just as Merrick Fountain's fist collided with her cheekbone and knocked the back of her head against the wall.

She braced herself for another blow and heard the same taunting laugh that rang in her ears just before she had lost consciousness. Her memory came flooding back with terrifying clarity. How had Merrick managed to catch David off guard and elude the other two officers? Then again, it probably hadn't taken him sixty seconds to tase David, knock her out with chloroform, and drive away with her. Had they figured out what vehicle he used and put out an APB?

"How does it feel to be helpless?" he said.

Brill kept still. She wasn't about to assume the role of victim for his pleasure.

"Hey, I'm talking to you!"

He slapped her across the face, and her mind flashed back to the pictures of his battered ex-wife that had been deemed inadmissible during the murder trial. The creep hated women. How could she engage him in conversation without playing his game?

"No one likes to be helpless," she finally said. "I'm sure you didn't either."

He put his face just inches in front of hers. "You're right. And it's your fault I went to prison, you and your ex-partner—and that arrogant Jason Cromwell."

"We were doing our jobs, Merrick. That's what we were paid to do."

"*Were*—that's right. They're dead. You'll be dead soon. But getting even feels so good. I'm not ready to be done with it yet."

"I'm curious … why didn't you go after Trent?"

"Because that's what you expected me to do. You think I'm stupid?" He grabbed her by the hair.

She looked him squarely in the eyes and fought not to wince. "Hardly. You're cunning. No one would dispute that."

"You have no idea *how* cunning. But you will before it's over." He shoved her head against the wall and let go of her hair. "I'm going after someone close to you, all right. But it ain't Captain Norris. Not when I can get a *two*fer." He raised his eyebrows.

Brill felt her neck muscles tighten. Was he planning to go after Emily and Vanessa? He'd never gone after any family member before. Why was he changing now? Were her officers on his tail? Were they still watching the house?

"Cat got your tongue?" he said.

"What do you want, Merrick? Why don't you just cut to the chase?"

"That'd be boring, don't you think?"

Brill scanned the room. It appeared to be a small basement with two boarded-up windows and a wood staircase.

"Don't even think about it." He kicked her knee with his heel. "You're never getting out of here. I want you to die, knowing what it feels like to be helpless."

"Will it change anything? Will you really feel any better?"

He grinned. "It's working so far. Did you know that Vanessa sneaks out of the house and walks down to that park at the end of your street—alone? The cops planted outside your house are clueless."

Was he lying? How could Vanessa pull that off with two officers watching the house? Why would she? How long had he been stalking her?

"What does Vanessa have to do with anything?"

"Oh, she's the big payback." Merrick's eyes lit up. "You took fifteen years of my life from me. Now I'm going to take something of yours."

"You've got a score to settle with me. I get that. But leave my daughter out of it. She's pregnant, for heaven's sake."

Merrick grabbed her ear, his jaw clenched. "Don't tell me what to do. That badge is useless. You're the victim now."

"That's right. And you're famous. Why change your MO?"

"Because I feel like it." He pulled her ear until she was sure it would fall off.

Brill finally whimpered, and he let go, laughing the same creepy laugh she remembered from his trial.

"I'm going to the park now and wait for Vanessa to come out and play."

"I'm the one you want. Let's settle it right here."

"Oh, we will. I'm going to bring your daughter back and cut her throat right over there. And then I'm going to finish you off."

Brill felt a chill crawl up her spine. What if he really could get to Vanessa?

Lord, help me get out of here. Please protect Vanessa. Give David and Trent wisdom and help them catch this guy before he hurts anyone else.

Vanessa glanced at the kitchen clock. It had been ten minutes since her dad and Emily left for Pigeon Forge. They wouldn't be back for hours. Would there ever be a better time to go to the park?

She took three one-dollar bills out of her purse and tucked them in the pocket of her sundress. She had been craving hot dogs all day. Surely the vendor was in the park on Wednesdays.

She set the security alarm and went out the back door. She scratched Rinnie's chin, then slipped out the back gate and turned right in the alley—out of Tessa's line of vision. She went around the block and circled back to Azalea Lane, then walked to the end of the street.

The park was more crowded than she thought it would be on a weekday. A little boy who looked to be about Emily's age occupied her tree swing, and a young woman and several preschool-age children sat at the nearby picnic table. Vanessa ambled past them, wondering how it would feel when she came to the park with her baby in a stroller.

She thought about Ethan giving up his lunch break to bring her blue daisies. How good it felt to have such a sensitive and thoughtful friend—one she could talk to and who seemed to understand.

She strolled down the earthen path that snaked through a grove of towering shade trees, enjoying the sounds of nature—the cawing of a crow … the wind in the trees … the clear, crisp song of a Carolina wren. It felt good to get out of the house and out from under the watchful eye of the police department—and her nosy neighbor.

She stayed on the earthen path and passed only two other people before she came out into the open again and headed across the rolling grounds to the duck pond.

She heard footsteps pounding the ground behind her, and then something grabbed her around the throat. A hairy arm. She scratched and clawed and tried to scream, but the more she fought, the less air she had.

"Make a sound, and you won't live to see that kid born."

Vanessa felt something sharp pressed against her neck. Her heart hammered, her mind racing with every awful thing this man might do to her.

"We're going to walk nice and easy to that white van parked at the curb. Make a sound—any sound—and I'll slice you so you'll bleed out before help can arrive. *And* I'll kill your mother. Yeah, I've got her, too. She's waiting for us."

Vanessa felt light-headed, her knees weak. David was supposed to be watching her mother's back. How could anyone have gotten close enough to kidnap her?

The attacker pushed her toward the van, one hand clutching her wrist, the other holding a knife to her throat. The only other person she saw was an elderly man walking a schnauzer, and he seemed oblivious to what was happening.

Vanessa thought her heart would beat out of her chest. If she got in the van, would she ever be found alive? Was she better off fighting and taking her chances? Would he really kill her mother?

A loud popping noise shattered her thoughts, and her attacker let go and fell to the ground, holding his chest and yelling obscenities. A black sedan sped away, its tires squealing as it rounded the corner.

She stood frozen, staring at the face of the man who had accosted her and was now writhing on the ground, his hands bloody from the chest wound.

He tried to grab her ankle, and she took off running toward home, never once glancing over her shoulder. He was a dead ringer for Merrick Fountain. She'd seen his mug shot. It had to be him. And if he kidnapped her mother, he intended to kill her whether or not Vanessa had cooperated.

She ran as fast as she could, then stumbled and fell on the sidewalk. She picked herself up, her knees scraped and bleeding, and kept going. Finally she saw the black Impala parked out in front of her house and headed straight for it.

"Help!" she cried. "Help! He's got my mother!"

She ran up to the driver's side window and banged on it.

The officer looked startled. He opened the door and got out.

"Vanessa, where have you been? We searched the house, looking for you."

"I was at the park. He tried to kidnap me. He's got my mother. He's going to kill her!"

The officer put a hand on each of her shoulders and looked into her eyes. "Who has your mother?"

"Merrick Fountain. He just tried to kidnap me."

"Start at the beginning, and tell me what happened."

Vanessa caught her breath and explained that she had gone for a walk in the park and Merrick Fountain had accosted her, threatened her, and tried to kidnap her. And then someone in a black car had shot him, and she escaped while he lay wounded on the ground.

"He said he had my mother, and if I made a sound, he'd kill her."

"Vanessa, listen to me," the officer said. "Someone tasered Special Agent Riley and kidnapped your mother. We called your dad. He was on his way to Pigeon Forge and turned around. He'll be home shortly. We called you, and when there was no answer, we went in the house and discovered you were gone. We reported you missing, too."

"I'm sorry," she said, aware that the other officer was already on the police radio, relaying information. "I just wanted fresh air and some time by myself. I'm so sorry."

"We'll need a description of the white van and the black car. We've already dispatched officers to the park. If the guy's still there, we'll get him."

Vanessa heard a sing-songy voice and turned toward it. Tessa Masino was in the middle of the street, walking briskly toward her, her hand waving in the air.

"Yoo-hoo … Vanessa … are you all right, dear?"

"Please don't touch her, ma'am." The police officer held out his palm. "We need to process Vanessa's clothes for DNA evidence."

"The man who's been threatening Mom tried to kidnap me." Vanessa put her hand over her mouth and tried not to cry. "If the man in the black car hadn't shot him, he would've succeeded. But he's got Mom ..."

"Heaven help us," Tessa said. "I need to go call the prayer chain."

Brill heard footsteps walking across the floor upstairs, and then the light came on, and she heard someone coming down the stairs.

Fountain rounded the staircase and marched over to her, his expression angry, his chest blood-soaked. He punched her in the face.

"You're not getting out of here alive just because your daughter got away. She was an afterthought anyhow."

Vanessa got away?

He grabbed his chest and groaned, and then let out a string of curse words. "Who was in the black car?"

"If it was an Impala, it was probably the officers who've been watching my house."

"It wasn't no Impala. It was some foreign job."

Brill shook her head. "I don't know."

Merrick kicked her in the ribs and then groaned, his hands grabbing his chest. "Don't lie to me. How'd your cops know I'd be in the park?"

"I don't know what you're talking about."

"Your people were waiting for me. Look what they did." He moved his hands and she could see the wound oozing blood.

"I've been right here, Merrick. No phone. No way to communicate. I have no idea what happened in the park."

"Someone shot me, and your daughter bolted. That's what happened!"

Good for her. Thank You, Lord.

Merrick put his face in front of Brill's. "It ain't over till I say it's over." He wrapped his fingers around her neck and squeezed, but his grip was weak and he let go.

"What do I need to put on this wound?" he said.

"What you *need* is a doctor."

"Well, I ain't going to the emergency room. So what's your second choice? And don't tell me you don't know. I read in the paper that you helped save that detective after I stuck him."

"You need to stop the bleeding and get the bullet out of there."

"I ain't removing it myself, and I sure ain't giving you the knife."

Merrick's face turned a peculiar shade of gray. He put his hand over his mouth, stumbled over to the corner of the basement, and retched until he emptied his stomach. He wiped his mouth with a handkerchief, and then sat against the far wall, hugging himself and rocking.

"You need medical attention, Merrick. You've lost a lot of blood. You could die."

"Like I care. You think I want to go back to that hellhole?"

It would be better than the hell that awaits you when you die.

She studied him: the epitome of evil suddenly fragile. Merrick Fountain was somebody's baby. How had he ended up at the bottom of the heap? Maybe his parents abused him or exposed him to violence at a young age. But what had caused him to hate women so? Had a woman broken his heart? Or crushed his spirit? Perhaps his mother? Was he hopelessly lost? Did God see him that way?

Could she afford to care? The guy planned to kill her daughter. He'd killed one of her best officers and her former partner. And he had one mission left in life: to stick a knife in her gut. This was not the time to care about where he was going to serve out his eternal sentence.

CHAPTER 34

VANESSA sat on the couch between her father and Emily, her scraped knees bandaged and throbbing, the baby kicking even more than usual.

Because they were now dealing with a kidnapping, the FBI had officially taken over the case. She wondered if David Riley would ever stop asking her questions and let her go to her room and think.

"Just to be clear," David said, "did the guy actually *say* he was Merrick Fountain?"

Vanessa shook her head. "I recognized him from the mug shot, but not until after he fell on the ground and I saw his face. I'm sure it was him."

"And he didn't give you any idea where he planned to take you or where your mother was being held?"

"No, he just said she was waiting for us. I wasn't even sure I believed him, but I wasn't about to argue with a guy holding a knife to my throat."

"Did he say how he knew you were at the park?"

"No."

"Vanessa, tell me again what you did at the park the times you snuck out."

"Nothing much. I swung on the tree swing. Watched people. Enjoyed the view of the mountains. Ate hot dogs. Talked to Micah."

"Yes, the elderly gentleman I met at the department store. Tell me again what you remember about him."

Vanessa told David how she met Micah Harvey, gave an overview of their conversations, and explained how she was surprised the day she saw him sprinting.

"I got paranoid because I'd never seen an old person move that fast. But Micah said he used to run marathons and that's why he was so limber."

David made a note on his pad. "Tell me again why he wore blue contacts?"

"He didn't say *why*. But I think he was embarrassed I made a big deal out of it."

"And what about the Carter House?"

"He said he wasn't listed as a resident because he was moving the next day, and they'd already taken him off their listing. That's when he told me about his bad diagnosis."

David lifted an eyebrow. "Was Micah the same height as Merrick Fountain?"

"I never really saw Fountain on his feet, so I can't say. But Micah was a lot thinner and didn't have a big belly. He really was a nice old man. I feel so bad that he's dying."

"So you believed his story that he had three to six months to live and was moving to Nashville to live with his son?"

Vanessa nodded. "You should've seen his face. He wasn't lying. It shouldn't be that hard to find him. If I remember right, his son's name is Charles."

"I'm curious about the black sedan you said his grandson was driving. Could it have been the same car you saw today? Could Micah's grandson have shot Merrick Fountain?"

"Maybe. It could've been the same car. I'm not sure. But if Micah's grandson was trying to protect me, why didn't he stop?"

David sat forward in the chair, his feet planted on the floor, his hands clasped between his knees. "Good question. Tell me what you know about the grandson."

"Just that he came to Sophie Trace to try to pressure Micah into giving him drug money. I guess it's possible he could've seen what was happening to me and shot Fountain. If he's into the drug culture, that would explain why he didn't want to get involved with the police. I don't see why you care *who* shot Merrick Fountain. He did you a favor."

"I'm afraid it doesn't work that way."

"Vanessa, Mom said regular people aren't allowed to take the law into their own hands." Emily looked up at her. "I still can't believe you snuck out and let everyone think you were at home. That's the same as lying."

Emily's words stung. Nothing like being reprimanded by the little sister she should have set a good example for.

"We'll talk about this later," Kurt said. "All I care about right now is finding your mother."

"Me, too." David slapped his knee and stood. "And Micah's grandson might know something that'll help us do that. I'm going to have my agents check with the Carter House and see if they have a forwarding address for Micah Harvey. Maybe he can put us in touch with his grandson. Why don't the three of you go rest? I'll call you if anything breaks."

Brill could see that Merrick was getting weaker and more agitated. How long could she keep him talking before he decided to do what he'd brought her here to do?

At least Vanessa had gotten away. The black car was a mystery, but whoever shot Merrick probably saved her daughter's life. She had to believe that Vanessa made it home safely and told David, Kurt, and Emily of her narrow escape.

Poor Emily would probably need counseling after this. Kurt's blood pressure was likely off the charts. The FBI would have taken over the case since it now involved a kidnapping. She hoped David might be allowed to work the case even though he'd been victimized.

She knew firsthand how it felt to be tasered. When Taser guns were introduced to law enforcement, she had asked to be shot so that she would understand its effectiveness. The pain was forever ingrained in her memory.

So far she had endured the pain Merrick had inflicted. But what could she expect as he became more anxious? How much meaner would he get before he finally came at her with a knife?

Merrick struggled to his feet, the T-shirt he was holding over the wound almost completely soaked in blood.

Lord, help me get out of here. Or give me the grace to endure whatever's next.

"You need a doctor," she said.

"I ain't giving myself up. Forget it."

"My officers will figure out where we are anyway. You can make demands. They'll listen."

"Not interested." Merrick grabbed her around the throat and then let go with a shove and a groan. "I'm going upstairs to get a clean shirt."

Brill was relieved as he walked away but dreaded his coming back. He'd waited fifteen years to get even, and he wasn't about to let the moment be stolen from him.

Her thoughts turned to Kurt. How she loved him! And how ironic it was that she was going to die just when the two of them had finally reestablished the trust that had been broken because of his affair with Victoria. The shrill pitch of betrayal had shattered two decades of happiness into a million sharp fragments that only God could put back together. And He had done it so beautifully. Why did it have to end like this?

Lord, why am I here? Why have You allowed this moment in my life? There has to be a reason.

The thought of being murdered terrified her. But she held on to the assurance that soon she would be looking into the face of Jesus.

What would happen to her kids? Would Ryan recover? He was unstoppable. He would grieve through the loss and graduate from Vanderbilt and go on to law school. He had a bright future.

What about Emily? Would she get over the horror of losing her mom this way? Not without God's help. But if Brill could forgive Kurt and let God restore her marriage, surely Emily could let God heal the deep wound that would be there. Her close relationship with her dad and her growing faith would be her anchor.

But Vanessa was much more complicated. What about the unresolved resentment between them? Brill realized she had unwit-

tingly reinforced Vanessa's insecurities, though she never expected
any more of Vanessa than she expected of herself or the other kids.
Why couldn't she have followed Kurt's lead and just appreciated
that Vanessa wasn't competitive or wired to excel scholastically?
Ryan and Emily thrived on the challenge. But Vanessa felt increas-
ingly doomed to fail. She had a sweet, giving spirit and was amazing
with children. She was well on her way to getting her degree in
elementary education. Did it really matter that she didn't make the
dean's list?

Brill blinked the stinging from her eyes. What she wouldn't give
to pull Vanessa into her arms and tell her how sorry she was for
expecting her to be something she wasn't. To tell her that she was
wonderful just the way God made her—and that her son would soon
be the joy of the family.

Or would he? Would Vanessa change her mind about being a
single mom if her family was torn apart by Brill's murder? Wasn't it
the support of the family that had given her the courage to take on
the responsibility of raising her son?

Brill's eyes clouded over, and she was suddenly overwhelmed.
She didn't want to die. Her family needed her. But the Lord knew
that. Whatever happened, He would use it for His good purpose.
But did that negate her regrets? Her unfinished business? The words
she never got around to saying?

Lord, I'm not ready to die. I need more time.

She heard Merrick coming down the stairs and lamented that her
hands were tied and she couldn't wipe the tears off her face. Showing
weakness was a sure way to invite more abuse. She wondered how
battered wives lived with the fear day after day.

Vanessa lay across her bed and heard a knock on her door.

"Come in."

The door opened. "It's Dad."

Kurt came over and sat on the side of the bed. "How're you doing?"

"Terrible." She wiped her eyes and turned over, her pulse racing. "Did they find Mom?"

"Not yet."

"I'm so scared …" Vanessa's voice failed.

Kurt brushed her cheek with his hand. "I'm praying they'll find her alive and well. She's resilient. And she's smart."

Smarter than a guy who's eluded police and killed two cops, wounded two others, killed a DA, and tasered Mom's bodyguard?

"I know what you're thinking," Kurt said. "Let's not go there. I just looked at the pictures David took in the park. There's a very distinct blood trail from the place where Fountain got shot to where they believe he got into the van. He was bleeding pretty badly. It's possible he never even made it back to where he was holding your mother. He might be dead." Kurt brushed the hair off her wet face. "Your mom could be safe and working on how to free herself."

"What if she can't? What if no one ever finds her?"

"Honey, have faith—in God, in law enforcement, and in your mother. She's one resourceful lady."

Vanessa wanted to ask what would happen if Fountain *did* make it back, but she couldn't make herself say the words out loud.

"Dad, I'm sorry I snuck out."

"What were you thinking, Vanessa? You knew Merrick Fountain was out there. We were trying to protect you, not smother you."

"I know. But having cops following me everywhere was oppressive. I honestly didn't think slipping out the back and going to the park would be much of a risk since Fountain hadn't gone after anyone else's family members. How was I supposed to know I'd be the first?"

"What really frosts me is that you deceived me. You looked me straight in the eyes, knowing you were going out as soon as I left the house. I thought we were closer than that."

"We are. But I'm almost twenty-one, and Mom treats me like I'm still a teenager. I wasn't trying to be rebellious. I just needed air. I'm an adult. I should be allowed to think for myself."

"Then why didn't you tell us that? We could've at least discussed it."

Vanessa sighed. "I probably should've, but I never get very far discussing things with Mom. I'm not sure what my place is at home now that I've been away at college. I'm used to making my own decisions."

"They haven't all been good ones, Vanessa."

"Neither have yours. But that doesn't mean Mom gets to make all your decisions now."

Kurt's face turned red.

"I didn't mean that the way it sounded." Vanessa sat up and threw her arms around him. "What I'm trying to say is just because we messed up doesn't mean we're forever incapable of making good decisions."

"Fair enough," Kurt said. "But we need to trust your mother's judgment when it comes to police work. She was just trying to keep us safe."

"I know. I'm sorry. Please don't make me feel worse than I already do. Why did Merrick Fountain have to come after me when he never bothered anyone else's kids?"

Kurt pulled back and looked in her eyes. "I don't know, honey. But at least we now know that he's the one who kidnapped your mother—and that he's seriously wounded. Maybe Micah's grandson knows something. Let's hope David can find him."

Brill saw Merrick round the stairwell. She had hoped he would collapse and never make it back. His breathing seemed labored, but his stamina surprised her. He had padded his shirt with something and was carrying what appeared to be a bottle of whiskey.

That's all she needed. History had shown him to be a mean drunk. And a broken bottle could make a dangerous weapon.

Merrick grabbed her by the hair, his face covered in perspiration.

"When I've finished this bottle of Jack Daniels, we're both going to die."

His breath already reeked of whiskey. The bottle was two-thirds empty. Hard to tell how much he had drunk when he was upstairs. He let her go, then slapped her face, laughing derisively.

"Feeling helpless, are you, without your Glock and the boys in blue watching out for you?"

Lord, You're watching out for me, aren't You? Give me the grace to die with dignity.

Merrick took a swig of whiskey. Whatever he'd stuffed under his shirt hadn't stopped the bleeding.

"You've got a fever," she said. "You need a doctor."

"Ain't gonna happen."

"Do you really want to die?"

"After I kill you."

"And then what? What happens when you die? Will it be over? Will you find peace?"

"How should I know?"

"Well, aren't you even curious about it?"

He waved the whiskey bottle in front of her. "No. What will be, will be. End of story."

"Do you really believe it's the end?"

"Shut up. I don't want to talk about it."

"Yes, you do. We all do."

"I said I don't."

"I'd be a lousy Christian if I didn't care what happens to you."

Merrick scoffed. "Why would you care? You're a cop, and I'm a loser ex-con. A drain on society."

"Not in God's eyes."

"*Especially* in God's eyes! Shut up, or I'll knock those perfect teeth right out of your head."

Brill had no doubt he was capable of it. The pictures in Mrs. Fountain's case file were still vivid in her memory. But what did she have to lose by keeping the conversation going? He was going to kill her anyway.

"I have a question for you," she said.

"What is it about 'shut up' you don't understand?"

"If you knew someone loved you more than life itself, would it make any difference?"

"How should I know? No one ever has."

"Actually, someone *always* has."

"Yeah, right. Who would that be—my old man, who beat the tar out of me just for existing, or mommy dearest, who turned her back while I screamed for help?"

"God loved you before you were ever born, Merrick. He created you to *be* something. He has a plan for your life. It's never too late to do what's right."

"I told you to shut up!" Merrick stomped on her leg. "God doesn't give a rip about me. Where was He when I needed Him?"

"He was always there. You just didn't know it."

"Then why didn't He *make* me know? I was a helpless little kid, for crying out loud."

"But you're not helpless now."

"No, *you* are." He grabbed her by the hair and pulled until her eyes watered. "How does it feel?"

"Probably as awful as when you were helpless."

"Good answer." He let go and shoved her head against the wall. "Still think God loves me?"

"I know He does—and like no one else ever could."

"I'm a killer."

"He knows that, Merrick. Everything's forgivable if you're truly sorry."

"Who says I'm sorry? What if I've enjoyed every sweet moment of revenge?" He smirked. "Trust me, there ain't no way God could love me when I get done with you."

Merrick drank the last of the whiskey, then set the bottle on the floor and pulled a knife out of his sock. His eyes had the same wild look they had at the murder trial.

Brill broke out in a cold sweat, her heart pounding frantically. In a matter of seconds, she would be face-to-face with the Creator of the universe, her Lord and Savior. And Merrick would enter a hell worse than the tortured existence he'd made for himself, separated from God by a chasm of unbelief. And there was nothing she could do about it.

CHAPTER 35

VANESSA sat with her dad, Emily, and Ryan at the kitchen table, the heaviness in her heart rendering her almost mute. What were the odds that her mother was still alive? There had been no ransom note. No demands. Hadn't Merrick Fountain made it clear what he intended to do? Since no reports had come in that he had run his van off the road or been involved in an accident, wasn't it logical to think he went back to her mother and made good on his threat?

Her dad's face was pallid and expressionless, his eyes vacant. It was as if a part of him were missing.

"I'm going to be strong." Emily folded her arms across her chest. "Mom would expect us to be."

"Just because we don't feel like talking doesn't mean we're not strong," Ryan said.

Emily sighed. "But it's depressing just sitting around."

The doorbell rang.

"That's the Masinos." Emily raced out of the kitchen.

Vanessa heard voices, and then Tessa strolled into the kitchen, Antonio on her heels and carrying several plastic containers.

"My sweetheart made dinner." Antonio set the containers on the countertop.

"There's sliced ham," Tessa said, "and au gratin potatoes, and fresh green beans. Everything's hot, but it can be reheated if you'd rather have it later. There's chocolate cake, too."

Her dad got up and put his arm around Tessa. "Thanks. That's so thoughtful of you. I hadn't even begun to think of dinner, but we really should eat something."

Tessa cupped his cheek in her hand. "I called the prayer chain at our church and yours. Hundreds of people are standing with you."

"I can't thank you enough. How do people get through things like this when they don't know that God is in control?"

"But He is, isn't He?" Tessa stroked Emily's ponytail. "Just like He was with us."

Emily nodded.

Antonio went over to Vanessa and put his hand on her shoulder. "How are you feeling, honey? Are your knees sore?"

"I haven't moved much, but they hurt when I bend them. Considering what almost happened, scraped knees are no big deal."

"Did Special Agent Riley figure out who shot your attacker?"

Vanessa looked into Antonio's kind eyes. "No, just someone in a black sedan. He's following up on a lead, but he asked us not to discuss it with anyone right now."

Nick stood behind the counter at the Grill, listening to the six o'clock news on the flat-screen TV mounted on the wall.

The FBI has now confirmed that Police Chief Brill Jessup is believed to have been kidnapped by Merrick Fountain, the fifty-six-year-old ex-con who, fifteen years ago, when he was convicted of second degree murder in the stabbing death of his brother-in-law, threatened to come after the chief, her former partner, Zack Rogers, and District Attorney Jason Cromwell.

Fountain was released from Holbrook State Penitentiary less than four weeks ago. Since that time, authorities believe he has been on a revenge spree and has stabbed and killed both Rogers and Cromwell.

Authorities believe Fountain is also responsible for attacks on two officers on the Sophie Trace police force: Detective Sean O'Toole, who died after being stabbed and later poisoned, and Detective Beau Jack Rousseaux, who survived the stabbing and is expected to make a full recovery.

Authorities here believe these officers were targeted to intimidate Chief Jessup, and had taken strong measures to ensure her safety.

The FBI would not comment on specific details surrounding Chief Jessup's kidnapping, citing the open investigation, but an unnamed source in the sheriff's department told WSTN News that Merrick Fountain used a Taser gun to disable an off-duty FBI official who had accompanied Chief Jessup to lunch at a local restaurant.

The source also stated that Fountain later went to Cherokee Valley Park where he accosted Vanessa Jessup, the chief's pregnant twenty-year-old daughter, and tried to force her into a late-model white Dodge Caravan. According to the daughter, Fountain was shot by someone driving a black sedan, possibly an Acura or a Toyota Avalon.

As of this hour, authorities are not saying whether they have any leads in the case, whether they know who shot Fountain, or even what the motivation might have been.

Meanwhile, the congregation at Cross Way Bible Fellowship, where Chief Jessup and her family attend church, is holding a candlelight vigil.

For now, it's a watch-and-wait situation. WSTN will bring you breaking news as it happens.

In other news tonight …

"What a mess," Gus said. "It's a sad state of affairs when a criminal can get his hands on a Taser gun. Tough break for the chief."

Maggie nodded. "It's downright depressing. I wonder if we should cancel our reservations to *Phantom of the Opera*."

"You say that like you're expecting bad news," Nick said.

Maggie shrugged. "I hope not. But except for Detective Rousseaux, this monster hasn't left any survivors."

Nick looked up and did a double take at the Masinos walking toward him. "Welcome, friends. I didn't expect to see you twice today."

Tessa sat at the counter, Antonio next to her. Nick could tell by their faces that they'd heard the news.

"I'm sorry about Chief Jessup," he said. "I know she's a personal friend."

"The whole family is very dear to us." Tessa sighed. "Antonio and I didn't want to be alone."

"I'm glad you came here."

Gus nodded and took Maggie's hand. "You know anything they're not tellin' on the news?"

"Not really," Antonio said. "Tessa and I took dinner over to the Jessups, but they're not supposed to discuss the case. They all looked grim."

"How's their daughter?"

"Vanessa's going to be all right," Antonio said. "But she's been through quite an ordeal. Poor kid. Fountain told her outright that he'd kidnapped her mother, and he was holding a knife to her throat when someone shot him."

"And we're worried about Emily." Tessa lifted her eyes. "She's still not over the last episode."

Antonio shook his head. "It's not looking good. I'd feel better if Fountain had made some kind of contact. I'm not sure that this is a 'no news is good news' situation."

"I don't want to think the worst," Maggie said. "But this could be tragic all the way around."

Nick saw Tessa's eyes brimming with tears and looked away. None of it seemed real.

Kurt sat with David at the kitchen table, listening to the sound of the clock ticking and the slow drip of the faucet. The pinkish glow of the western sky was quickly fading.

"I feel like I should be doing something besides just sitting here while my wife is …" Kurt's voice broke, and he took a sip of water. "What are the odds she's still alive? Tell me the truth."

"I don't play the odds with people I care about," David said. "I'm giving the case a hundred and ten percent. Let's stay focused on that."

Kurt studied the tough FBI man who had worked with Brill on numerous cases over the years. A five o'clock shadow covered his face and head, and deep ridges had formed above his eyebrows. This David looked a decade older than the one he'd shared breakfast with.

"You care a lot about Brill, don't you?" Kurt said.

"She's a good friend. A great cop. I'd do anything for her."

Kurt took his index finger and traced the pattern on the ceramic fruit bowl in the center of the table. "Just so you know … she told me about the kiss."

"I'm sorry it happened. I'd just broken up with Patricia and was feeling lost. Brill put me in my place. I hope she told you that, too."

"She did. But my affair left her vulnerable, and I know the kiss wasn't one-sided. We all made mistakes. Brill and I let it go. The only reason I'm bringing it up now is so you and I can clear the air."

"So we're okay?"

"On the past, yeah." Kurt raked his hands through his hair. "I'm not sure how to deal with the present, though. I feel like I'm trapped in a nightmare that I can't allow to end or I'll be dealing with the unthinkable."

David held his wrist. "Don't go there. Cops don't come any more intuitive than Brill. If there's a way to get out alive, she'll find it."

Big if. Kurt understood the implications of Brill's capture becoming Fountain's finale. She had no firearm, no way to protect herself from a murdering misogynist who reveled in physical abuse and marital rape and outweighed her by a hundred pounds. He could use her as a piñata, if he wanted. He blinked away the images that popped into his mind.

Lord, be with her. Don't let her suffer. If she's going to die, let her die with dignity.

Kurt swallowed the ball of emotion in his throat. "I hate being out of control. I felt this same way when I couldn't protect Emily."

"I remember," David said. "I'm so sorry you have to feel this kind of fear and helplessness again. I never saw it coming, Kurt. Fountain fired the Taser gun before I even saw him. He outsmarted me. And believe me, the *O* word is hard for a fed to admit."

"I don't blame you or the officers who sat outside Nick's and didn't see what Fountain was doing. He outsmarted everyone. Revenge is a powerful incentive. I'm convinced he would've gotten to Brill no matter what defenses she put in place." Kurt choked back the fear that tore at his heart. "I'm just afraid that he'll unleash all the rage he has left on her."

Kurt's cell phone rang and he looked at the screen. "Excuse me. I want to take this … Hi, Tessa."

"I hope you'll forgive the intrusion," she said. "I felt impressed to call and say, 'The battle is the Lord's.'"

Tessa's words seemed to echo in his spirit. "I really do know that. But I needed to hear it. Thanks."

"There's an army praying for Brill. She's not alone, no matter what."

Kurt swallowed hard. "You're right. Thanks for reminding me."

"That's really all I had to say. Antonio and I are on our knees. Call us if we can do anything. We love you."

"I know. We love you, too."

Kurt bowed his head and sat for a moment in the peace that seemed to lift him above the fray.

"I overheard the conversation," David said. "Sorry. I think you had it on speakerphone."

"That's all right."

There was a long pause, and then David said, "You know, I don't understand this whole faith thing. But I've seen it work too many times to deny there's something to it. How do you Christians just turn it on?"

"We don't. Faith takes practice. It starts out fragile and gets stronger each time we use it. If we learn to trust God with the little things, the more we're able to trust Him with the big stuff."

"Are you saying you trust God to get Brill out alive?"

"I'm saying I trust God, period. And I know He'll use this awful situation for good, regardless of how it turns out." Why was he trying to explain faith while he sat there, trembling? How could David understand that in the flesh he was terrified—but in his spirit, he was confident the Lord was in control?

David's cell phone rang. "Sorry to interrupt, but I've been waiting for this." He put the phone to his ear. "Special Agent Riley … Good, what'd you'd find out …? You're sure? Did you run it through the computer …? Well, that's certainly not what I was expecting. Okay, thanks."

David put his phone in his pocket. "The forwarding address Micah Harvey gave the Carter House is not his son's Nashville residence. In fact, it's bogus. We checked every variation of the numerals and the spelling of the street name and cross-referenced it with *every* Harvey listed—not just Charles—and came up blank."

Kurt sighed. "Which means you can't find his grandson."

"I have serious doubts it was his grandson in that black sedan. It's hard to say how much of what Micah Harvey told Vanessa was a lie. I need to talk to her again and see what else she can remember. There might be something true in his litany of lies that would point to whoever was in the black sedan. I'm just not sure the shooting is connected to the kidnapping."

"This gets weirder by the minute."

David patted Kurt on the shoulder. "Let me worry about it. Why don't you go do something to get your mind off the waiting? It might be a long night."

CHAPTER 36

VANESSA lay in bed, Emily asleep in her arms, and watched the ceiling fan go round and round. Had she ever felt this empty? Maybe she did when Ty left, but she had only known him for a couple months. Her mother had been there all her life. The thought that she might never see her mother again was almost more than she could bear.

"Your tears are getting me wet." Emily dabbed Vanessa's face with the sheet.

"Sorry, Shortcake."

"Are you thinking about Mom?"

Vanessa wasn't sure what to say. She didn't want to worry Emily, but her little sister was so perceptive that it was futile to talk around it.

"That's okay," Emily said. "I know you are. Me, too. Did I tell you I prayed for a guardian angel to protect Mom? He—I guess it's a *he*—won't let anything happen to her."

Vanessa didn't say anything. Maybe Emily would just keep talking and answer all her own questions.

"Oh, brother. It's already dark outside." Emily sighed. "I wanted us to get in the car and go look for Mom. Where would we look? Everywhere, I guess. It's better than just waiting around. I wonder what Dad's doing. Maybe he needs us."

Vanessa glanced at the clock. It was ten forty-five. He was probably gearing up for the eleven o'clock news.

Emily pressed her ear against Vanessa's tummy. "The baby's kicking. And I hear gurgling in there."

How would the family handle a new baby if her mother was dead and each of them was grieving? All her emotional energy had gone into the decision to keep him, and she felt as if she would die if anything happened to change it now. She pictured the family sitting around the Thanksgiving and Christmas table—a high chair replacing the empty straight-back chair that would have been her mother's.

"You're crying again." Emily sat up and plucked a tissue from the box on the nightstand and wiped Vanessa's tears. "I don't want you to be sad. And it might make the baby sad. You need to have happy thoughts."

"I'm all for that. I sure didn't ask to feel this way."

"Me, either. I know what it feels like for someone to threaten to kill you if you don't stay quiet."

Vanessa stroked Emily's hair. "I know you do. You were very brave."

"Mom taught me to be brave when all those people started disappearing, so I practiced being brave and knew how when I had to. Now it's her turn. The guardian angel will help her."

We can only hope. Lord, send a multitude.

Kurt sat in the overstuffed chair and watched the news. He didn't hear anything new reported or even a spark of hope in the voices of the news anchors.

"Why don't you go to bed?" David said. "The kids are all sacked out. It's a good time to rest. Brill would want you to."

Kurt looked at the flowers on the entry hall table. She was the only woman he'd ever loved. And he wanted to spend the rest of his life making up for his brief and completely stupid affair that had almost destroyed his family. But there hadn't been enough time yet.

Lord, please don't punish me by taking Brill away from me. Not now. Not when we finally have things together again.

"Did she tell you we met in college?" Kurt said.

"Yeah, but she didn't elaborate."

"We were in the same political science class our senior year. She was impossible to ignore—a sassy redhead with a temperament to match." Kurt smiled. "Did you know her real name is Colleen?"

"I did, but I'd forgotten. I know she got the nickname Brill when she was at the police academy."

"Short for brilliant. I think the powers that be knew she'd be going up the ranks. She always wanted to be in law enforcement—well, after she got over wanting to be a lion tamer. That ended in about the third grade."

David chuckled. "Why am I not surprised?"

"Brill was the only student in our political science class who had the guts to challenge the views of the liberal professor. He was amused. I was *impressed*. I finally got the nerve to ask her out. I couldn't believe she said yes. I found out we had a lot in common. And we were both Christians, so we weren't into drinking and partying."

"Clear back then, eh?"

Kurt nodded. "Brill more than me. We spent a lot of time hanging out at the Baptist Student Union. And she got me involved in Campus Crusade for Christ. In the beginning, I only got involved because she did. But that's when I got serious about my faith."

"When did you get married?"

"A month after we graduated. We were crazy in love. We caught a plane after the reception and flew to New York for our honeymoon. That was my parents' wedding gift to us."

Kurt's mind flashed back to that first morning when he woke up next to his bride, the morning sun filtering through the sheers that covered the wall of windows in their fancy hotel room. Brill looked beautiful, her long red hair and bright blue eyes a contrast to the white sheets. He remembered thinking she looked like a storybook princess but thought it would sound corny if he told her so.

"We had kids right off the bat. Ryan was born on our first wedding anniversary."

"You're kidding."

Kurt arched his eyebrows. "Vanessa came thirteen months later. Brill gave it another year and then entered the police academy. We juggled schedules, but we were young and energetic. I never felt like the kids missed out with both of us working. Most of the time, they were with one of us and not a babysitter."

"Now *I'm* impressed. Patricia and I don't have kids. I've never understood how you manage career and family."

"You learn as you go. It was doable. By the time Emily came along ten years later, Ryan and Vanessa were more help than trouble. Brill stayed out of the field when she was pregnant, then went right back to it. She was partners with Zack then."

"That's when I met her," David said. "We worked a few cases together when she was a detective."

Kurt's mind raced in reverse, so many highlights vivid in his memory. He shuddered to think that, by this time tomorrow, memories might be all he had left of Brill.

Vanessa left Emily asleep in the double bed and went out to the bathroom. Through the wall, she could hear Ryan snoring. She wondered if he felt funny sleeping in a bed with a lavender ruffle or if he was too depressed to care.

She pressed the auto dial on her cell phone and hoped she didn't get Ethan's voice mail. It seemed almost cruel, calling him at this hour, especially when he had to get up at five.

"Hello," said a sleepy voice.

"Ethan, it's Vanessa."

"Are you all right?" Suddenly he sounded wide awake. "I've been worried sick about you. I started to call a couple times but then I hung up. I didn't think I should bother you right now."

"I've been walking around in a daze, but everything is starting to sink in. I'm so scared ..." Her voice failed, and she took a slow, deep breath and tried to relax. "The FBI has no idea where my mother is, or even if she's alive. It's like a morgue around here."

"I heard on the news that your church was holding a vigil. I went over there for a while. You wouldn't believe how many people showed up and are praying. It was very touching."

"I'd love to go thank them, but I can't seem to get past myself at the moment."

"That's understandable. Are you hurt at all? From what I

heard on the news, the creep got shot in the act of kidnapping you."

"He did. But he held a knife to my throat and threatened to kill my mother and me if I made a sound. I just hope this kind of stuff doesn't affect a baby in the womb."

"Man, I'd love to get my hands on this guy. Does the FBI have *any* leads?"

"Not exactly. But do you remember the old man I was talking to in the park? They think his grandson might've shot Fountain."

"Are you serious?"

Vanessa gave Ethan a quick overview of Micah Harvey, the odd things that had made her suspicious, and how bad she felt when she found out he was terminally ill. She also told Ethan about the black sedan, and what Micah had told her about his grandson asking for drug money.

"I'm pretty sure it was the same black car I saw both times. The FBI wanted to contact Micah at his son's in Nashville to see if he knew how to reach his grandson, but the forwarding address he gave the Carter House is either wrong or phony." Vanessa sighed. "I don't know that it matters that much if they find his grandson. I doubt he knows anything about Mom."

CHAPTER 37

BRILL sat slumped, her back pinned against the basement wall under the weight of Merrick's passed-out body. His head lay heavy on her shoulder and was turned sideways facing her, his mouth open.

The stench of stale whiskey thickened the air with every breath he exhaled. She had tried repeatedly to get enough leverage to move his body or to wiggle out from under it. But with her hands and feet bound, she just couldn't do it.

His blood had seeped into her clothes, but it appeared to be dried, and she couldn't tell if he was still bleeding. Every time he stirred, she feared he would wake up, realize he had failed to kill her, and finish the job.

Brill tried not to think about the pain—as much as she could ignore two hundred fifty pounds of crushing dead weight pinning her down. How exasperating it was that, while her captor was finally defenseless, she was rendered helpless. A murderous drunk had fallen on her like a mountain. She had enough faith to move the mountain—just not enough strength.

Okay, Lord. It's Your call. There's nothing more I can do.

She thought of Kurt and the kids. How scared they must be, and how angry, that all the protections she put in place had not stopped Merrick Fountain from getting to her.

She blinked the moisture from her eyes, her mind racing through all the events she would miss: Vanessa's giving birth; Ryan's passing the bar; Emily's childhood. Holidays. Weddings. Spoiling her grandkids. Growing old with Kurt …

Merrick let out a loud snort and then smacked his lips. Her heart pounded so fast that she could hardly breathe. His left eye flew open, and he rolled over on his back and hit the floor, letting out an agonizing scream.

"What'd you do to me?" His eyes looked like those of a wounded animal.

"I didn't do anything. You passed out hours ago and fell on top of me."

He tried again to get up and cried out in pain.

"Take it easy," she said. "You have a gunshot wound in your chest."

"I think my ribs are busted."

She eyed the knife on the floor. Could he reach it? Could she convince him to cut her loose instead of end of her life?

"I ain't dying till you're dead." He grabbed for the knife and missed, then hugged himself, his face contorted, his lips spewing profanity. Finally, he quieted down and let out a low moan, flat on his back on the floor, his arms at his side.

"Your chest wound is bleeding again," she said. "If you cut me loose, I'll go get you help. You're going to die without medical attention."

"I ain't going back to prison."

"Would you rather go to hell? I guarantee you it's worse than prison. And you'll never get out."

"Don't start on that again. I don't want to hear it."

"Well, God doesn't want you to die *without* hearing it."

"How do you know hell even exists?"

"How do you know it doesn't?"

"Why do you care what happens to me, anyway?"

"Because God cares, and I'm His voice at the moment."

Lord, tell me what to say. I have no idea what I'm doing.

Merrick tried to rise up on his elbows and groaned, then fell back on the floor, his face dotted with perspiration. "If there *is* a hell, I'm doomed. There's no way God's letting me off the hook after what I've done."

"You're still going to jail, Merrick. But Jesus' death on the cross can get you an eternal pardon—heaven instead of hell. Life instead of death. No lawyer can cut you that kind of deal."

"Why would He do that?"

"I don't pretend to understand His kind of love. I'm a cop. I'm into punishing the guilty, not wiping their slate clean."

"What's the catch? There's gotta be a catch. Sounds too easy."

"It's simple. I never said it was easy. You have to tell God you're a sinner. And acknowledge that His Son, Jesus, died to pay the penalty for your sins. You need to ask His forgiveness, and let Him into your heart."

"I don't even know what 'let Him into my heart' means."

"It means the God of the universe wants a *relationship* with you. He wants to change you from the inside out."

"Why would He want *me?*"

"I've asked myself the same question. Why me? But He made the choice to save us before the world began. He wants to be in relationship with us. He loves you and me equally and doesn't want us to spend eternity separated from Him. That's what hell is. I'm not making this up. It's all in the Bible."

"No one can change what I am." Merrick coughed, blood trickling out of his mouth.

"How do you know? I've seen guys in prison who were totally different after they opened their hearts and invited Jesus Christ to come in. They found purpose. They actually enjoyed getting up in the morning."

"Shut up! You're just stalling. Time's up." He stretched out his arm and screamed with pain as he finally managed to grab the knife.

Brill tried to slide her hands out of the rope tied round her wrists, but it was too tight.

Merrick pressed the knife blade against her gut. "What did being a Christian do for you? You're going to die just like all the others."

Brill closed her eyes, peace wrapping itself around her like a warm blanket. "You can kill my body, Merrick. But you can't touch my spirit. I'll be with God the second I die."

Kurt shuddered, his heart pounding. He thought he heard Brill call his name and realized he must've been dreaming. He slid out of bed and went over to the window and pulled back the sheers. The sun was up. Had she survived the night?

Lord, I can't face this day without You.

There was a gentle knock. He turned around and saw Emily standing in the doorway, dressed in her pink baby-doll pajamas.

"I knew you'd be awake," she said. "I thought you might want company."

"Sure. Come in."

Emily climbed up in the bed and sat cross-legged, hugging her mother's pillow. "I couldn't sleep last night. Every time I closed my eyes, I had a bad dream."

"Is your sister asleep?"

"Finally. We talked and talked, hoping it would make us feel better. It didn't." Emily sighed. "I know it doesn't do any good to worry, but I don't feel like doing anything else."

Kurt got in bed and sat next to Emily, stroking the long tresses that draped her shoulders. How he wished he could tell her that everything was going to be all right.

"Hey, did they find Mom?" Ryan shuffled in the room, bare-chested and wearing jean shorts, his hair disheveled.

"No, son. Nothing yet."

"How did you like my lavender bed?" Emily said.

"I felt like a Ken doll." Ryan flopped on the bed, his hands behind his head, and smiled wryly at Emily. "If you tell anyone outside the family that I slept in your room, all your dolls will come to life when you're sleeping—and pluck out your eyebrows."

"That's creepy." Emily threw the pillow at him.

Vanessa stood in the doorway. "I heard voices. Why didn't you come get me? Did they find Mom?"

"They haven't found her yet, honey." Kurt patted the bed. "Might as well crawl in and get comfortable."

Vanessa went around to the foot of the bed and climbed in, then lay facing Ryan.

Kurt couldn't remember the last time all the kids were in his bed—probably Christmas morning years ago. He pulled Emily close to him and blinked to clear his eyes. All this togetherness seemed empty without Brill.

The room was suddenly pin-drop still, and he wondered if his kids were thinking the same thing.

CHAPTER 38

AN hour later, Kurt sat at Brill's desk and took in the sights and sounds and smells of her office—the old leather of the desk chair she had inherited from Chief Hennessey, the musty smell of the antique rug, the gold paint he had spread on the walls, the woody smell of the old oak desk, the faint scent of lemon oil. And coffee.

Through the blinds on the glass wall, he could see that the detective bureau was bustling with activity, but the only law-enforcement person he recognized was Trent. All the others were deputy sheriffs or FBI special agents.

He got up and stood at the window. Sun filtered through the leafy branches of the shade trees that formed a canopy over Main Street. The media presence was heavy, and all the meters in front of city hall were taken. Automatic sprinklers showered the manicured grounds with a fine mist, and grackles bathed in the wet grass.

The Great Smoky Mountains looked as though a child had cut them out of chalky-blue poster board and glued them behind the hazy foothills.

Brill, where are you?

"Want me to get you more coffee?" David said.

Kurt glanced over at the conference table where David sat, the case file open in front of him. "No, thanks."

"You sure you want to just sit around and wait?"

"I can't concentrate on anything else."

"I understand."

Kurt picked up the nail file in Brill's pencil cup and held it in his hands.

He heard a stir out in the detective bureau and realized the officers had gathered around a woman and were talking to her. They stepped aside and let her through. She limped toward Brill's office, disheveled, her face cut and bleeding, her eyes sunken in puffy mounds of black and blue.

Kurt stood, his heart hammering, his gaze fixed on the woman.

He pushed back the chair and nearly stumbled as he ran around the desk and raced to the door.

Oh, Lord … You did it! You brought her home!

The love of his life hobbled slowly toward him, her uniform bloody and torn, her face battered, unrecognizable except for the red hair and the four stars on her collar.

Brill put one foot in front of the other and trudged across the detective bureau, every muscle and bone in her body aching, throbbing. Her eyes so badly swollen it was hard to see where she was going.

Lord, don't let me faint. Not after I made it this far. Not until I feel Kurt's arms around me.

Could she make it a few more steps? She had to. Wanted to. Not because her officers were watching. But because she had so much to live for, and every minute of the rest of her life was a gift.

She spotted a familiar figure walking toward her. Her heart leapt and her eyes clouded over, Kurt's arms enfolding her as gently as a summer breeze, and as surely as the grace of God.

A tear trickled down her cheek, and she whispered in his ear, "I just knew you'd be waiting. That's all I could think about all the way here."

"I'd almost given up hope that I'd ever see you alive again …" Kurt stifled a sob. "What did that monster do to you?"

"I'm okay now. I've got quite a story to tell you. Is Vanessa all right?"

Kurt nodded and held her, almost as if he were afraid to let her go.

She lost herself in her husband's arms and allowed herself to feel safe. Was this really happening? Had she survived the ordeal and made it back to him? Would she soon be hugging her children? Waking up in the morning without the threat of death hanging over her? Suddenly, she was aware of people applauding and David standing next to her.

"You gave us quite a scare," David said. "I knew if there was a way to break free, you'd find it. Any idea where Fountain is?"

"Yes. He's in the basement of a house for sale two blocks from here. 215 Melody Lane. He needs an ambulance. He confessed to each of the stabbings. I'm sure you'll find him totally cooperative."

David snickered. "Oh, yeah. I can tell by looking at you just how cooperative he is."

Brill reached over and gripped David's arm. "Don't hurt him. Merrick could've killed me. He didn't. Let's do this by the book."

"*Merrick?* You're on a first-name basis with this slimeball?"

She shifted her gaze to Kurt, and then back to David. "Let's just say I promised his Father I'd treat him with respect."

Kurt opened the front door and Brill stepped inside, the scent of roses filling her senses.

All three kids rushed over to her, their expressions registering their horror at how battered she looked.

"I guess nothing your dad said could prepare you for all this black and blue. The emergency-room doctor said it'll look worse before it looks better, but I don't have any serious injuries."

Emily gingerly put her arms around Brill, and Vanessa and Ryan each took her by the hand.

"I knew you'd come home," Emily said. "I prayed and prayed for a guardian angel."

Brill kissed the top of Emily's head. "He was there."

She looked into Vanessa's eyes. "I was so worried about you. Merrick told me he tried to kidnap you at the park and someone shot him. I could only hope and pray you made it home and were safe."

Vanessa's eyes brimmed with tears. "He said he was going to kill you, that he planned to kill us both."

"But look at us. We're fine."

"You don't exactly look *fine,* Mom," Ryan said. "I wish I could get my hands on that creep."

Emily leaned back and looked up at her. "Dad didn't tell us how you got away. He said *you* wanted to."

"I do. Let's go in the living room."

Brill sat on the couch with the three kids, and Kurt sat on the overstuffed chair facing them.

"It started out pretty awful," she said. "There was no doubt in my mind that Merrick was going to kill me …"

Without being too graphic, Brill told the kids what had happened from the time she realized David had been tasered until Merrick woke up after being passed out for hours.

"At that point, I didn't have much hope. I knew that unless I could talk Merrick into cutting me loose so I could get him medical help, he was going to kill me and then himself."

Brill told them how she had implored him to think about hell, that dying without Christ wouldn't free him from anything, that it would ensure his eternal separation from God.

"You actually *witnessed* to him?" Vanessa said.

"I did. And it's the last thing I ever expected to do. I'll be honest, at first I was just saying the words out of desperation. I didn't really care what happened to Merrick. But then the power behind the words hit me right between the eyes, and I realized that this was a divine appointment and God was using me. Suddenly getting through to Merrick seemed more important than anything he might do to me."

"Wow," Ryan said. "That's awesome."

"Not that he seemed receptive at that point. In fact, he wanted me to stop talking and finally got his hand on the knife and held it to my stomach. He asked me what being a Christian had done for me, since I was going to die like all the others. I really thought I was. But instead of being afraid, I remember feeling warm all over and totally peaceful. I told him that he could kill my body but he couldn't touch my spirit—and that I'd be with God the moment I died."

Emily's eyes were wide. "What did he do?"

"He pushed the knife until he broke the skin, and then his hand began to shake. He dropped the knife and started to weep. He said he didn't want to go to hell, that he wanted to believe God could forgive him. He said he didn't know why he kept hurting people, but he was sorry and he wanted to stop."

Brill looked at Kurt, a tear spilling down her cheek. "I told him Jesus died so he didn't have to be a slave to violence. That's all Merrick needed to hear. He wanted to know how he could be free of it. I'm a little blurry on what we said after that, but I remember leading him in a simple sinner's prayer."

Emily squeezed her hand. "Tell us the prayer."

"Sweetie, I don't recall the exact words, but Merrick said he believed that Jesus is God's Son and that because of His death and resurrection our sins can be forgiven and we can receive the gift of eternal life. He spent a few moments silently confessing his sins, and then we both cried when he asked Jesus to come into his heart and change him."

Emily reached up and wiped the tear off Brill's cheek. "It must've been something, Mom. You hardly ever cry."

"It was. I'm not sure I've ever felt closer to God than I did at that moment."

Vanessa laid her head on Brill's shoulder. "I can hardly believe we're talking about the same man."

"How'd you get away?" Ryan said.

"After we prayed, Merrick cut me loose, but I stayed a while longer. I told him I forgave him for hurting me. It was so strange— police chief and criminal on equal footing. We talked about forgiveness and how God removes our sins as far as the east is from the west—and doesn't remember them anymore. I also told him about the prison ministry Antonio Masino is involved in. I promised that Antonio would come see him and bring him a Bible and some reading material that would help him understand the significance of his having put his faith in Christ. There's no doubt in my mind that Merrick's repentance was sincere."

Emily linked arms with Brill and looked up at her. "What did Agent David say about all this?"

"Oh, I think David is scratching his head big time. He knows I wouldn't make this up, but it doesn't make sense to him either."

CHAPTER 39

A week later Vanessa finally got up the courage to walk through Cherokee Valley Park and past the place where Merrick Fountain had accosted her. Though she found it amazing that God could take someone as mean as he and turn his life around, she shuddered to think what might have happened if he hadn't been shot.

Would the authorities ever know who shot Merrick? He told them that he didn't have any enemies and hadn't made any acquaintances since getting out of prison. But how likely was it that the shooting was random?

She waved to the hot-dog vendor and walked past the duck pond, her thoughts turning to Micah. It hardly seemed possible that someone that vibrant might be gone in three to six months.

She strolled down the sidewalk toward Azalea Lane and heard footsteps behind her. She moved over to one side and, a few seconds later, a man walked up next to her, keeping perfect stride. She did a double take.

"Micah! For heaven's sake, I was just thinking of you. I thought you were in Nashville. The police were looking for you, hoping you could help them find your grandson. But the forwarding address you gave was wrong."

"Come sit with me for a minute." He took her by the arm and led her over to an empty park bench.

Vanessa lowered herself to a sitting position, glad to get off her feet.

Micah sat next to her. "I have something to say to you."

"Your voice is different."

"Not different. Just not phony. Look at me." He peeled off his gray eyebrows and mustache and turned to her, his eyes deep brown and unmistakably Ty Nicholson's.

She sucked in a breath and couldn't seem to exhale.

"I'm sorry to shock you like this, but you deserve to know the truth, and it's now or never. I really am leaving, and I don't want you spending the rest of your life thinking I rejected you or our son."

"What would you call it?"

"Vanessa, listen to me. I never wanted to hurt you. I'm in witness protection and—"

"I know. My mother hired someone to find you and ran into a brick wall."

"Really? That's great news."

"I'm glad *you* think so. You could've at least said good-bye."

"Look, I left Memphis in a panic when you decided to keep the baby, because I thought having his name linked to mine on a birth certificate could put you both at risk. Turns out I overreacted. The feds assured me that it's next to impossible for someone to find me under the name Ty Nicholson. But since I walked away from my job and couldn't go back, they changed my identity again."

"What happened? Why are you in witness protection?"

"I'm a psychologist. I testified against a gangster who murdered a patient of mine, who was also a gangster. I shouldn't even be here, but I didn't want to write you, email, call, or come to your home. I didn't want to leave any trail leading to you."

"How did you know where I was?"

"I figured you'd stay with your parents till you had the baby, so I came to Sophie Trace, looking for you. I had to be absolutely sure no one had followed me before I made contact with you. When I saw the car staked out in front of your parents' house, I thought the mob had their eye on you and were waiting for *me* to show. Then I listened to the news and realized Chief Jessup is your mother and figured they were cops."

"So you know what's going on with my family?"

Ty nodded. "I'm really sorry to lay this on you. You've really been through the mill."

Vanessa wiped the tears off her cheeks. "Do you have any idea what *you've* put me through?"

"I think I do, but I never meant to hurt you. Things would have been a lot simpler if you'd just gotten the abortion."

"Simpler for whom?" She took his hand and held it on her abdomen so he could feel the baby kicking. "You're the psychologist. Do you really think destroying this child would simplify my life?"

"I just wanted you to finish college and not be saddled with all the responsibility."

"Well, *Micah* … I've already told you how I'm going to do all that."

"I wish I could be involved in the baby's life, but it's out of the question."

Vanessa sighed. "Why didn't you tell me all this the first time you followed me to the park?"

"Too risky. I wasn't sure how you'd react, and I needed us to look like 'just acquaintances' in case we were being watched. I had to see you a few times to be absolutely sure no one was following us."

Vanessa looked up at a white-haired couple pushing a stroller. "You obviously don't have a grandson. Who was in the black car?"

"A retired U.S. marshal who's watching my back and wanted me out of here a week ago."

"So did he shoot the guy who tried to kidnap me?"

Ty shook his head. "*I* did. I'm sorry I couldn't stop, but I knew I hit him and saw you run away. Getting arrested would have put me in a very precarious situation, but I couldn't let the guy hurt you. I heard on the news that he's the man who was stalking your mother."

"I didn't even know you could shoot."

"In my situation, you never know when you might need to defend yourself."

"I have so many questions, I hardly know where to start. How should I list the baby's father on the birth certificate?"

"Ty Nicholson. That's who I was when we were together."

"What do you want me to tell the baby about you?"

"I'll leave that up to you. I'd like to think you'd tell him I cared very much what happened to him."

Vanessa sighed. "Do you?"

"Sure. It's killing me that I can't watch him grow up."

"Did you have a family before?"

"I've never been married. No other kids. I've never seen or contacted my parents, siblings, or anyone in my extended family since the day I went into witness protection. It's been torture."

"You talked about Eleanor and your son Charles and your grandsons with such ease. How could you lie to me like that? None of that was necessary."

"I'm sorry. I needed to come across as believable."

"Well, you can feel proud of yourself. I felt sorry for you and believed you were dying. I've actually been praying for you."

There was a long pause, and then Ty said, "Maybe your prayers are doing some good. I told you the truth about my reading the book of John, and I'm halfway through the book of Acts."

"I can't believe you baited me into that discussion. I only bit because I thought you were an eighty-six-year-old man who didn't have much time to make peace with his Maker."

"Maybe that's why I listened objectively. You made some good points … and, truthfully, even though it turned my life upside down, I respect you for standing by your beliefs when I pressured you about the abortion."

"You do?"

"Vanessa, before we broke up, the last thing you said to me was, 'I have to do what's right. I'm accountable to my Lord and Savior, and I love Him even more than I love you.' I don't understand that kind of relationship. But that's what I want." Ty's eyes were suddenly dark pools. "If there is a God, it seems to me that He's the only person that we can count on, no matter what. I really need that. If you hadn't been bold enough to challenge a feisty old man, I never would've picked up the Bible and taken a closer look."

A man behind the wheel of a white Ford Taurus parallel-parked along the curb honked and motioned for Ty to come.

Ty put his arm around her and held her gaze. "I have to go. We can't have any more contact after this. Do you have any more questions?"

She shook her head, tears trickling down her cheeks.

"Now you can get on with your life. Get your teaching degree. Marry some young guy who loves you and your little boy and who deserves the special person you are. I'll never forget you, and I wish you the best of everything." He picked up her hand, brought it to his lips, and then handed her an envelope and rose to his feet.

She sat in a daze and watched him walk over to the car, get in, and drive away.

Brill lowered the blinds on the glass wall in her office and sat at the conference table with Mayor Roswell. If he was determined to fire her, there was nothing she could do to stop him.

"Well, Mr. Mayor, I trust you heard that the DA's investigators cleared Rick Ulman of all charges?"

"I did. That's not why I'm here."

Brill studied his expression. "Why *are* you here?"

"First of all, let me say I'm sorry for all you and your family have been through in the ordeal with Merrick Fountain. It's quite amazing that you're alive."

"It is. Thank you."

"I also owe you an apology for the caustic tone I used with you the last time I was here. It was wrong of me—and the city council—to make you a scapegoat because revenues were down. You cleaned out the gangs.

Crime is down across the board. And you played some very difficult hands with leadership and courage. It's obvious your department is behind you, and I don't know who told the media otherwise. I want you to know I'm standing by my original decision. Hiring you was absolutely the right move. I've made my feelings clear to the city council."

"You might be boarding a sinking ship."

The corners of the mayor's mouth turned up. "I've got a life raft. It's called integrity."

"Thank you. It means more than you know."

The mayor seemed to study her face. "You're starting to look more like *you* again. I'm glad your injuries weren't serious. I still don't know how you talked your way out of it, but I'm glad you did."

"So am I. I believe everything happens for a reason."

"When will Officer Ulman be reinstated?"

"I told him to take some time off. It's demoralizing for any officer to have his integrity and competence questioned publicly. I'll do everything I can to help him regain his confidence and stay in law enforcement. He's a good cop."

The mayor stood and extended his hand. "I know this is a day late and a dollar short, but I respect the job you're doing. I can't control the city council, but I promise you have an advocate in the mayor's office."

After dinner, Vanessa sat with her mother on the side of her parents' bed and told her of the conversation she'd had with Ty Nicholson.

"That's it. Ty got in the car and left. I opened the envelope and found the cashier's check for ten thousand dollars and the unsigned note saying it was all he had and he hoped it would help. And that he could never contact me again."

"Must've been emotional."

"It was. I have mixed feelings. I still love him, but I love who I thought he was, and not who he really is. It's hard to explain."

Brill squeezed her arm. "You don't have to explain. I understand."

"I'm not sorry he showed up. I mean, it hurts. But now I know for sure why he left. Actually, it's better that he didn't show up till after I made the decision to keep the baby. I'm so confident it's the right move that all I really needed from Ty was closure. But the money is certainly appreciated. I still can't fathom that he listened to anything I said about God. I thought I was talking to a stone wall."

"Just goes to show that God's Word doesn't return empty. We both experienced that in different but dramatic ways."

"It's so weird, Mom. The only reason I opened up with Micah was because I felt sorry for him."

"As well you should. If we really care about the lost we should never be ashamed of the gospel. What struck me is that neither of us started out with pure motives. And yet when it came down to eternity and what was at stake, we started to care more about them than our own circumstances."

Vanessa locked gazes with her mother. "At least my situation wasn't life threatening. I still can hardly believe the mean, awful man who threatened to kill us both got saved because you dared to get in the last word."

"Speaking the truth gave *me* strength. Maybe that's another way the Word doesn't come back empty."

"I'm just so thankful we both found closure and can move on."

Her mother paused for a few moments and then said, "Speaking of closure, Vanessa … I have something I need to say to you. I did a lot of thinking when I thought I was going to die. I can't tell you how desperately I wanted to put my arms around you and tell you I'm sorry for pushing you so hard. My expectations of you have been unrealistic. You're wonderful just the way you are. And I don't care if you ever make the dean's list."

Vanessa paused, emotion tightening her throat. "I probably needed a little pushing, Mom."

"Maybe a nudge now and then." Brill put her arm around Vanessa and kissed her cheek. "I love you, honey. I'm proud to be your mother. I just wish you could know how much."

"You're not ashamed of me because I'm pregnant?"

"It was never about shame. I was shocked. Disappointed. I knew you were going to have to grow up really fast, and all my dreams for you would have to change. But there's no doubt in my mind that you're going to be a wonderful mother. And I want to be there for both of you."

Vanessa rested in the comfortable silence that followed and let her mother's words of acceptance gently knead the knots of resentment and insecurity.

"I think we should keep today's visit with Ty among the adults in the family," Brill finally said.

"*And* Ethan, since he already knows you tried to find Ty. I trust him not to say anything."

Brill picked up a lock of Vanessa's hair. "I'm sorry you haven't had the happily-ever-after you'd hoped for, honey."

"I've got the rest of my life for that, Mom. The only happily-ever-after I care about right now is having you home safe and sound."

CHAPTER 40

ON a muggy Sunday evening in mid-July, Vanessa strolled with Ethan on the sidewalk along Azalea Lane, glad to finally have the freedom to explore the neighborhood.

"I'm beginning to like Sophie Trace," she said. "It's a pretty town."

"I loved growing up here." Ethan looked over at the foothills that were cloaked in sheer white haze. "I have some great memories."

"Did you like being an only child?"

"Sure. What's not to like? I got *all* the attention." He grinned. "Have you picked out a name for the baby yet?"

"Not really. I want to see him first."

"Are you thinking of naming him after the professor?"

Vanessa shook her head. "My son needs his own name. I can hardly wait to see him and hold him in my arms. With all the support I'm getting from my family now, I just know this was the right decision."

"I'm so glad you didn't do what Professor Nicholson wanted. Who's to say this little boy might not change the world?"

"Ethan, why do I sense this is a personal thing with you?"

He picked up his pace and didn't answer.

"I didn't mean to put you off"—she kept stride with him—"but it's not the first time I've sensed it."

"I'm not put off, Vanessa. It's just that I've never told anyone what I'm working up the nerve to tell you. Though it *is* something I've pondered a great deal."

"What?"

Ethan glanced over at her and then looked straight ahead. "I'm the product of a botched abortion. My biological mother decided in the eighth month of her pregnancy that she didn't want me."

"Oh, Ethan …"

"Hey, don't feel sorry for me. My adoptive parents are wonderful. They've given me the chance to live life to the fullest. And I've given them twenty-one years to love a child they might not have had otherwise. How different things would've been if I had been left for dead in that dirty trash can at the abortion clinic."

"Who found you?"

"I don't know. Maybe an angel." Ethan smiled. "I was in children's intensive care for a while and then placed in child protective services. The doctors said there were no guarantees that I wouldn't have physical problems down the road. Mom and Dad wanted an infant, and they were willing to risk it. I turned out healthy, but if it had gone the other way, I doubt it would've changed anything. They knew I was meant to be theirs."

Vanessa linked arms with him. "Wow, did God ever have His hand on you. He must have something important for you to do."

"I'm sure He does. But isn't that true of all believers? I have a feeling we're all going to be shocked when we get to heaven and see how involved He was in every aspect of our lives. Each one of us is chosen, handpicked by the Father for a specific purpose. I don't know if that turns your crank, but it does mine. I guess that's why

I'm so pro-life. I mean, look at Merrick Fountain. Everyone wrote him off as a total loser, but God didn't let go of him."

"Yeah, but what purpose would a guy like that have?"

Ethan shrugged. "We're about to find out. But your mother's life has been impacted for the better. You said yourself she's softened."

"Yes, but what about the people whose lives he ruined? I doubt Mrs. O'Toole has any warm fuzzies for her husband's killer."

"Vanessa, I don't pretend to have all the answers. All people sin, and they either come to Christ for forgiveness or they don't. I just know that when they do, the angels rejoice—even for a guy like Merrick Fountain."

Brill sat on the glider on the screened-in porch, knitting an afghan for her grandson.

"Kurt, do you realize Vanessa's due date is less than two weeks away?"

"Yeah, but I don't know what more we can do to get ready except get plenty of sleep. I'm disappointed that Emily's baby bed and dresser didn't need painting."

"Why? It was one less thing to do."

"That's not the point, honey. You girls like to knit and shop and have baby showers. I want to contribute something."

Brill laughed. "You'll get your chance, buster. Vanessa and I aren't worth two cents without sleep. Someone's got to get up with the baby."

"Yoo-hoo!"

Brill looked up and spotted Tessa and Antonio coming in the gate, each carrying a big plastic container.

Kurt stood and walked over to the door. "Hi, neighbors."

"We just sliced a watermelon," Tessa said, "and had to share it. It's a *really* good one."

"Sounds great." Kurt opened the screen door and held it. "Come in. It's cool under this big fan."

Emily seemed to come out of nowhere, her eyes wide. "You always bring something I'm in the mood for. I *love* watermelon."

Antonio winked. "She's a mind reader."

Vanessa came out on the porch, Ethan on her heels. "I heard voices and was hoping it was you. You remember my friend Ethan."

"Of course we do."

Ethan shook hands with Antonio and was a good sport when Tessa hugged him and fussed over his curly hair.

"I want you to see how darling the baby's corner in my room looks," Vanessa said. "Dad got the crib set up and hung the Babies of the Bible mobile you gave me. It's perfect."

Brill set down her knitting. "Why don't you all go take a look and I'll get out the watermelon bowls."

They all went in the house, and while Kurt and the kids took the Masinos upstairs, Brill got the watermelon bowls, napkins, forks, and a saltshaker and put them on the round table on the porch.

Ten minutes later, each of them had a slice of watermelon and was oohing and aahing over how good it tasted.

"This is my favoritest fruit." Emily giggled as she picked out some seeds from the slice in her hand. "I'm not sure *favoritest* is even a word."

"It won't work for Scrabble," Tessa said, "but I think it says it all. I can't get over how adorable the baby's corner is. Your old baby bed is perfect."

Emily smiled. "I knew it would be."

"By the way, I saw Merrick yesterday." Antonio salted his slice of watermelon. "He's already shared his faith with two other inmates, and they want Bibles. Isn't that great?"

"And amazing," Brill said.

"He's also going to write a letter to each of the victims' families and ask their forgiveness." Antonio arched his eyebrows. "I'm not sure how open *they* will be, but Merrick is determined to make peace with them if it takes the rest of his life."

"I've forgiven him," Emily said. "It feels better than being mad."

Brill studied her younger daughter, proud of the way she handled herself during the kidnapping ordeal, surprised and pleased the nightmares that started last fall had stopped.

"Thanks for the watermelon," Vanessa said. "It really hit the spot. Ethan and I are going to go water the flowers."

"You're welcome, dear."

Ethan stood and held the door and followed Vanessa down the steps to the backyard.

When they were out of sight, Tessa said, "He is such a nice young man. And handsome, too."

"We've really enjoyed having him around," Kurt said. "He and Vanessa are the best of friends these days."

Emily jumped up. "May I please be excused? I want to show Ethan how tall my morning-glory vines are getting. I'll be back."

"Would you mind taking the empty bowls and rinds to the kitchen first?" Brill said.

"Okay." Emily gathered the bowls and carried them inside, then came back out, opened the screen door, and skipped down the steps.

"She seems much more at ease," Tessa said.

Brill nodded. "She hasn't had a bad dream since the whole ordeal with Merrick. She's fascinated that at the moment I thought he was going to kill me, I felt peace. I think knowing that has taken away her fear."

Tessa looked over at Antonio. "We had such a strong sense that the battle was the Lord's. We're just so grateful."

"We are too," Kurt said.

A high-pitched shriek caused Brill's heart to stop and then pound wildly with relief as she heard male laughter and the sound of Emily's giggling.

A split second later, Ethan came around the side of the house, Emily in pursuit with the garden hose. She chased Ethan to the corner of the yard, where he stopped and turned around, dripping from head to foot, and wrestled Emily for the hose.

Emily's shrieks of protest turned to belly-laughing as Ethan pried the hose from her hands, then turned the stream on Vanessa.

"Listen, you two, I came out here to water the flowers!" Vanessa crossed her arms in front of her face, her laughter exuberant and contagious. "Enough! Will you stop? All right, you asked for it …"

Vanessa snatched the hose from Ethan and took several steps backward, dousing the front of him till he finally took off his glasses and retreated.

Emily jumped up and down, clapping her hands and giggling until she made no sound.

Brill, fully engaged, looked over at Kurt. "Are you game?"

"Definitely."

"Excuse us for a moment," Brill said to Tessa and Antonio, "but this is just too good to pass up."

Brill went out the screen door and down the steps and trudged over to where the three kids were now tussling for possession of the garden hose. Before they realized what she was doing, she had the nozzle firmly in hand and pointed at Vanessa, evoking piercing screams of delight she was sure could be heard at Cherokee Valley Park.

Brill heard herself chortling like a schoolgirl, Kurt making loud whooping sounds, and her daughters laughing with gleeful abandon. She immersed herself in the moment, unaware that someone had taken the hose until she felt a cold gush of water pouring over her head.

She stood soaking wet, her arms held out to the side, and her face turned upward.

"Mom, what are you doing?" Emily said.

"Enjoying."

"Enjoying what?"

"*Everything*, sweetie. Absolutely everything."

... a little more ...

When a delightful concert comes to an end,

the orchestra might offer an encore.

When a fine meal comes to an end,

it's always nice to savor a bit of dessert.

When a great story comes to an end,

we think you may want to linger.

And so, we offer ...

AfterWords—just a little something more after you

have finished a David C. Cook novel.

We invite you to stay awhile in the story.

Thanks for reading!

Turn the page for ...

- **A Note from the Author**
- **Discussion Questions**

A NOTE FROM THE AUTHOR

I AM NOT ASHAMED OF THE GOSPEL,
BECAUSE IT IS THE POWER OF GOD FOR THE
SALVATION OF EVERYONE WHO BELIEVES:
FIRST FOR THE JEW, THEN FOR THE GENTILE.
ROMANS 1:16

Are we, the body of believers, ashamed of the gospel? Why are we so easily intimidated into silence—into letting those whose hearts are blinded by unredeemed sin remake our holidays, determine what is politically correct, and remove any mention of God from our schools, our government buildings, and our national treasures?

Perhaps we lack the passion to safeguard what is sacred because we've lost the courage to share our faith in our daily lives. Do we believe that Jesus is the way, the truth, and the life, and that no one comes to the Father except through Him—that without Him, and Him alone, unbelievers are doomed to hell? Are we deeply concerned for their eternal welfare?

I confess to you that this was a difficult book to write. I did not start out writing a story that made a bold statement about the choice we all have to spend eternity with God or without Him. But my characters fought me the whole way and forced my hand to proclaim the truth, even at the risk of sounding preachy.

As I'm writing this afterword, the war against Christmas is raging all over America. How dare we "offend" the godless by holding to a blessed tradition that pays homage to the Word made flesh who gave

His life so that we don't have to live in darkness. These well-meaning individuals believe they can find peace on earth without turning to Him who is our peace. It can never happen. The only light in this dark world was lit in Bethlehem two thousand years ago and continues to burn today in the hearts of believers. He is both the Giver *and* the Gift, our only hope.

Most of us will never have a divine appointment like Brill's, when our faith will be tested to the death. But almost every believer will face situations when, like Vanessa, we must choose to stand firm on that which cannot be compromised, even if it costs us dearly.

I have a feeling most of us don't have to look past our own family, friends, and coworkers to find people who need to hear the message of the cross. Have you lamented that if these should die without a saving knowledge of Jesus, they would be doomed to a fate far worse than death? Perhaps you've tried to broach the subject but have been rebuffed?

Are you bold enough to try again? Or to give this book to them because you care more about their eternal future than the possibility they'll figure out why you gave it to them? When we stand before God and give an account of our lives, it won't matter if our efforts to share the gospel were met with jeering and rejection. What *will* matter is that we were obedient to the Great Commission.

Isaiah 55:11 promises that the Word of God never returns empty and that it will accomplish His purpose. Brill certainly experienced that, and so did Vanessa. Only the Holy Spirit can bring a person to the place of repentance and faith. Our job as believers is to tell the good news, and I loved being able to weave it into this story. If it touched you, please pass it on to someone you care about.

And if you read this story and would like to know more about how to become a Christian and begin a personal relationship with God, feel free to contact me through my guestbook page on my Web site (listed below).

I can hardly believe we've finished book two. Join me in the final book of the trilogy, *The Right Call*, where we go back to Sophie Trace and see how the Jessups are doing—and what Vanessa decided to name the baby. And whether Ethan's friendship with Vanessa turns into something more. But don't get too comfortable. Mystery and suspense abound!

I would love to hear from you. Feel free to drop by my Web site at www.KathyHerman.com and leave your comments on my guest book. Or look me up on Facebook. I read and respond to every email and greatly value your input.

In Him,

Kathy Herman

DISCUSSION QUESTIONS

1. In Romans 1:16, the apostle Paul makes a bold declaration: "I am not ashamed of the gospel, because it is the power of God for the salvation of everyone who believes: first for the Jew, then for the Gentile." What do you think it means to be ashamed of the gospel?

2. Is there ever a legitimate reason not to share the gospel? Can you give examples of what might be a legitimate reason and what would be an excuse?

3. Can you think of times you've been bold about sharing your faith and times when you've been reluctant—or even ashamed? Can you explain what motivated you either way? Do you think God wants us to share our faith, even if we haven't been called to the "mission field" as it's generally understood? What might be a broader definition of mission field?

4. First Corinthians 1:18 tells us, "For the message of the cross is foolishness to those who are perishing, but to us who are being saved it is the power of God." What do you think this means? Do the words make you feel more inclined or less inclined to share your faith with an unbeliever? And why?

5. Do you know people who see the salvation message as foolishness? Have you ever tried to explain to an unbeliever what the Christian life is all about, only to be ridiculed? Patronized? Made to feel defensive?

6. Have you ever tried to hold an unbeliever to the same

moral standard as yours? Should you? Who or what brings a person to a saving knowledge of Christ? Without the mind of Christ, can that person even understand he or she is lost?

7. If you found yourself in Brill's circumstances, dialoguing with your attacker, do you think you would have the courage to share your faith? Do you think Brill's firm belief that when she died she would be with the Lord gave her strength?

8. Why do you think Brill's persistence in the face of death made an impression on Merrick Fountain—was it just what she said about God, or was it more than that?

9. Do you agree with Brill's assertion that everything happens for a reason—even the really difficult things? If so, can you give a Scripture that supports it? Have you ever seen evidence of this in your own life? Could you believe God would use it for good even without seeing evidence?

10. Romans 8.28 makes a strong statement of faith: "And we know that in all things God works for the good of those who love him, who have been called according to his purpose." How did God use Brill's dire circumstances for good in this story? If she had been murdered, would that have negated the truth of Romans 8:28? Is it possible that a believer's suffering, even at the hands of a killer, might serve God's higher purpose? Is that hard for you to accept? Be honest.

11. Vanessa's sinful choices resulted in an unwanted pregnancy, and her choice not to abort the baby resulted in a severed relationship. Both choices, one wrong and one right,

initially brought her sorrow. What was it that motivated her to make the right choice and not abort the baby? Do you believe she could have been happy for long if she had gotten an abortion? Or if Ty had changed his mind about breaking up with her?

12. Do you think God can use even our mistakes for His higher purpose? How did He use Vanessa's good and bad choices to bring Ty to the place of realizing he needed God?

13. Which do you think is the better teacher: blessing or suffering? Does God use both? Which has made a bigger impact in your life?

14. Which do you think is more important if we are to be ambassadors of the gospel—what we say or what we do? Or can the two be separated? Which do you think is more likely to offend an unbeliever—our sin? Our hypocrisy? Our apathy?

15. If you could meet one of the characters in this story, which one would it be? What would you talk about? What did you take away from this story?